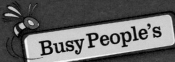

Busy People's

fast & frugal
cookbook

Published in Nashville, Tennessee, by Thomas Nelson. Thomas Nelson is a registered trademark of Thomas Nelson, Inc.

Thomas Nelson, Inc., titles may be purchased in bulk for educational, business, fund-raising, or sales promotional use. For information, please e-mail SpecialMarkets@ThomasNelson.com.

Photography on pages iv, vi, xii, 13, 29, 46, 55, 64, 75, 77, 86, 92, 109, 122, 151, 194, 213, 215, 222, 228, 240, 245–46, 249–50, 263, 280, 289, and 291 by Danielle Adams.

Library of Congress Control Number: 2009934420

ISBN-13: 978-1-59555-290-7

Printed in the United States of America

09 10 11 12 QW 6 5 4 3 2 1

Busy People's

fast & frugal cookbook

Dawn Hall

THOMAS NELSON
Since 1798

NASHVILLE   DALLAS   MEXICO CITY   RIO DE JANEIRO   BEIJING

Raspberry and Cheese Crescents (page 240)

Contents

Chopped Italian and Rye Salad (page 76)

Watching My Weight and Counting My Pennies

I feel like I was born watching my weight and counting my pennies. It is a part of who I am. I have learned to do the best I can with what I have and to be content. For me, this life lesson has been a gift.

Please don't get me wrong. I would never choose to be born watching my weight or counting my pennies; but much good has come from it, and for those life lessons that I have learned, I am grateful!

I have struggled to be within my ideal body weight as far back as I can remember. We grew up on a farm and took pride in how much we could eat. You can eat six ears of corn? I can eat seven! As children, we were proud that our hefty dad won the "Hog Trough Award" for eating too much at the ice cream parlor. Even now, there is nothing a hot fudge brownie can't make feel better. But I also remember the not-so-proud feeling of my little white gym shorts being too tight in the first grade. It is no wonder I struggle with food. Can you relate to anything I am saying here?

I have learned the hard way that, for me, the price I was paying by being unhealthy is a LOT higher emotionally, mentally, and physically than the sacrifices I pay of eating less calories and healthier foods so I can be within my healthy weight range. I wish I could tell you that after all of these years it is now easy for me to be within my ideal weight, and that I have no desires to ever "pig out," but I cannot. It is still a daily challenge for me. Sometimes I feel as if there is this obese woman in me, just wanting to eat her way out.

To help fight the battle of the bulge, along with exercising, I count my daily caloric intake as if each calorie has one dollar value, and I only have so many caloric dollars to spend a day. Eating low-fat and healthier food choices instead of unhealthy junk food has helped me stretch and enjoy daily caloric restriction. As if shopping at a great sale on clothing, I try to get a great value with my limited daily caloric dollars, thus one of the reasons why I eat low-fat. Of course, reducing the risks of cancer, heart disease, and diabetes, which all thrive on a high-fat diet, are other reasons I try to eat low-fat. I try to eat 80 percent of my daily calories from healthy food choices and allow the remaining 20 percent to come from what I call unhealthy food choices (also known as junk food or foods with little nutritional value).

On a financial note: I am the oldest of seven children, and we grew up living on my father's modest income. I was very fortunate and blessed to learn from my mother how to stretch a dollar!

As my life transitioned from a single lady in my early twenties living on my own, to a stay-at-home-mom in my late twenties, to the financial provider for our family while my loving husband was fighting brain cancer for six and a half years, until now as a widow, I have ALWAYS counted my pennies! I believe that what we make of our money is every bit as important as how much we make!

About a year ago I was literally fighting back tears as I was grocery shopping because it just seems as though financially it is getting more and more difficult to stretch my grocery budget eating healthier choices. I thought to myself, *If I am feeling the pinch, surely others are also!* That is when I decided to write *Busy People's Fast & Frugal Cookbook.* My goal was to create home-style recipes that busy people could quickly and easily afford to make in the comfort of their own homes using inexpensive and easy-to-find grocery store ingredients. I wanted the recipes to taste and look as though we had slaved over them all day, but in all honesty each recipe had to be effortlessly made with seven or fewer ingredients, be low-fat, and be finished in five to thirty minutes!

The Cost Factor: The Bottom Dollar vs. Fat and Fiber Content— Choices You'll Need to Make for Yourself

Throughout this cookbook you will see that I had to make choices regarding the higher costs of fat-free and higher-fiber products compared to the lower costs of using products higher in fat and lower in fiber. Prime examples are in cheeses, butters, salad dressings, breads, and pastas. *My choices:*

Higher-Cost Ingredients: For most recipes I chose to pay the higher cost to use fat-free cheeses, low-fat butter or light margarines, fat-free salad dressings, low-calorie sliced breads and only the egg whites. *Why?* Because for me, the extra money I am paying seems worth it for the amount of fats, cholesterol, and unwanted calories I am saving.

Lower-Cost Ingredients: For the most part I chose to pay less for regular pastas and did not use whole-grain pastas which have more fiber. *Why?* Because for me, I did not feel the extra costs to use whole-grain pastas were worth the benefits. However, I do try to eat 25 grams of fiber a day. Now if the whole-grain pastas were on sale, and I was able to purchase it at a price comparable to the lower-fiber pastas, by all means I recommend using the higher-fiber pastas! You may have to cook them for just a little bit longer, but the time is well worth the effort.

For the most part I choose to save on cholesterol, unwanted fats, and calories by using only the egg whites of eggs in my recipes. You'll save more than 300 milligrams of cholesterol per egg by using just the whites, plus oodles of calories and fats. I have found that purchasing eggs by the dozen is usually less expensive than buying liquid egg substitute (aka Egg Beaters). However, If you like the ease of using liquid egg substitute, then by all means, go ahead and substitute it in my recipes for the egg whites.

2 egg whites = $\frac{1}{4}$ cup liquid egg substitute = 1 whole egg

$\frac{1}{4}$ cup liquid egg substitute = 1 whole egg = 2 egg whites

If you prefer to use the entire egg, then substitute 1 whole egg for 2 egg whites in recipes.

TIP: Adding a few drops of yellow food coloring to the egg whites (before beating them) makes the color look as if you used whole eggs.

You will need to make these choices for yourself, but I recommend substituting an ingredient that has greater nutritional value whenever you are able to do so *at the same price* as a lower-nutritional ingredient. (Example: whole-grain pasta instead of regular pasta.) In order to do this you will need to be on the lookout for sales.

Saving on Groceries

❯ See what is on sale before deciding what to eat. Make sale items (that are a great value) the featured ingredients in your meals.

❯ Stock up on ingredients you know you will use when they are on sale. Store paper products under the bed in plastic containers.

❯ Shop with a grocery list. Have an ongoing grocery list for family members to write down when an ingredient is either running low or is out. This is a life saver for me! When children complain (which is usually after I have already done my shopping) that we are out of a certain item, all I have to say is, "It wasn't on the list."

❯ Don't shop when you are HUNGRY! Studies show that people spend more on groceries when they shop hungry.

❯ Don't shop with children; they are compulsive buyers and tend to spend money on things none of us need—junk food.

- Know what you can afford to spend on groceries each pay period. This is called a "grocery budget."
- *Shop with cash:* When the cash is gone, you know you've reached your limit. This is especially helpful with children! Children do not understand the concept of credit cards, debit cards, or checks; but they do understand when the cash is gone we have no more money for extras.
- Don't go down junk food isles unless you have to. It is easier to avoid temptation than to resist it.
- Food is money! Throwing out food is like throwing out money. Keep a bag of leftover vegetables in the freezer that you can add to. When the bag is full, make a pot of vegetable soup out of the leftover frozen vegetables by cooking them in chicken or beef broth.
- Rotate your inventory at home. Yes, just like they do at grocery stores! When unloading your groceries, bring the older ingredients to the front of the cupboard, and place the new ingredients in the back. Do the same thing in the refrigerator: move opened ingredients to the front, and place the new ingredients behind the partially used or older ingredients.
- Organize your cupboards so you know what you have. Too often we purchase ingredients we don't need simply because we do not know what we already have. Then, down the road we end up throwing away ingredients because they are past their expiration dates.
- When donating your pantry items to churches or food pantries write down a list of the donated ingredients, along with the price you paid and the date and address of where you are donating them. If you have a receipt, keep it and staple it to the list. Have the contact person who accepted your donation sign and date your list. This is a legitimate tax-deductible donation.

Smoked Sausage and Cheddar Egg Bake (page 28)

Breakfast and Brunch

MINI INDEX

SUPPLIES LIST FOR
SUGGESTED MEAL
Microwave-safe plate

GROCERY LIST FOR
SUGGESTED MEAL
*Ingredients for the Bacon,
Egg and Cheese Sandwich

PACKAGED
*English muffin (1 needed)

PRODUCE
Any desired fruit

MEAT
*Canadian bacon
(1 slice needed)

DAIRY
*Egg (1 egg needed)
*Fat-free American or
fat-free Swiss cheese
(1 slice needed)

PANTRY
Mustard, or honey mustard—
optional
*Hot sauce—optional

Bacon, Egg, and Cheese Sandwich *3 minutes*

This baby is less than half of the price of the packaged store versions, which makes this twice as nice! For extra flavor, use your favorite condiment after the muffin is cooked. I suggest either: mustard or hot sauce. My favorite is honey mustard!

Ingredients

1 English muffin
1 medium egg
1 slice fat-free American or fat-free Swiss cheese
1 slice Canadian bacon

Instructions for entrée:

▶ If the English muffin is not presliced, then slice 1 English muffin in half horizontally (to make a sandwich).

▶ Make a shallow bowl out of the bottom of the English muffin. Place on a microwave-safe plate.

▶ Crack the egg into the center of the hollowed-out muffin. Puncture the egg yolk with a fork, and stir until well mixed.

▶ Cover with wax paper and cook in the microwave on high for 45 seconds, or until fully cooked.

▶ While the egg is cooking, place 1 slice of cheese on the other half of the muffin, and top with 1 slice of Canadian bacon.

▶ Remove the English muffin half with the cooked egg from the microwave and set aside.

▶ Cover the cheese-and-bacon half of the muffin with wax paper, place in the microwave, and cook for 15 seconds.

▶ Put the two halves together to form a sandwich.

Yield: 1 sandwich **Calories per serving:** 262 (24% fat); **Total fat:** 7 g; **Cholesterol:** 226 mg; **Carbohydrate:** 29 g; **Dietary Fiber:** 2 g; **Protein:** 19 g; **Sodium:** 965 mg **Diabetic Exchanges:** 2 starch, 2 lean meat

Instructions to prepare the suggested meal

Set the timer for 3 minutes.

3 minutes before the meal

- ▸ Prepare the Bacon Egg and Cheese Sandwich according to the directions.
- ▸ Pour the fruit juice or wash your fruit while the sandwich is cooking.

**MEAL SUGGESTION:
3 MINUTES FOR
TOTAL MEAL:**
1 (8-ounce) glass 100-percent
fruit juice or 1 piece of fruit

HELPFUL HINTS

❷ To make a shallow bowl out of the English muffin: with fingers, scoop out enough muffin to make a circle $1/4$-inch deep into one half of the muffin.

❷ Leave a $1/4$-inch rim around the edge of the English muffin.

❷ Save 30 calories per sandwich by substituting light English muffins.

Greek Egg Scramble *10 minutes*

Simplicity is the name of the game in this super-easy scramble! No need to fuss with omelet preparations when a scramble tastes this good and is so much easier to make than an omelet!

Ingredients

18 egg whites (or 2 1/4 cup Egg Beaters)
Yellow food coloring (enough drops to make it
    look like whole eggs are being used)
1/2 cup grape tomatoes
1 teaspoon Italian seasoning
1/4 cup feta cheese crumbles

Instructions for entrée:

▸ Spray a 12-inch or large nonstick saucepan with butter-flavored cooking spray and preheat over high heat.
▸ While the pan is preheating, whisk the egg whites in a medium mixing bowl. Add enough yellow food coloring to make the whites look like whole eggs.
▸ Cook the eggs in the preheated pan.
▸ Add the grape tomatoes, Italian seasoning, and feta cheese. Cook over high heat stirring constantly until well mixed and thoroughly cooked.
▸ Turn off the heat and cover until ready to eat.

Yield: 6 (1/2-cup) servings **Calories per serving:** 68 (19% fat); **Total fat:** 1 g;
Cholesterol: 6 mg; **Carbohydrate:** 2 g; **Dietary Fiber:** 0 g; **Protein:** 12 g;
Sodium: 236 mg **Diabetic Exchanges:** 2 lean meat

Instructions to prepare the suggested meal

Set the timer for 30 minutes.

30 minutes before the meal

- Preheat the oven to 375 degrees.
- Prepare the Raspberry and Cheese Crescents. Set aside, and do *not* put into the oven at this time.

20 minutes before the meal

- Make the Honeydew Chutney according to the directions. Set aside.

15 minutes before the meal

- Place the crescents in the preheated oven on the middle rack to bake for 11-12 minutes or until golden brown.
- Continue making the Ham with Honeydew Chutney, but do *not* cook the ham yet.

10 minutes before the meal

- Make the Greek Egg Scramble.

3 minutes before the meal

- Cook the ham in a carousel microwave for 2 to 3 minutes or until fully heated.
- Remove the crescents from the oven. Let cool a couple of minutes before serving.
- Once the ham is fully heated, pour the Honeydew Chutney over the cooked ham and serve along with the rest of the meal. Enjoy!

MEAL SUGGESTION:
30 MINUTES FOR TOTAL MEAL:
Ham with Honeydew Chutney (page 126)
Raspberry and Cheese Crescents (page 240)

HELPFUL HINTS:

❯ You save on fats and calories by substituting egg whites for whole eggs and adding a few drops of yellow food coloring for color.

❯ You could substitute Egg Beaters for the egg whites in this recipe.

❯ If you are not concerned about cholesterol, fats, or calories you can substitute 9 whole eggs for the 18 egg whites and leave out the yellow food coloring.

5

**SUPPLIES LIST FOR
SUGGESTED MEAL**
Microwave-safe bowl
Electric mixer
Cutting board
Knife
8 x 8-inch baking dish
Carousel microwave
Small bowl
Butter knife

**GROCERY LIST FOR
SUGGESTED MEAL**
*Ingredients for the
Reuben Egg Bake*

PACKAGE
*Seeded hearty rye bread
(2 slices needed)
*1 (14.5-ounce) can
sauerkraut
*Fat-free Thousand Island
salad dressing, optional

DAIRY
*Eggs (8 needed)
*Fat-free sour cream
(1/4 cup needed)
*Sliced Swiss cheese
(1 slice needed)

MEAT
*1 (2-ounce) package corned
beef (Carl Buddig)

PRODUCE
Tomatoes (2 needed)

PANTRY
Dried parsley
Light Miracle Whip
Fat-free Miracle Whip
Ketchup
Sweet relish
*Nonfat cooking spray

Reuben Egg Bake   *15 minutes*

If you're a fan of the Reuben sandwich you are going to love this dish.

Ingredients

8 egg whites (or 1 cup Egg Beaters)
1/4 cup fat-free sour cream
2 slices seeded hearty rye bread
1 (2-ounce) package corned beef (Carl Buddig brand)
1 (14.5-ounce) can sauerkraut
1 slice natural Swiss cheese
Thousand Island Salad dressing, preferably fat-free, optional
    (not figured into nutritional info)

Instructions for entrée:

▸ In a microwave-safe bowl beat egg whites and the fat-free sour cream with an electric mixer for 1 minute on high speed.
▸ Cut the bread into bite-sized pieces and add to the egg mixture, making sure the bread is saturated with the egg mixture.
▸ Cut the corned beef into bite-sized pieces and add to egg mixture.
▸ Open and squeeze the sauerkraut dry. Stir 1/2 cup of the sauerkraut into the egg mixture. (Save remaining sauerkraut to use in another recipe.)
▸ Spray an 8 x 8-inch glass baking dish with nonstick cooking spray. Put the egg mixture into the prepared baking dish.
▸ Cut into julienne strips 1 slice of natural Swiss cheese. Lay the strips on top of egg mixture.
▸ Cook in a carousel microwave for 5 minutes, or until the egg is fully cooked.
▸ Cut into 4 servings.

Yield: 4 servings **Calories per serving:** 129 (20% fat); **Total fat:** 3 g; **Cholesterol:** 17 mg; **Carbohydrate:** 12 g; **Dietary Fiber:** 1 g; **Protein:** 14 g; **Sodium:** 551 mg
Diabetic Exchanges: 1 starch, 1 1/2 very lean meat

Instructions to prepare the suggested meal

Set the timer for 15 minutes.

15 minutes before the meal

> ▶ Make the Reuben Egg Bake according to the directions.

5 minutes before the meal

> ▶ Make the Tomato Slices with Homemade Thousand Island Dressing according to the directions.

MEAL SUGGESTION:
15 MINUTES FOR TOTAL MEAL:
Tomato Slices with Homemade Thousand Island Salad Dressing (page 213)

HELPFUL HINTS:

❯ I recommend serving this entrée with the Tomato Slices with Homemade Thousand Island Salad Dressing recipe on page 213, but if you do not prepare the side dish, add fat-free Thousand Island salad dressing to the Reuben Egg Bake as a condiment.

❯ The easiest way to squeeze the sauerkraut dry is to pour it into a strainer and squeeze it dry with your hands.

**SUPPLIES LIST FOR
SUGGESTED MEAL**
Griddle or large frying pan
Large mixing bowl
Large saucepan or soup pan
Jelly-roll pan
Small mixing bowl
Cutting board

**GROCERY LIST FOR
SUGGESTED MEAL**
*Ingredients for the Potato
Pancakes with Sour Cream
and Chives Topping*

PRODUCE
*Fresh chives (1/4 cup
fresh or 2 tablespoon
dried chives needed)
Sweet onion (2 tablespoons
finely chopped needed)

MEATS
1 (16-ounce) package baked
sliced ham

DAIRY
*Eggs (3 needed)
*Fat-free sour cream
(1 cup needed)
1 (8-ounce) package fat-free
cream cheese
Fat-free skim milk
(3/4 cup needed)

PACKAGED
*1(15-ounce) can diced
potatoes
*Heart Smart Bisquick
reduced-fat baking mix
(11/2 cups needed)
*Instant mashed potato flakes
(1/2 cup needed)

FROZEN
1 (12-ounce) container frozen
concentrated orange juice

*Grocery list continued
on next page*

Potato Pancakes with Sour Cream and Chives Topping *15 Minutes*

Sour cream and chives top thick pancakes loaded with hearty chunks of potatoes. The complete suggested meal could be served for breakfast, brunch, or dinner.

Ingredients

1 (15-ounce) can diced potatoes, undrained
$1^1/2$ cups Heart Smart Bisquick reduced-fat baking mix
3 egg whites (or 6 tablespoons Egg Beaters)
$1/2$ cup instant mashed potato flakes
$3/4$ cup fat-free milk
1 cup fat-free sour cream
$1/4$ cup chopped fresh chives

Instructions for entrée:

- Preheat on high heat a griddle or large frying pan.
- In a large mixing bowl, stir the undrained can of diced potatoes, Bisquick, egg whites, instant mashed potato flakes, and fat-free milk until well blended.
- Generously spray the griddle or large preheated frying pan with fat-free cooking spray.
- Drop batter by $1/2$ cups onto the preheated griddle or frying pan. Spread the batter out to make a $4^1/2$-inch to 5-inch in diameter pancake.
- Cook until the bottom is golden brown, flip, and cook the other side until it is golden brown.
- Keep an eye on the pancakes, but while they are cooking, make the sour cream and chives topping. In a small bowl mix the fat-free sour cream and chives.
- When the pancakes are done cooking, top each pancake with 2 tablespoons of the sour cream and chive mixture.
- If you have leftover chives, sprinkle them on top of the sour cream mixture if desired.

Yield: 8 (1 pancake) servings; 8 (2 tablespoon) servings of sour cream and chives topping; **Calories per serving:** 161 (9% fat); **Total fat:** 2 g; **Cholesterol:** 5 mg; **Carbohydrate:** 30 g; **Dietary Fiber:** 2 g; **Protein:** 6 g; **Sodium:** 425 mg **Diabetic Exchanges:** 2 starch

Instructions to prepare the suggested meal

Set the timer for 30 minutes.

30 minutes before the meal

- Preheat the oven to 350 degrees.
- Make the Ham and Onion Cheese Rollups according to the directions.

15 minutes before the meal

- Make the Citrus Cider according to the directions.

10 minutes before the meal

- Make the Potato Pancakes according to the directions.

1 minute before meal

- Remove the Ham and Onion Cheese Rollups from the oven and serve the meal.

PANTRY
Ground allspice
Splenda Brown Sugar Blend
(2 tablespoons needed)
Ground cinnamon
Dried parsley
*Butter-flavored cooking spray

MEAL SUGGESTION:
30 MINUTES FOR
TOTAL MEAL:
Ham and Onion Cheese
Rollups (page 58)
Citrus Cider (page 289)

HELPFUL HINTS:

❷ If you don't have fresh chives, use 2 tablespoons of dried chives instead.

❷ Butter-flavored cooking spray has a tendency to scorch the pancakes when cooked on high heat. Use regular cooking spray for this recipe to keep your pancakes from burning.

**SUPPLIES LIST FOR
SUGGESTED MEAL OVEN**
Medium-size mixing bowl
Griddle
Cutting Board
Jelly-roll pan
Large microwavable (4-cup)
measuring cup or pitcher
Whisk
Microwave oven
Timer

**GROCERY LIST FOR
SUGGESTED MEAL**
*Ingredients for the
Hawaiian French Toast*

MEATS
1 (16-ounce) package 97%
fat-free honey-ham

DAIRY
*Fat-free vanilla yogurt
(1/3 cup needed)
* Eggs (5 needed)
1 (8-ounce) package fat-free
cream cheese
Fat-free skim milk
(4 cups needed)

PACKAGED
*Shredded coconut
(3 tablespoons needed total)
*1 (16-ounce) package King's
Hawaiian Sweet bread
(1/2 package needed)
1 (8-ounce) can pineapple
tidbits
Sugar-free butter-flavored
syrup (1/2 cup needed)

PANTRY
*Coconut extract
*Nonstick cooking spray
Splenda granular
Banana extract

Hawaiian French Toast *15 minutes*

This is one of my favorite French toast recipes!

Ingredients

1/3 cup fat-free vanilla yogurt
1/2 teaspoon coconut extract
5 egg whites
2 tablespoons firmly packed shredded coconut
1/2 of 1 (16-ounce) package King's Hawaiian Sweet bread

Instructions

▶ Preheat the griddle to high.
▶ In a medium mixing bowl, whisk together the yogurt, coconut extract, egg whites, and coconut until well blended. Set aside.
▶ Cut the King's Hawaiian Sweet bread in half. Save the other half for use at another time.
▶ Cut the half loaf of bread into 8 (1/2-inch thick) palm-size slices.
▶ Dip the bread slices in the egg mixture, coating both sides of the bread.
▶ Spray the preheated griddle with nonstick cooking spray.
▶ Cook the slices on the prepared griddle until golden brown on both sides.

Yield: 4 (2-piece) servings **Calories per serving:** 203 (19% fat); **Total fat:** 4 g; **Cholesterol:** 8 mg; **Carbohydrate:** 30 g; **Dietary Fiber:** 1 g; **Protein:** 10 g; **Sodium:** 347 mg **Diabetic Exchanges:** 2 starch, 1/2 lean meat

---

Instructions to prepare the suggested meal

Set the timer for 30 minutes.

30 minutes before the meal
- ▸ Preheat the oven to 350 degrees.
- ▸ Begin making the Pineapple Ham Rollups according to the directions.

15 minutes before the meal
- ▸ Preheat the griddle to high.
- ▸ Make the Hawaiian French Toast according to the directions.

7 minutes before dinner
- ▸ While the French toast is cooking, make the Banana Cream Steamers according to the directions.
- ▸ Keep an eye on the French toast, and turn over to cook the other side.

2 minutes before the meal
- ▸ Pour the Banana Cream Steamers into coffee cups.
- ▸ Make coconut syrup according to the directions.
- ▸ Take the Pineapple Ham stacks out of oven.

Just before serving
- ▸ Plate the Hawaiian French Toast and Pineapple Ham Stacks.

BREAKFAST AND BRUNCH

MEAL SUGGESTION: 20 MINUTES FOR TOTAL MEAL:
Pineapple Ham Stacks (page 62)
Coconut Syrup (sugar-free) (page 220)
Banana Cream Steamer (page 293)

HELPFUL HINT:

❷ Discard any leftover egg mixture after dipping the bread

Hawaiian Ham Breakfast Bake *15 minutes*

Tender chunks of Hawaiian bread are adorned with sweet pineapple and ham.

Ingredients

1 (20-ounce) can pineapple chunks, drained, juices reserved for punch
4 egg whites
1 teaspoon coconut extract
8 slices from 1 (16-ounce) package 97% fat-free baked ham
1/2 of 1 (16-ounce) package King's Hawaiian Sweet bread

Instructions

‣ Drain 1 cup of juice from the can of pineapple. If desired, save to use it in the punch recipe for the suggested meal.
‣ In a large mixing bowl, stir together the egg whites, coconut extract, and the pineapple chunks. Set aside.
‣ Cut 8 slices of ham into bite-size pieces. Save the remaining ham for another recipe.
‣ Cut half of the King's Hawaiian Sweet bread into 1-inch chunks. Save the other half for another recipe.
‣ Stir the ham and bread into the egg and pineapple chunks. This is easiest to do with your hands, making sure the bread is completely saturated with the egg mixture.
‣ Spray a 2-quart round glass microwaveable dish with nonstick cooking spray.
‣ Place the egg mixture in the glass dish.
‣ Cover with wax paper and cook in a carousel microwave for 5 minutes.

Yield: 4 (1 1/4-cup) servings **Calories per serving:** 312 (16% fat); **Total fat:** 6 g; **Cholesterol:** 29 mg; **Carbohydrate:** 44 g; **Dietary Fiber:** 2 g; **Protein:** 20 g; **Sodium:** 1059 mg **Diabetic Exchanges:** 2 starch, 1 fruit, 2 lean meat

---

Instructions to prepare the suggested meal

Set the timer for 15 minutes.

15 minutes before the meal

▸ Make the Hawaiian Ham Breakfast Bake according to the directions.

10 minutes before the meal

▸ Begin making the Polynesian Fruit Salad according to the directions.

2 minutes before the meal

▸ Begin making the Fruit Punch according to the directions.

MEAL SUGGESTION:
15 MINUTES FOR TOTAL MEAL:
Tropical Fruit Punch
(page 292)
Polynesian Fruit Salad
(page 81)

HELPFUL HINT:

❷ Have all of your fruit juices for the entire suggested meal already pre-chilled by storing the canned fruits in the refrigerator.

**SUPPLIES LIST FOR
SUGGESTED MEAL**
Timer
12-inch nonstick oven-safe
saucepan with lid
Large bowl
Cutting board
Large microwave-safe (4-
cup) measuring cup
or pitcher
6 champagne glasses or
small glasses

**GROCERY LIST FOR
SUGGESTED MEAL**
*Ingredients for Italian
Breakfast Pizza*

PRODUCE
3 apples

MEAT
*1 package turkey pepperoni
(19 slices needed)

DAIRY
*Eggs (6 needed)
*1 (8-ounce) package fat-
free shredded mozzarella
cheese (1 cup needed)

PACKAGED
*1 (6-ounce) box Italian
stuffing mix
*1 (8-ounce) can tomato
sauce
1 (33.8 fl. ounce) bottle
virgin Bloody Mary mix

PANTRY
*Italian seasoning
*Nonfat cooking spray

Italian Breakfast Pizza *20 minutes*

For those of us who love Italian foods, the comfort of a relaxing Italian-inspired breakfast is only 20 minutes away.

Ingredients

1/2 cup plus 2 tablespoons water
1 (6-ounce) box of Italian stuffing mix
6 large eggs
2 1/2 teaspoons Italian seasoning, divided
19 slices turkey pepperoni
1 (8-ounce) can tomato sauce
1 cup fat-free shredded mozzarella cheese

Instructions *for entrée:*

▸ Preheat the oven to 400 degrees.
▸ Spray a 12-inch nonstick, oven-safe saucepan with nonfat cooking spray.
▸ Turn heat on high. Place 1/2 cup water in the pan; stir in the Italian stuffing mix. (I used Stove Top brand.)
▸ Reduce heat to medium. With a pancake turner, press the stuffing into the pan to form a crust.
▸ Cover and continue cooking over medium heat while preparing the egg mixture.
▸ In a large bowl mix the large eggs with 2 tablespoons water and 1 teaspoon Italian seasoning until well blended.
▸ Pour the egg mixture on top of the stuffing.
▸ Place 19 slices of turkey pepperoni on top of the egg and stuffing mixture.
▸ Cover and cook over medium heat for 5 minutes or until the eggs are dry on top.
▸ Remove from the heat and spread 3/4 of the can of tomato sauce over the egg and stuffing mixture, and then sprinkle with 1 teaspoon Italian seasoning.
▸ Sprinkle the top of the tomato sauce with 1 cup fat-free shredded mozzarella cheese and the remaining 1/2 teaspoon Italian seasoning.
▸ Generously spray the cheese with nonfat cooking spray.
▸ Place the pan in the preheated oven on the top rack for 1 minute or until cheese is melted.

Yield: 6 servings (1/6 of pan) **Calories per serving:** 234 (26% fat); **Total fat:** 7 g; **Cholesterol:** 224 mg; **Carbohydrate:** 25 g; **Dietary Fiber:** 1 g; **Protein:** 18 g; **Sodium:** 976 mg **Diabetic Exchanges:** 1½ starch, 2 lean meat

Instructions to prepare the suggested meal

Set the timer for 20 minutes.

20 minutes before the meal

- ‣ Preheat the oven to 400 degrees.
- ‣ Begin making the Italian Breakfast Pizza according to the directions to the point of cooking for 5 minutes in the pan or until the eggs are fully cooked.

5 minutes before the meal

- ‣ Make the warm Italian Virgin Mary according to the directions.

3 minutes before the meal

- ‣ Continue making the Italian Breakfast Pizza according to the directions.

MEAL SUGGESTION: 20 MINUTES FOR TOTAL MEAL:
Apple Slices
Warm Italian Virgin Mary
(page 282)

SUPPLIES LIST FOR
SUGGESTED MEAL
2 12-inch or larger nonstick
saucepans with lids
Cutting board
Knife
Mixing bowl
Electric mixer
Microwave-safe glass
measuring cup or pitcher

GROCERY LIST FOR
SUGGESTED MEAL
*Ingredients for the Onion
and Rye Skillet Egg Bake*

PACKAGE
*Rye bread with seeds
(4 slices needed)
*French-fried onions
(3 tablespoons needed)
1 (12-ounce) can roast beef
(I used Hormel)
2 (14.5-ounce) cans whole
green beans
2 (15-ounce) cans sliced
new potatoes
1 (7-ounce) can mushroom
stems and pieces
1 jar diced pimentos
1 jar minced garlic
1 (33.8 fl. ounce) bottle virgin
Bloody Mary mix

DAIRY
*Eggs (12 needed)
*Fat-free cottage cheese
(1/2 cup needed)

PRODUCE
*1 medium sweet
yellow onion
*1 bunch fresh green onions
(1 tablespoon needed)

PANTRY
*Onion salt
*Buttered flavored
cooking spray
Steak seasoning

Onion and Rye Skillet Egg Bake *20 minutes*

Even people who aren't egg fans like this meal! The light onion flavor united with the rye makes for an elegant brunch combination. It is so satisfying and filling that you could serve it for dinner. My neighbor says she thinks it'd be good cut into smaller servings for an upscale appetizer.

Ingredients

1 medium sweet yellow onion
4 slices of Rye bread with seeds
12 egg whites (or 1 1/2 cup Egg Beaters)
1/2 teaspoon onion salt
1/2 cup fat-free cottage cheese
1 tablespoon finely chopped green onion tops
3 tablespoons French fried onions

Instructions for entrée:

▸ Preheat a 12-inch or larger nonstick saucepan over high heat.
▸ While pan is preheating, chop 1 medium sweet yellow onion onto make 1 cup.
▸ Spray the preheated pan with butter-flavored nonfat. Add the chopped onions, spray with butter-flavored cooking spray again and brown.
▸ While onions are browning, lay 4 slices Rye bread with seeds on a cutting board. Spray both sides of bread with butter-flavored cooking spray. Sprinkle 1/2 teaspoon of onion salt evenly over one side of bread slices.
▸ Stack the bread and cut into bite-sized chunks.
▸ Over medium heat add the bread to the browned onions and spray with butter-flavored spray. Mix well.
▸ In a large mixing bowl, beat 12 egg whites, 1/2 teaspoon onion salt, and cottage cheese until well mixed.
▸ With a spatula move the onions and bread to the side of the pan. Spray the bottom of the pan with butter-flavored spray. Pour the egg mixture into the pan making sure it covers all of the ingredients. Spread the ingredients evenly in the pan.
▸ Sprinkle green onions on top.
▸ Cover and cook over medium heat.

- While the eggs are cooking, place the French-fried onions in a small bowl and crush them into small pieces with your thumbs.
- When the eggs are done cooking, sprinkle with the crushed onions.
- Transfer the Onion and Rye Skillet Egg Bake to a serving platter; then cut into quarters and serve.

Yield: 4 (1/4 size) servings **Calories per serving:** 179 (12% fat); **Total fat:** 2 g; **Cholesterol:** 1 mg; **Carbohydrate:** 21 g; **Dietary Fiber:** 3 g; **Protein:** 17 g; **Sodium:** 732 mg **Diabetic Exchanges:** 1 1/2 starch, 2 medium-fat meat

---

Instructions to prepare the suggested meal

Set the timer for 30 minutes

30 minutes before the meal
- Make the Onion Rye Skillet Egg Bake according to the directions.

15 minutes before the meal
- While the Onion Rye Skillet Egg Bake is cooking, begin making the Beefy Green Beans, according to the directions.
- While the Beefy Green Beans and Potatoes are cooking, make the Warm Italian Virgin Mary according to the directions.

10 minutes before the meal
- Remove the Onion Rye Skillet Egg Bake from the stove. Cover and set on a trivet. The Onion Rye Skillet Egg Bake will stay warm in the pan.
- Finish cooking the Beefy Green Beans and Potatoes and Warm Italian Virgin Mary.

BREAKFAST AND BRUNCH

MEAL SUGGESTION: 30 MINUTES FOR TOTAL MEAL:
Beefy Green Beans and Potatoes (page 160)
Warm Italian Virgin Mary (page 282)

HELPFUL HINTS:

❷ You will save more than 300 milligrams of cholesterol by using only egg whites, plus oodles of calories and fats! You can also substitute liquid egg substitute, but it is usually more expensive than using only the egg whites.

❷ If you prefer to use the entire egg, then substitute 6 whole eggs for the 12 egg whites in this recipe.

❷ Add a few drops of yellow food coloring to the egg whites (before beating them) to make the color look like you used whole eggs.

**SUPPLIES LIST FOR
SUGGESTED MEAL**
Cutting board
Knife
Cookie sheet
Jelly-roll pan
Round cookie cutter, biscuit
cutter, or glass

**GROCERY LIST FOR
SUGGESTED MEAL**
*Ingredients for the
Sunshine in a Pond*

PACKAGE
Splenda Brown Sugar Blend
Ground allspice

DAIRY
*Eggs (6 needed)

PRODUCE
3 navel oranges

BREADS/BAKERY
Loaf light bread
(12 slices needed)

PANTRY
*Buttered flavored cooking
spray

Sunshine in a Pond *20 minutes*

*Here's a fun way to get children involved in making and eating a healthy breakfast!
Have the children use a 2-inch cookie cutter to cut the circles out of the centers of
six slices of bread.*

Ingredients

12 slices light bread
6 eggs

Instructions for entrée:

▶ Place the oven rack on the lowest shelf of the oven. Preheat the oven to 400
degrees.
▶ Line a jelly-roll pan with aluminum foil for easier cleanup.
▶ Spray both sides of 12 slices of light bread with butter-flavored cooking spray.
▶ Place 6 slices of the bread on the lined jelly-roll pan.
▶ Using a biscuit or cookie cutter, cut a circle out of the center of the other
slices and place the slices on top of the 6 slices already on the pan, to make
sandwiches.
▶ Break one egg on top of each cutout bread.
▶ Sprinkle the tops of the eggs with salt and pepper to taste.
▶ Place the jelly-roll pan into the oven. Bake for 7–10 minutes, until the eggs are
done to your liking.

Yield: 6 (1 piece) servings **Calories per serving:** 152 (30% fat); **Total fat:** 5 g;
Cholesterol: 212 mg; **Carbohydrate:** 18 g; **Dietary Fiber:** 7 g; **Protein:** 10 g;
Sodium: 300 mg **Diabetic Exchanges:** 1 starch, 1 medium-fat meat

---

Instructions to prepare the suggested meal

Set the timer for 30 minutes.

30 minutes before the meal

▶ Place one oven rack on the top shelf of the oven, and the other rack on the
bottom shelf of the oven. Preheat the oven to 400 degrees.
▶ Prepare the Spiced Baked Oranges according to the directions. Do not place
in the oven at this time.

MEAL SUGGESTION:
30 MINUTES FOR
TOTAL MEAL:
Spiced Baked Oranges
(page 225)

20 minutes before the meal

> ‣ Make the Sunshine in a Pond according to the directions.
> ‣ Place the Spiced Baked Oranges into the oven on the top rack. Bake according to the directions.

10 minutes before the meal

> ‣ Place the Sunshine in a Pond in the oven on the bottom rack. Bake according to the directions.

HELPFUL HINTS:

❷ If you don't have a biscuit or cookie cutter, a glass works perfectly well also.

❷ Don't throw out those bread centers! Save them in a freezer-safe container, and use them for croutons or stuffing

Sausage Gravy over Biscuits *20 minutes*

This recipe will feed a whole family for less than the cost of one serving at a restaurant! (Plus this is a lot lower in fat and calories.)

Ingredients

1 (16-ounce) package turkey breakfast sausage
    (Honeysuckle White brand)
1 (7.5-ounce) can buttermilk biscuits
2½ cups fat-free milk
2 tablespoons cornstarch
⅛ teaspoon ground pepper

Instructions for entrée:

▸ Place the oven rack in the middle of the oven. Preheat the oven to 400 degrees.
▸ Preheat a large 12-inch nonstick saucepan over high heat. Brown and crumble the sausage.
▸ While the meat is browning, place the biscuits on a cookie sheet. Set aside.
▸ Once the meat is browned and crumbled, reduce the heat to medium.
▸ In a small bowl add the fat-free milk and cornstarch. Stir together with a fork until the cornstarch is completely dissolved.
▸ Pour into the browned sausage and stir well.
▸ Add the ground pepper, stir well, and let simmer, stirring occasionally.
▸ Place the biscuits in the the oven and bake for 10-12 minutes or until golden brown.
▸ Reduce heat to medium under the gravy, cover and stir occasionally until the biscuits are done.

Yield: 5 (2/3 cup over 2 biscuits) servings **Calories per serving:** 299 (28% fat);
Total fat: 8 g; **Cholesterol:** 47 mg; **Carbohydrate:** 28 g; **Dietary Fiber:** 1 g;
Protein: 21 g; **Sodium:** 1026 mg **Diabetic Exchanges:** 1½ starch, ½ fat-free milk,
2 lean meat

Instructions to prepare meal:

Set the timer for 20 minutes.

20 minutes before the meal

- Preheat the oven to 400 degrees.
- Make the sausage gravy.
- Prepare the biscuits to bake. Set them aside. Do not bake yet.
- Continue making the sausage gravy.

12 minutes before the meal

- Bake the biscuits in the preheated oven.
- While the biscuits are baking and the gravy is thickening, occasionally stir the gravy.
- Make your coffee or tea.
- Slice your fresh oranges.

2 minutes before the meal

- Remove the biscuits from the oven and serve with the sausage gravy.

BREAKFAST AND BRUNCH

MEAL SUGGESTION: 20 MINUTES FOR TOTAL MEAL:
Sliced oranges
(1 orange per person)
Coffee or tea

**SUPPLIES LIST FOR
SUGGESTED MEAL**
Large mixing bowl
8 x 8-inch baking dish
Microwave oven

**GROCERY LIST FOR
SUGGESTED MEAL**
*Ingredients for the White
Cheese Strata*

PACKAGE
*Light reduced-calorie white
bread (8 slices needed)
Cherry cola
Sugar-free peach
drink mix
Cinnamon red-hot candies

DAIRY
*1 dozen eggs
*Fat-free skim milk
(1/4 cup needed)
*1 (8-ounce) package
shredded fat-free
mozzarella cheese
*Shredded parmesan cheese
(1/3 cup needed)

MEAT
8 (2-ounce) slices lean
cooked ham steaks

PRODUCE
Grapefruit or oranges
(1 per person)

PANTRY
*Ground black pepper
Allspice
Splenda Brown Sugar Blend
*Buttered flavored
cooking spray

White Cheese Strata *20 minutes*

This is a special treat for cheese lovers. They will never know this recipe is low-fat.

Ingredients

12 eggs, divided
1/4 cup fat-free skim milk
8 slices light reduced-calorie white bread
1 (8-ounce) package shredded fat-free mozzarella cheese
1/3 cup shredded parmesan cheese
Ground black pepper

Instructions for entrée:

▸ Place oven racks in the middle of the oven and preheat the oven to 350 degrees.
▸ In a large mixing bowl, beat together with an electric mixer 4 whole eggs, 8 egg whites*, and the fat-free skim milk.
▸ Generously spray an 8 x 8-inch baking dish with butter-flavored cooking spray.
▸ Pour half of the egg mixture in the bottom of the pan.
▸ Place 4 slices of bread on top of the egg mixture and press the bread into the egg mixture.
▸ Place the mozzarella cheese on top of bread and egg.
▸ Place 4 more slices of bread on top of the cheese.
▸ Pour the remaining egg mixture on top of the bread.
▸ Place the shredded parmesan cheese on top of the egg mixture.
▸ Sprinkle lightly with ground black pepper.
▸ Bake in the oven for 17 minutes.
▸ Remove from the oven and place in microwave for 2 minutes to finish cooking.

Yield: 4 servings (using whole eggs and egg whites) **Calories per serving:** 320 (21% fat); **Total fat:** 8 g; **Cholesterol:** 226 mg; **Carbohydrate:** 26 g; **Dietary Fiber:** 6 g; **Protein:** 38 g; **Sodium:** 1184 mg **Diabetic Exchanges:** 2 starch, 5 lean meat

Instructions to prepare the suggested meal

Set the timer for 30 minutes.

30 minutes before the meal

▸ Place the oven racks in the middle of the oven, and preheat the oven to 350 degrees.
▸ Begin making the White Cheese Strata according to the directions.

20 minutes before the meal

▸ Place the White Cheese Strata in the oven.
▸ Make the Spiced Ham Steaks according to the directions.

15 minutes before the meal

▸ Place the Spiced Ham Steaks in the oven to bake.
▸ Make the Cinnamon and Spice Candied Peach Punch according to the directions. Serve warm.

3 minutes before the meal

▸ Remove the strata from the oven, and finish cooking in the microwave for 2 minutes.
▸ Cut the grapefruits (or oranges) into wedges and place them on a plate to serve with the meal.
▸ Remove the ham steaks from oven.

<hr/>

BREAKFAST AND BRUNCH

MEAL SUGGESTION: 30 MINUTES FOR TOTAL MEAL:
Spiced Ham Steaks (page 140)
Fresh Grapefruit or Orange Wedges
Cinnamon and Spice Candied Peach Punch (page 287)

HELPFUL HINTS:

❯ This strata will rise and get puffy in the microwave. Once removed from the oven, it will deflate.

❯ As a tasty garnish place wedges of grapefruit on the sides of the plates.

❯ When making this recipe with the 4 whole eggs, you can use 1 cup Egg Beaters as a substitute for the egg whites.

❯ I like the consistency the egg yolks gave this recipe, but it adds a lot of cholesterol. To reduce the cholesterol substitute 2 cups of Egg Beaters for the whole eggs and egg whites.

**SUPPLIES LIST FOR
SUGGESTED MEAL**
Large mixing bowl
Whisk
8 x 8-inch baking dish
Cutting board
Knife
Carousel microwave
4-quart nonstick saucepan

**GROCERY LIST FOR
SUGGESTED MEAL**
*Ingredients for the Ham
and Cheese Breakfast Bake

PACKAGE
*Light wheat bread
(8 slices needed)
2 (15-ounce) cans
no-sugar-added chunky
mixed fruits
1 (15-ounce) can mandarin
oranges in light syrup
Sugar-free spiced cider
apple flavor drink mix
(10 pouches per box)
Maraschino cherries

DAIRY
*Eggs (9 needed)
*Fat-free skim milk
* 1 (8-ounce) package
shredded fat-free cheddar
cheese (1½ cups needed)

MEAT
*1 (16-ounce) package honey
ham lunch meat slices
(8 slices needed)

PANTRY
*Yellow mustard
* Buttered-flavored
cooking spray

Ham and Cheese
Breakfast Bake *20 minutes*

You won't want to limit this entrée to only breakfasts and brunch!

Ingredients

9 eggs
½ cup fat-free skim milk
1 teaspoon yellow mustard
8 slices light wheat bread
½ pound 97% fat-free sliced honey ham (8 slices)
1½ cups shredded fat-free cheddar cheese (divided)

Instructions for entrée:

▸ In a large mixing bowl, whisk 3 whole eggs, 6 egg whites, fat-free skim milk, and yellow mustard until well blended.
▸ Generously spray an 8 x 8-inch baking dish with butter-flavored cooking spray. Set aside.
▸ Cut the bread and ham into bite-size pieces.
▸ Add the bread pieces, ham pieces, and 1 cup of the cheese to the egg mixture.
▸ Pour into the prepared 8 x 8 inch baking dish.
▸ Put into a carousel microwave oven and cook for 5 minutes.
▸ Remove from the microwave, sprinkle the remaining ½ cup of cheese on top of the casserole, and spray the top of the cheese with butter-flavored cooking spray.
▸ Cook in the microwave for an additional 3 minutes, or until it no longer looks wet.

Yield: 6 servings **Calories per serving:** 209 (20% fat); **Total fat:** 5 g; **Cholesterol:** 122 mg; **Carbohydrate:** 16 g; **Dietary Fiber:** 5 g; **Protein:** 27 g; **Sodium:** 890 mg
Diabetic Exchanges: 1 starch, 3½ very lean meat

Instructions to prepare the suggested meal

Set the timer for 20 minutes.

20 minutes before the meal

▸ Begin preparing the Ham and Cheese Breakfast Bake according to the directions.

10 minutes before the meal

▸ Make the Warm Fruit Cocktail according to the directions.

MEAL SUGGESTION: 20 MINUTES FOR TOTAL MEAL:
Warm Fruit Cocktail (page 210)

HELPFUL HINT:

❯ To save time, stack the bread up before cutting it into bite-size pieces.

**SUPPLIES LIST FOR
SUGGESTED MEAL**
1 medium mixing bowl
1 (8 x 8-inch) glass
baking dish
4 juice glasses
Wax paper
Microwave oven
Serving plate
Toothpicks
Timer

**GROCERY LIST FOR THE
SUGGESTED MEAL**
*Ingredients for the
Upside-Down French Toast
and Ham Bake*

MEATS
*1 (16-ounce) package
97% fat-free honey ham
(4 slices needed)

DAIRY
*Light butter
(2 tablespoons needed)
* Eggs (4 needed)
*Fat-free skim milk
(2 tablespoons needed)

PACKAGED
*Light white bread
(8 slices needed)
24 ounces diet cranberry
juice
Maraschino cherries

PANTRY
Splenda Brown Sugar Blend
(1/4 cup plus -2 tablespoons
needed)
Ground cinnamon
Sugar-free hazelnut coffee
creamer

Upside-Down French Toast and Ham Bake *20 minutes*

A combination of sweet roll, French toast, and breakfast bake all delightfully combined in one! You won't need syrup—this unique dish makes its own.

Ingredients

2 tablespoons light butter
1/4 cup plus 2 tablespoons Splenda Brown Sugar Blend, divided
1 teaspoon ground cinnamon plus a dash, divided
4 egg whites
2 tablespoons fat-free skim milk
8 slices light white bread, divided
4 slices of 97% fat-free honey ham

Instructions for entrée:

▸ In the bottom of an 8 x 8-inch glass baking dish, cook the light butter in the microwave for a few seconds until it is melted.
▸ Use a fork to mix the melted butter, 1/4 cup Splenda Brown Sugar Blend, and 1/2 teaspoon cinnamon until well combined.
▸ Spread the mixture on the bottom of the glass baking dish. Set aside.
▸ In a medium mixing bowl, whisk together the egg whites, the remaining 1/2 teaspoon ground cinnamon, 1 tablespoon Splenda Brown Sugar Blend, and the milk.
▸ Lightly dip 4 slices of light white bread in the egg mixture and place in the prepared baking dish.
▸ Place 4 slices of 97% fat-free honey ham on top of the bread. The ham slices will overlap.
▸ Lightly dip 4 additional slices of light white bread in the egg mixture and place them on top of the ham. You will use the entire egg mixture.
▸ Sprinkle 1 tablespoon Splenda Brown Sugar Blend on top of the dipped bread.
▸ Lightly sprinkle ground cinnamon on top.
▸ Cover with waxed paper and cook in a carousel microwave for 5 minutes.
▸ Remove from the microwave and let rest for 2 minutes before serving.
▸ Invert onto a serving plate.
▸ Cut into 4 servings.

Yield: 4 servings **Calories per serving:** 249 (20% fat); **Total fat:** 5 g; **Cholesterol:** 18 mg; **Carbohydrate:** 37 g; **Dietary Fiber:** 5 g; **Protein:** 13 g; **Sodium:** 670 mg **Diabetic Exchanges:** 2¹/₂ starch, 1¹/₂ lean meat

Instructions to prepare the suggested meal

Set the timer for 20 minutes.

20 minutes before the meal

> ▸ Make the the French Toast and Ham Bake according to the directions.

5 minutes before the meal

> ▸ While the French toast is cooking, make the Cranberry Cream Cocktails according to the directions.

MEAL SUGGESTION: 20 MINUTES FOR TOTAL MEAL: Cranberry Cream Cocktails (page 290)

HELPFUL HINTS:

❷ When the bread is slightly wet with the egg mixture it will easily squeeze together to fit inside the prepared dish without overlapping.

❷ To invert onto the serving plate: place a serving plate upside-down on top of the baking dish. Hold the baking dish and serving plate firmly together. Turn over so the upside down French Toast and Ham Bake inverts from the baking dish onto the serving plate. The juices of the French toast will ooze down the sides.

SUPPLIES LIST FOR
SUGGESTED MEAL
2-quart pitcher
Cutting board
Large mixing bowl
Whisk
2-quart glass microwavable
casserole dish
Timer

GROCERY LIST FOR THE
SUGGESTED MEAL
*Ingredients for the
Smoked Sausage and
Cheddar Egg Bake

MEATS
1 (14-ounce) package Healthy
Ones skinless smoked
sausage

DAIRY
*Eggs (7 needed)
*Fat-free skim milk
(1/3 cup needed)
*1 (8-ounce) package fat-free
shredded cheddar cheese

FROZEN
1 (12-ounce) can frozen
concentrated lemonade
1 (16-ounce) bag frozen
blueberries

PACKAGED
*1 (16-ounce) loaf of French
bread (1/2 loaf needed)

PANTRY
*Dried chives
*Nonstick cooking spray
Splenda granular

Smoked Sausage and Cheddar Egg Bake *20 minutes*

Warm, thick chunks of French bread smothered with melted cheddar cheese and smoked sausage deliver a gratifying meal.

Ingredients

7 eggs
1/3 cup fat-free skim milk
1 tablespoon dried chives
1 (8-ounce) package fat-free shredded cheddar cheese, divided
1 (14-ounce) package Healthy Ones skinless smoked sausage
1 (16-ounce) loaf of French bread (use only half)

Instructions for entrée:

- In a large mixing bowl, whisk together 3 whole eggs, 4 egg whites, milk, dried chives, and 1 1/2 cups cheese until well blended. Set aside. Reserve the remaining 1/2 cup cheese to use later.
- Cut the sausage into thin, bite-sized pieces and add to the egg mix.
- Cut half of a 16-ounce loaf of French bread into 1-inch-thick chunks. Add to the egg mixture. Save the other half of the loaf for another recipe.
- Using your hands mix all the ingredients together until the bread is saturated with the egg and cheese mixture.
- Generously spray a 2-quart glass microwavable casserole dish with nonstick cooking spray.
- Pour the egg and bread mixture into the casserole dish. Sprinkle the reserved 1/2 cup cheese on top.
- Spray the top of the casserole with nonstick cooking spray.
- Cover with wax paper and cook in the microwave for 6 minutes or until the egg is no longer wet looking.

Yield: 6 (1-cup) servings **Calories per serving:** 300 (15% fat); **Total fat:** 5 g; **Cholesterol:** 136 mg; **Carbohydrate:** 32 g; **Dietary Fiber:** 1 g; **Protein:** 30 g; **Sodium:** 1142 mg **Diabetic Exchanges**: 2 starch, 3 1/2 very lean meat

Instructions to prepare the suggested meal

Set the timer for 20 minutes.

20 minutes before the meal

▸ Make the Smoked Sausage and Cheddar Egg Bake according to the directions.

5 minutes before the meal

▸ Make the Blueberry Lemonade according to the directions.

**MEAL SUGGESTION:
20 MINUTES FOR
TOTAL MEAL:**
Blueberry Lemonade
(page 291)

HELPFUL HINT:

❷ We discarded some of the yolks in this recipe to lower the fat content.

SUPPLIES LIST FOR
SUGGESTED MEAL
2 medium mixing bowls
1 8 x 8-inch microwave-safe
baking dish
1 coffee maker
Cutting board

GROCERY LIST FOR
SUGGESTED MEAL
*Ingredients for the Cheesy
Mushroom Bake

PACKAGE
*1 (10.34- ounce) can
Campbell's Healthy Request
Cream of Mushroom Soup
*1 (16-ounce) bottle fat-free
ranch salad dressing
(1/2 cup needed)
1 (16-ounce) bottle fat-free
Italian salad dressing
(1/4 cup needed)
*1 (11.5-ounce) package
fat-free flour tortillas
(10 tortillas per package,
only 9 used)
1 box of 10 packages Diet
Hot Cocoa Mix (Swiss Miss
Sensible Sweets)
1 bag red hot cinnamon
candies (1/4 cup needed)

DAIRY
*1 (8-ounce) package
shredded fat-free
mozzarella cheese
*Eggs (2 needed)
*Finely shredded
Parmesan cheese
(2 tablespoons needed)

PRODUCE
*1 (8-ounce) package
sliced fresh mushrooms
2 large Bartlett pears
1 large red delicious apple

Grocery list continued
on next page

Cheesy Mushroom Bake *25 minutes*

Ideal for breakfast, brunch, or lunch, yet filling and satisfying enough for dinner!

Ingredients

1 (8-ounce) package shredded fat-free mozzarella cheese, divided
1 (10.34-ounce) can Campbell's Healthy Request Cream of
   Mushroom Soup
1/2 cup fat-free ranch salad dressing
2 egg whites (or 1/4 cup Egg Beaters)
1 (11.5-ounce) package flour tortillas
1 (8-ounce) package sliced fresh mushrooms
2 tablespoons finely shredded parmesan cheese

Instructions for entrée:

▸ Set aside 1/2 cup of the mozzarella cheese to use later.
▸ In a medium-size mixing bowl, stir together the remaining mozzarella with the cream of mushroom soup, salad dressing, and egg whites until well mixed. Set aside.
▸ Spray the bottom of an 8 x 8 inch baking dish with nonfat cooking spray.

Assembling the entrée:

▸ Tear 3 of the flour tortillas in half. Cover the bottom of the baking dish with the torn tortillas.
▸ Spread 1/3 of the mixture on top of the tortillas.
▸ Sprinkle 1/3 of the (8-ounce) package of sliced mushrooms on top of the cream mixture.
▸ Repeat the layering two more times. You will only use 9 of the tortillas.
▸ Sprinkle the top layer with the reserved mozzarella and the finely shredded parmesan cheese. Top with the remaining sliced mushrooms.
▸ Spray the top with nonfat cooking spray, cover with wax paper, and cook in a carousel microwave for 6 to 7 minutes on high until heated through.
▸ Remove from the microwave and let rest for a few minutes before serving.

Yield: 4 servings **Calories per serving:** 384 (9% fat); **Total fat:** 4 g; **Cholesterol:** 18 mg; **Carbohydrate:** 56 g; **Dietary Fiber:** 6 g; **Protein:** 30 g; **Sodium:** 1894 mg **Diabetic Exchanges:** 4 starch, 3 very lean meat

Instructions to prepare the suggested meal

Set the timer for 30 minutes.

30 minutes before the meal

▸ Make the hot chocolate according to the directions.

25 minutes before the meal

▸ Make the mushroom bake according to the directions.

10 minutes before the meal

▸ Make the Pear and Apple Chutney according to the directions.

PANTRY
Ground cinnamon
Splenda granular
Dried chopped chives
Bac-Os Bits (imitation bacon, 2 tablespoons needed)
*Nonfat cooking spray

MEAL SUGGESTION: 30 MINUTES FOR TOTAL MEAL:
Cinnamon and Spice Hot Chocolate (page 288)
Pear and Apple Chutney (page 218)

HELPFUL HINT:

❷ Pre-sliced mushrooms save time and are usually the same price as whole mushrooms.

SUPPLIES LIST FOR SUGGESTED MEAL
Large nonstick skillet with lid
Medium mixing bowl
Whisk
6-8-inch nonstick skillet
4-cup measuring cup
or mixing bowl
Paper towels

GROCERY LIST FOR THE SUGGESTED MEAL
Ingredients for theBanana Cream Crepes

PRODUCE
*2 small bananas

MEATS
1 (14-ounce) package skinless smoked low-fat sausage (Healthy Ones)

DAIRY
*Fat-free skim milk (1³/4 cups needed)
* Eggs (2 needed)

FROZEN
*1 (8-ounce) container fat-free dessert (about 3 cups total needed)

PACKAGED
*1 (1.34-ounce) box Sugar-free French vanilla instant pudding
Sugar-free butter-flavored syrup (¹/2 cup needed)
*Powdered sugar (3 tablespoons needed)
*Heart Smart Bisquick reduced-fat baking mix (¹/2 cup needed)

PANTRY
Ground cinnamon
*Nonstick cooking spray

Banana Cream Crepes *25 minutes*

Don't be intimidated by this recipe. Once you make it, you'll see how easy (and delicious) it is to make crepes.

Ingredients

1 (1.34-ounce) box sugar-free French vanilla instant pudding
1³/4 cups fat-free skim milk, divided
1 cup fat-free dessert whipped topping, plus additional for topping
2 tablespoons plus 1 tablespoon powdered sugar
2 small bananas
¹/2 cup Heart Smart Bisquick baking mix
2 egg whites

Instructions for entrée:

Crepe filling:

▶ In a medium mixing bowl, whisk together the Sugar-free French vanilla instant pudding mix and 1 cup milk. Whisk until well blended.
▶ Add whipped topping and 2 tablespoons powder sugar to pudding mixture and whisk.
▶ Thinly slice the bananas and add three-fourths of the sliced bananas to the pudding mixture; reserve the remaining slices.
▶ Put the pudding mixture into the refrigerator.

Crepes:

▶ Preheat a 6 to 8-inch nonstick skillet over high heat.
▶ In a 4-cup measuring cup or mixing bowl, whisk together the Bisquick, 3/4 cup milk, and the egg whites.
▶ When the nonstick skillet is hot, spray with nonstick cooking spray. Pour 2 tablespoons of crepe batter into the preheated skillet. Lift and tilt the skillet to spread the batter. Brown on one side. The top of the crepe will be full of bubbles. With pancake turner lift the cooked crepe from the pan and place on a plate with a paper towel. Watch closely because it only takes about 1 minute for each crepe to cook. Place a paper towel or wax paper between each crepe to keep from sticking together.

Assembling Crepe:

▸ Put 1/4 cup of the filling in the center of
1 crepe and roll up jelly-roll–style; squeeze
to flatten slightly.
▸ Repeat until all of the crepes are filled.
▸ Sprinkle the tops of the crepes with reserved
sliced bananas and 1 tablespoon of
powdered sugar.
▸ Makes 10 crepes.

Yield: 5 (2 filled crepes) servings **Calories per serving:** 88 (5% fat); **Total fat:** <1 g;
Cholesterol: 1 mg; **Carbohydrate:** 18 g; **Dietary Fiber:** 1 g; **Protein:** 3 g; **Sodium:**
260 mg **Diabetic Exchanges:** 1 starch

Instructions to prepare the suggested meal

Set the timer for 30 minutes.

30 minutes before the meal

▸ Begin making the Cinnamon Glazed Smoked sausage by cutting the sausage
into bite-size pieces and heating the sausage in the pan with the lid on, to
brown.

25 minutes before the meal

▸ Begin making the banana crepes filling.

20 minutes before the meal

▸ Turn the sausage over and continue with the sausage recipe, reducing the
heat to medium.

18 minutes before the meal

▸ Make the crepes according to the directions.

8 minutes before the meal

▸ Assemble crepes and serve with sausage.

**MEAL SUGGESTION:
30 MINUTES FOR
TOTAL MEAL:**
Cinnamon-Glazed Smoked
Sausage (page 57)

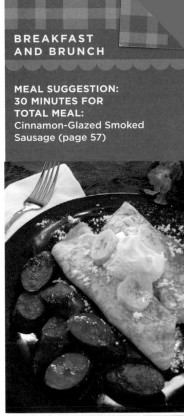

HELPFUL HINTS:

❷ If your cooking spray
browns when you spray the
skillet, your skillet is too
hot. Turn the heat down to
medium-high.

❷ Unfilled crepes freeze well.
Place a piece of waxed paper
between crepes and then
place them in a zip top plastic
freezer bag. They will freeze
for up to 4 months.

❷ If you do not have a 4-cup
measuring cup you can
make the batter in a bowl.
However, making the batter in
a 4-cup measuring cup makes
it super simple to pour the
batter onto the skillet.

**SUPPLIES LIST FOR
SUGGESTED MEAL**
12-inch or larger nonstick
saucepan with lid
Mixing bowl
Blender
Toaster

**GROCERY LIST FOR
SUGGESTED MEAL**
*Ingredients for the Farmer's
Breakfast Frittata*

PRODUCE
*1 green pepper (1/2 needed)
*1 medium sweet onion
(1/2 needed)

MEAT
*1 (14-ounce) package lean
smoked turkey sausage

DAIRY
*Nonfat plain yogurt
(2 tablespoons needed)
*Fat-free shredded cheddar
cheese (1/2 cup needed)
*Eggs (10 needed)

PACKAGED
1 (11-ounce) can
mandarin oranges
1 (15.5-ounce) can
sliced peaches
Whole-wheat fat-free bread

PANTRY
*Ground black pepper
Splenda granular
Ground cinnamon
Nonfat cooking spray

Farmer's Breakfast Frittata *30 minutes*

Ordinary ingredients are combined to make a special morning meal.

Ingredients

1 (14-ounce) package lean smoked turkey sausage
1/2 fresh green pepper
1/2 medium sweet onion
5 whole eggs plus 5 egg whites (or 1 3/4 cup Egg Beaters)
2 tablespoons nonfat plain yogurt
1/4 teaspoon ground black pepper
1/2 cup fat-free shredded cheddar cheese

Instructions *for entrée:*

▸ Slice 1 (14-ounce) package lean smoked turkey sausage into thin slices and cook in a large nonstick saucepan (12 inch or larger) over medium heat, stirring occasionally.

▸ While the meat is cooking, finely chop the green pepper and onion (to make 1/2 cup of each). Stir into the cooked sausage; then cover and continue to cook over medium heat.

▸ In a medium-sized bowl beat 5 whole eggs, 5 egg whites, yogurt, and ground black pepper together until well mixed. Set aside.

▸ With a pancake turner, scrape the bottom of the pan to release the juices, and then stir the cooked sausage, green pepper, and onions with the egg mixture until well mixed.

▸ Cover and continue to cook on medium heat.

▸ When the eggs are fully cooked, sprinkle the shredded cheddar cheese over the egg mixture. Spray the cheese with nonfat cooking spray, cover, and let cook for another 1 to 2 minutes or until the cheese is melted.

▸ Cut into pie-shaped servings.

Yield: 5 (pie-shaped) servings **Calories per serving:** 215 (30% fat); **Total fat:** 7 g;
Cholesterol: 242 mg; **Carbohydrate:** 12 g; **Dietary Fiber:** 1 g; **Protein:** 24 g;
Sodium: 891 mg **Diabetic Exchanges:** 1 carbohydrate, 3 1/2 lean meat

Instructions to prepare the suggested meal

Set the timer for 30 minutes.

30 minutes before the meal

  ▸ Prepare the Farmer's Breakfast Frittata according to the directions.

10 minutes before the meal

  ▸ Prepare the Spiced Nectar Smoothie according to the directions.

4 minutes before the meal

  ▸ Place whole-wheat slices of bread into the toaster; toast.

2 minutes before the meal

  ▸ Finish making the Farmer's Breakfast Frittata.

**MEAL SUGGESTION:
30 MINUTES FOR
TOTAL MEAL:**
Whole-wheat fat-free toast
Spiced Nectar Smoothie
(page 284)
Coffee or tea

HELPFUL HINTS:

❷ The moisture from the eggs, along with the coating of nonfat cooking spray over the cheese, makes the nonfat shredded cheese creamy.

❷ Once the eggs are in a bowl, use a slotted serving spoon to remove the yolks.

Home-Style Skillet Egg Bake *30 minutes*

This is like an omelet, a skillet dinner, and an egg bake all wrapped up in one.

Ingredients

7 ounces lean turkey breakfast sausage links (1/2 of 14-ounce package)
2 (15-ounce) cans diced potatoes
6 eggs
1/2 tablespoon Italian seasoning, plus 1/2 teaspoon
1 teaspoon garlic salt, divided
1 (7.5-ounce) can home-style biscuits

Instructions for entrée:

▸ Place the oven rack on the top shelf. Preheat the oven to 400 degrees.
▸ Spray a 12-inch or larger nonstick saucepan with butter-flavored nonfat cooking spray. Over medium heat brown the turkey links.
▸ Cover and cook, turning the sausages occasionally.
▸ While the meat is browning, drain and discard the juice from 2 cans of diced potatoes and set aside.
▸ Check the sausage.
▸ Separate 6 eggs, place the yolks in a small bowl, and set aside. Place the whites in a medium mixing bowl and beat on high speed until soft peaks form. Once you have soft peaks, add the yolks and beat into the egg whites. Set aside.
▸ Remove the sausage from the pan and set aside. In the same pan, stir in the drained potatoes, 1/2 tablespoon Italian seasoning, and 1/2 teaspoon garlic salt. Cook over high heat until most of the juices have evaporated
▸ Press the potatoes down into the pan with the back of a spatula.
▸ Pour the eggs on top of the potatoes. Arrange the sausages on the eggs in a flower or windmill pattern. Place the biscuits on top of the eggs. (The biscuits will sink, and the eggs will rise up during cooking.) Sprinkle with the remaining 1/2 teaspoon Italian seasoning and 1/2 teaspoon garlic salt.
▸ Place in the preheated oven on the top rack, and bake for 10 minutes.
▸ Move the pan to the middle of the oven and bake for an additional 5 minutes.
▸ After removing the pan from the oven, spray the top with butter-flavored nonfat cooking spray.
▸ Cut into 6 pie-shaped servings.

Yield: 6 (pie-shape) servings **Calories per serving:** 282 (24% fat); **Total fat:** 7 g; **Cholesterol:** 228 mg; **Carbohydrate:** 36 g; **Dietary Fiber:** 4 g; **Protein:** 16 g; **Sodium:** 1017 mg **Diabetic Exchanges:** 2¹/2 starch, 1¹/2 lean meat

Instructions to prepare the suggested meal

Set the timer for 30 minutes.

30 minutes before the meal

- ▸ Place oven rack on top shelf. Preheat the oven to 400 degrees.
- ▸ Prepare the Home-Style Skillet Egg Bake according to the directions.

15 minutes before the meal

- ▸ Make the Creamy Grape Salad according to the directions.

5 minutes before the meal

- ▸ Finish making the Home-Style Skillet Egg bake.
- ▸ Transfer the Home-Style Skillet Egg Bake to the middle of the oven.
- ▸ Finish making the Creamy Grape Salad.

MEAL SUGGESTION:
30 MINUTES FOR
TOTAL MEAL:
Creamy Red Grape Salad
(page 68)

SUPPLIES LIST FOR
SUGGESTED MEAL
Cutting board
12-inch nonstick saucepan
Baking sheet
Cupcake tin

GROCERY LIST FOR
SUGGESTED MEAL
*Ingredients for the Sausage
Gravy Egg Baskets

PACKAGE
*Light multi-grain English
muffins (4 needed)

DAIRY
*Fat-free skim milk
(2½ cups needed)
*Fat-free American cheese
(8 sices needed)
*Eggs (8 needed)

MEAT
*16-ounce package lean
turkey breakfast sausage
(Honeysuckle White)

PRODUCE
oranges (4 needed)
grapefruit (4 needed)

PANTRY
*Cornstarch
(2 tablespoons needed)
*Ground black pepper

Sausage Gravy Egg Baskets *30 minutes*

*WOW! My ultimate goal when creating a recipe is to serve up what I call "wow factor."
When my guests say, "Wow!" when they take their first bite, then I know it's a winner! This
recipe does just that!*

Ingredients

1 (16-ounce) package lean turkey breakfast sausage
2½ cups fat-free skim milk
2 tablespoons cornstarch
⅛ teaspoon ground pepper
4 light multi-grain English muffins
8 slices fat-free American cheese
8 large eggs

Instructions for entrée:

▸ Place the oven racks in the middle of the oven. Preheat the oven to 400 degrees.
▸ In a 12-inch nonstick saucepan brown and crumble the sausage.
▸ Once the meat is browned and crumbled, reduce the heat to medium.
▸ In a medium bowl use a fork to stir together the fat-free milk and cornstarch until the cornstarch is completely dissolved.
▸ Pour into the browned sausage and stir well.
▸ Add the ground pepper; stir well.
▸ Reduce the heat to medium, and stir occasionally.
▸ Once the gravy has thickened, reduce the heat to low, and cover to keep warm.
▸ Slice the multi-grain English muffins in half horizontally and place on a cookie sheet with the cut side up.
▸ Place 1 slice of fat-free American cheese on each half of the English muffins and set aside.
▸ Spray 8 wells of a muffin pan with nonstick spray.
▸ Crack one egg into each muffin cup.
▸ Place the muffin pan of eggs and the cookie sheet of the English muffins in the oven and bake for 5 minutes.
▸ After baking for 5 minutes remove the English muffins. but leave the eggs in the oven to continue baking for an additional 5 minutes or until baked to a soft set stage.

For each serving:

▸ Place a baked cheesy English muffin half on a plate. Place 1/3 cup of sausage gravy over each cheesy English muffin half.
▸ Take the eggs out of the oven and use a spoon to remove one baked egg at a time from the muffin pan, then place one baked egg in the center of each sausage gravy–covered English muffin.
▸ Serve immediately.

Yield: 8 **Calories per serving:** 247 (28% fat); **Total fat:** 7 g; **Cholesterol:** 243 mg; **Carbohydrate:** 17 g; **Dietary Fiber:** 0 g; **Protein:** 24 g; **Sodium:** 819 mg **Diabetic Exchanges:** 1 starch, 3 lean meat

---

Instructions to prepare the suggested meal

Set the timer for 30 minutes.

30 minutes before the meal

▸ Make the Sausage Gravy Egg Baskets.

10 minutes before the meal

▸ Put the eggs and cheesy English muffins in the oven to bake and start the coffee or tea (if desired). Also, slice 4 oranges and 4 grapefruit. Arrange on plates.

5 minutes before serving

▸ Remove the cheesy English halves from the oven and put on individual plates. Put 1/3 cup of the sausage gravy on top of each cheesy English muffin half

1 minute before meal

▸ Place 1 baked egg on the center of each sausage gravy–covered English muffin.

MEAL SUGGESTION: 30 MINUTES FOR TOTAL MEAL:
Oranges and grapefruit slices
Coffee or tea

SUPPLIES LIST FOR
SUGGESTED MEAL
2-quart round casserole dish
Electric mixer
Microwave oven
Microwave-safe bowl
4-quart saucepan

GROCERY LIST FOR
SUGGESTED MEAL
*Ingredients for the Crabby
Egg Bake Casserole

PACKAGE
*Light white bread
(4 slices needed)
2 (14.5-ounce) cans
asparagus cuts and tips
Low-fat slaw dressing
(I use Marzetti)
2 (15-ounce) cans no-sugar-
added Bartlett pear halves
Maraschino cherries
1 box sugar-free spiced cider
apple-flavor drink mix
(box of 10 pouches)

DAIRY
*Eggs (6 needed)
*Low-fat ricotta cheese
(1/2 cup needed)
*Light fat-free vanilla yogurt
(1/4 cup needed)
*Finely shredded parmesan
cheese (2 tablespoons
needed)

SEAFOOD
*1 (12-ounce) package
imitation crab meat

PANTRY
Lemon pepper
Garlic salt
*Butter-flavored cooking
spray

Crabby Egg Bake Casserole *30 minutes*

Don't let the grouchy title of this recipe scare you away from trying it.

Ingredients

6 eggs, divided
1/2 cup low-fat ricotta cheese
1/4 cup light fat-free vanilla yogurt
4 slices light white bread
1 (12-ounce) package imitation crab meat
1/2 teaspoon garlic salt
2 tablespoons finely shredded parmesan cheese

Instructions for entrée:

‣ Place the oven racks in the middle of the oven. Preheat the oven to 350 degrees.
‣ Generously spray a 2-quart round (microwave- and oven-safe) casserole dish with butter-flavored cooking spray.
‣ In the casserole dish beat together with an electric mixer 2 whole eggs, 4 egg whites, ricotta cheese, and yogurt.
‣ Cut the bread and imitation crab meat into bite-size pieces.
‣ Gently stir all ingredients together with garlic salt, making sure the bread is completely saturated.
‣ Sprinkle the top with parmesan cheese.
‣ Bake in oven for 17 minutes.
‣ Take out of the oven and cook in a carousel microwave for 3 minutes.
‣ Cut into 6 pie shaped wedges.

Yield: 6 servings **Calories per serving:** 164 (21% fat); **Total fat:** 4 g; **Cholesterol:** 105 mg; **Carbohydrate:** 16 g; **Dietary Fiber:** 2 g; **Protein:** 16 g; **Sodium:** 289 mg **Diabetic Exchanges:** 1 starch, 2 lean meat

---

Instructions to prepare the suggested meal

Set the timer for 30 minutes.

30 minutes before the meal

> ▸ Make the Crabby Egg Bake Casserole.

20 minutes before the meal

> ▸ Bake the Crabby Egg Bake Casserole in a preheated the oven.
> ▸ Make the Sweet Cherried Pears according to the directions.
> ▸ Once the pears are made reduce the heat to low to keep warm.

10 minutes before the meal

> ▸ Make the Lemon-Peppered Asparagus according to the directions.

3 minutes before the meal

> ▸ Remove the Crabby Egg Bake Casserole from the oven and cook in the carousel microwave for 3 minutes or until the eggs are fully cooked.

MEAL SUGGESTION: 30 MINUTES FOR TOTAL MEAL:
Lemon-Peppered Asparagus (page 209)
Sweet Cherried Pears (page 208)

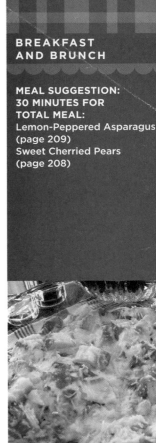

HELPFUL HINT:

❯ The quickest way to slice the 4 slices of bread and the imitation crab meat is to stack them up before cutting.

SUPPLIES LIST FOR
SUGGESTED MEAL
12-inch nonstick oven-safe
saucepan
Cutting board
Knife
Medium-size mixing bowl
4¹/2-quart saucepan

GROCERY LIST FOR
SUGGESTED MEAL
*Ingredients for the
Southwestern Egg
Bake Casserole

PACKAGE
*Whole-wheat light bread
(4 slices needed)
*1 (5-ounce) can green chilies
Sugar-free peach
drink mix
Cinnamon red hot candies

DAIRY
*Fat-free sour cream
(¹/2 cup needed)
*Eggs (6 needed)
*1 (8-ounce) package fat-free
shredded cheddar cheese
(1 cup needed)

MEAT
*1 pound extra-lean
ground beef

PRODUCE
Grape or cherry tomatoes

PANTRY
*Taco seasoning mix
(2 tablespoons needed)
*Butter-flavored
cooking spray

Southwestern Egg Bake
Casserole *30 minutes*

Morning, noon, or night—this is just right anytime!

Ingredients

1 pound extra-lean ground beef
2 tablespoons plus 1 teaspoon taco seasoning mix
4 slices whole-wheat light bread
¹/2 cup fat-free sour cream
6 eggs (or 1 cup total Egg Beaters for the eggs and egg whites)
1 cup shredded fat-free cheddar cheese
2 teaspoons chopped green chilies

Instructions for entrée:

▸ Preheat the oven to 400 degrees.
▸ Preheat a 12-inch nonstick oven proof saucepan over medium-high heat. Brown and crumble ground beef with 2 tablespoons taco seasoning mix. Stir occasionally.
▸ While the meat is cooking, cut the bread into bite-size pieces. Set aside.
▸ In a medium mixing bowl, beat the sour cream with 4 egg whites and 2 whole eggs until well blended.
▸ With a spatula stir the bread pieces into the egg mixture, making sure the bread is completely saturated with the egg mixture.
▸ Place the pieces of egg-soaked bread on top of the cooked meat. (Note: There will be gaps between the bread where you will be able to see the meat.)
▸ Sprinkle the top with the cheese.
▸ Spray the cheese with nonfat butter-flavored cooking spray.
▸ Sprinkle the top of the cheese with the remaining 1 teaspoon taco seasoning mix.
▸ Sprinkle chopped green chilies on top of the casserole.
▸ Bake for 20 minutes.
▸ Once fully baked cut into 6 pie-shaped wedges and serve.

Yield: 6 (1 wedge) servings **Calories per serving:** 219 (23% fat); **Total fat:** 6 g; **Cholesterol:** 119 mg; **Carbohydrate:** 12 g; **Dietary Fiber:** 2 g; **Protein:** 29 g; **Sodium:** 579 mg **Diabetic Exchanges:** 1 starch, 3¹/2 lean meat

Instructions to prepare the suggested meal

Set the timer for 30 minutes.

30 minutes before the meal

- ▶ Preheat the oven to 400 degrees.
- ▶ Start preparing the Southwestern Egg Bake Casserole.

20 minutes before the meal

- ▶ Place the Southwestern Egg Bake Casserole in the oven and cook for 20 minutes.
- ▶ Prepare the Green Chile Scones, but do not bake. Set aside.

10 minutes before the meal

- ▶ Bake the Green Chile Scones.
- ▶ Make the Cinnamon and Spice Candied Peach Punch.
- ▶ Place grape or cherry tomatoes in a serving bowl.

BREAKFAST AND BRUNCH

MEAL SUGGESTION: 30 MINUTES FOR TOTAL MEAL:
Grape or cherry tomatoes
Green Chile Scones (page 242)
Cinnamon and Spice Candied Peach Punch (page 287)

HELPFUL HINT:

❯ Salsa makes an excellent condiment with this entrée.

SUPPLIES LIST FOR
SUGGESTED MEAL OVEN
Griddle
2 medium-size mixing bowls
Whisk
Cutting board
Baking dish
Aluminum foil
Timer
Large microwavable (4-cup)
measuring cup or pitcher
Microwave oven
Small saucepan with lid

GROCERY LIST FOR
SUGGESTED MEAL
*Ingredients for the Stuffed
French Toast with Sweet Egg
and Sausage Scramble

PRODUCE
1 pound fresh strawberries

MEATS
*1 (14-ounce) package
Healthy Ones skinless
smoked sausage
(1/2 package needed)

DAIRY
*Eggs (6 needed)
*Fat-free cream cheese
(4 tablespoons needed)
Fat-free skim milk
(4 cups needed)

PACKAGED
*1 (16-ounce) loaf of
unsliced French bread
(1/2 loaf needed)
Sugar-free butter-flavored
syrup (1 cup needed)

PANTRY
*Sugar-free hazelnut or
French vanilla coffee creamer
(21/2 tablespoons needed)
*Splenda granular
*Nonstick cooking spray
Almond extract
Ground cinnamon

Stuffed French Toast with Sweet Egg and Sausage Scramble *30 minutes*

Smooth and slightly sweetened cream cheese is stuffed between thick layers of French bread and then grilled to perfection. The remaining egg mixture (used for the French toast) is combined with low-fat smoked sausage, adding just a touch of sweetness to a traditional breakfast entrée. Served together these entrees are divine.

Ingredients

2 eggs
4 egg whites
2 1/2 tablespoons sugar-free hazelnut or French vanilla coffee creamer, divided
4 tablespoons fat-free cream cheese
1/2 tablespoon Splenda granular
1/2 of 1 (16-ounce) loaf unsliced French bread
1/2 of 1 (14-ounce) package skinless low-fat smoked sausage

Instructions
Stuffed French Toast:

- Preheat the oven to 375 degrees.
- Preheat the griddle on medium-high heat.
- In a medium mixing bowl, whisk together the eggs, egg whites, and 2 tablespoons coffee creamer. Set aside.
- In a separate medium mixing bowl, use a fork to mash together the cream cheese, 1/2 tablespoon coffee creamer, and Splenda until completely blended. Set aside.
- Cut 4 (1 1/2-inch-thick) slices of French bread. Save the rest of the loaf for another recipe.
- Cut the slices in half to form a pocket.
- Spread the cream cheese mixture on one side of each pocket.
- Spray the preheated griddle with nonstick cooking spray.
- Dip only the cut sides of the bread in the egg mixture; do not dip the rounded sides of the loaf.
- Place the dipped bread on the preheated griddle, and brown on both sides. The French toast will brown within 30 seconds on each side.

44

▸ Once browned on both sides place in a baking dish, cover with aluminum foil, and bake in a preheated oven for 10 minutes.

Sweet Egg and Sausage Scramble:

Make this part of the recipe while the Stuffed French Toast is baking.

▸ Cut half of the sausages into bite-size bites.
   Save the other half to use in another recipe.
▸ Cook the sausage pieces on the preheated griddle (that was used to cook the French toast.)
▸ Cook the remaining egg mixture (from the French toast) with the sausage, using a pancake turner to cook the scrambled eggs and sausage until the eggs are dry.

Yield: 4 (1/2 cup of sausage and scrambled eggs, along with one 1 piece of stuffed French toast) servings **Calories per serving:** 305 (19% fat); **Total fat:** 6 g; **Cholesterol:** 125 mg; **Carbohydrate:** 39 g; **Dietary Fiber:** 1 g; **Protein:** 22 g; **Sodium:** 963 mg **Diabetic Exchanges:** 2¹/2 starch, 2 lean meat

Instructions to prepare the suggested meal

Set the timer for 30 minutes.

30 minutes before the meal

▸ Make the Cinnamon Syrup according to the directions.

25 minutes before the meal

▸ Preheat the oven to 375 degrees.
▸ Preheat the griddle on medium-high heat.
▸ Start making the Stuffed French Toast according to the directions.

5 minutes before the meal

▸ Make the Almond Steamers according to the directions.
▸ Put Cinnamon Syrup in a small gravy boat or creamer container.

1 minute before meal

▸ Plate the French toast and eggs.
▸ Place the Almond Steamers in cups.
▸ Serve meal.

BREAKFAST AND BRUNCH

MEAL SUGGESTION: 30 MINUTES FOR TOTAL MEAL:
Fresh Strawberries
Almond Steamer (page 293)
Cinnamon Syrup (page 219)

Sweet-and-Sour Lettuce Wraps (page 60)

Appetizers

SUPPLIES LIST
Microwave oven
Medium-sized mixing bowl
Wax paper

GROCERY LIST

DAIRY
1 (8-ounce) package fat-free
cream cheese
1 (8-ounce) package
shredded fat-free mozzarella
cheese (1 3/4 cups needed)

PACKAGED
1 box low-fat crackers

PANTRY
Real bacon pieces
Horseradish
Liquid Smoke

Smoky Bacon and Horseradish Cheese Ball *5 minutes*

Here's the "quick fix" answer when you want to serve something homemade and you are in a pinch for time.

Ingredients

1/4 cup real bacon pieces (less-fat)
1 (8-ounce) package fat-free cream cheese
3 teaspoons prepared horseradish
1 3/4 cups shredded fat-free mozzarella cheese
1 teaspoon Liquid Smoke*
1 box of your favorite low-fat crackers

Instructions

▸ Place the bacon pieces in a medium-size mixing bowl. Cover with wax paper and cook in the microwave for 30 to 40 seconds, or until warm.
▸ Add the cream cheese, horseradish, mozzarella cheese, and Liquid Smoke to the bacon pieces, and mix with your hands until well mixed.
▸ Shape the cheese mixture into a ball with your hands.
▸ Place the cheese ball on the serving plate and serve with low-fat crackers.

Yield: 18 (2-tablespoon) servings (Crackers not included) **Calories per serving:** 37 (0% fat); **Total fat:** 0 g; **Cholesterol:** 6 mg; **Carbohydrate:** 2 g; **Dietary Fiber:** 0 g; **Protein:** 6 g; **Sodium:** 211 mg **Diabetic Exchanges:** 1 very lean meat

HELPFUL HINT:

*Liquid Smoke is found in the condiment aisle.

❷ Have your serving plate ready to put the cheese ball on before starting this recipe, otherwise you'll need to wash your hands before plating the cheese ball.

❷ Do not let the crackers touch the cheese ball until it is ready to eat, otherwise the crackers will get soggy.

Southwestern Black Beans and Beef Confetti (Dip) *10 minutes*

Not only is this a healthy appetizer; it is also a tasty filling for lettuce wraps!

Ingredients

1 (16-ounce) package of extra-lean ground beef
1 (8.75-ounce) can golden sweet whole kernel corn
1 (15.25-ounce) can black beans
1 cup salsa
1/4 cup taco sauce
1/4 cup fat-free red French salad dressing
1 bag baked tortilla chips or 2 heads iceberg lettruce

Instructions

▸ Spray a large nonstick saucepan with nonstick cooking spray.
▸ On high heat brown and crumble the ground beef.
▸ Open and drain the cans of corn and black beans.
▸ Stir the salsa, drained corn and black beans, taco sauce, and salad dressing into the browned meat.
▸ Reduce the heat to medium and let cook uncovered until heated through.
▸ Serve immediately with baked tortilla chips or as a filling for lettuce wraps.

Total Time: 10 minutes **Yield:** 18 (1/4 cup) servings (tortilla chips not included)
Calories per serving: 75 (20% fat); **Total fat:** 2 g; **Cholesterol:** 14 mg;
Carbohydrate: 7 g; **Dietary Fiber:** 2 g; Protein: 7 g; **Sodium:** 228 mg
Diabetic Exchanges: 1/2 starch, 1 very lean meat

SUPPLIES LIST
Large nonstick saucepan

GROCERY LIST

MEATS
1 (16-ounce) package of extra-lean ground beef

PRODUCE
2 heads iceberg lettuce, optional

PACKAGED
1 (8.75-ounce) can golden sweet whole kernel corn
1 (15.25-ounce) can black beans
1 (16 ounce) jar salsa
(1 cup needed)
Taco sauce (1/4 cup needed)
Fat-free red French salad dressing (1/4 cup needed)
1 bag baked tortilla chips, optional

PANTRY
Nonstick cooking spray

HELPFUL HINTS:

❷ If you're making this dish for a party, after you've cooked it completely, transfer it to a small slow cooker to keep it warm.

❷ If you like it hot, spice up this dish with hot taco sauce and salsa. Just remember to tell your guests how hot it is before they dig in.

SUPPLIES LIST
Microwave oven
12-inch or larger
nonstick saucepan
Cutting board

GROCERY LIST

MEATS
1 (9.6-ounce) package of
turkey sausage patties
(Jimmy Dean)

PACKAGED
1 (29-ounce) can 100%
pure pumpkin
2 (8-ounce) cans
crushed pineapple
Honey barbecue sauce
(1/2 cup needed)
Reduced-fat butter
flavored crackers

PANTRY
Ground cinnamon
Splenda granular
(2 tablespoons needed)
Sea salt
*Butter-flavored cooking spray

HELPFUL HINT:

❯ Regular salt or
reduced-sodium salt
can be used if desired.

Pumpkin Sausage Spread *10 minutes*

This spread was a huge hit at a holiday party I had.

Ingredients

1 (9.6-ounce) package of turkey sausage patties
1 (29-ounce) can 100% pure pumpkin
2 (8-ounce) cans crushed pineapple
1 1/2 teaspoon ground cinnamon
1/2 cup honey barbecue sauce
2 tablespoons Splenda granular
1 teaspoon sea salt
Reduced-fat butter-flavored crackers

Instructions

▸ On a plate covered with a paper towel or wax paper, cook the turkey sausage patties in the microwave for 1 1/2 minutes or until fully heated.

▸ Spray a 12-inch or larger nonstick saucepan with butter-flavored cooking spray.

▸ Add the pumpkin to the pan and heat over medium heat.

▸ Cut the sausage into tiny pieces and stir into the pumpkin.

▸ Drain the juice from both cans of crushed pineapple.

▸ Add the drained pineapple, ground cinnamon, honey barbecue sauce, Splenda, and sea salt to the pumpkin mixture, and stir to combine. Continue cooking over medium heat until fully heated.

▸ Serve immediately with reduced-fat butter-flavored crackers (Ritz) or keep warm in a small slow cooker.

Yield: 18 (1/4-cup) servings (Crackers not included) **Calories per serving:** 73 (23% fat); **Total fat:** 2 g; **Cholesterol:** 14 mg; **Carbohydrate:** 12 g; **Dietary Fiber:** 2 g; **Protein:** 3 g; **Sodium:** 242 mg **Diabetic Exchanges:** 1 carbohydrate, 1/2 lean meat

---

Cheesy Cranberry Spread *5 minutes*

This was a huge hit at a party I had! Everyone loved it!

Ingredients

1/3 cup dried cranberries
1/4 cup real bacon pieces (less-fat)
1 (8-ounce) package fat-free cream cheese
3 teaspoons prepared horseradish
1 3/4 cups shredded fat-free mozzarella cheese
1 cup fat-free vanilla yogurt
1 teaspoon Liquid Smoke*
1 box low-fat butter-flavored crackers

Instructions

▸ Chop the dried cranberries. Set aside to use later.
▸ Place bacon pieces in a medium-size mixing bowl. Cover with wax paper and cook in the microwave for 30 to 40 seconds or until warm.
▸ Add the cream cheese, horseradish, mozzarella cheese, chopped dried cranberries, fat-free yogurt, and Liquid Smoke to the bacon pieces, and mix until well combined.
▸ Place cheese spread in a bowl and serve with low-fat butter-flavored crackers.

Yield: 18 (2-tablespoons) servings (Crackers not included) **Calories per serving:** 51 (0% fat); **Total fat:** 0 g; **Cholesterol:** 7 mg; **Carbohydrate:** 5 g; **Dietary Fiber:** 0 g; **Protein:** 6 g; **Sodium:** 218 mg **Diabetic Exchanges:** 1/2 carbohydrate, 1 very lean meat

---

APPETIZERS

SUPPLIES LIST
Medium-size mixing bowl
Wax paper
Microwave oven
Cutting board
Medium-size serving bowl

GROCERY LIST

DAIRY
1 (8-ounce) package fat-free cream cheese
1 (8-ounce) package shredded fat-free mozzarella cheese (1 3/4 cups needed)
Fat-free vanilla yogurt (1 cup needed)

PACKAGED
Real bacon pieces (1/4 cup needed)
Horseradish
Dried cranberries (1/3 cup needed)
1 box low-fat butter-flavored crackers

PANTRY
Liquid Smoke

HELPFUL HINT:

*Liquid Smoke is found in the condiment aisle.

51

SUPPLIES LIST
Large mixing bowl
Electric mixer
Serving platter
Small microwave-safe bowl
Microwave oven

GROCERY LIST

DAIRY
Nonfat light vanilla yogurt
(2/3 cup needed)
1 (8-ounce) package fat-free
cream cheese

FROZEN
1 (8-ounce) fat-free dessert
whipped topping
(1 cup needed)

PACKAGED
1 (1.5-ounce) box sugar-free
chocolate instant
pudding mix
Mini semi-sweet chocolate
chips (2 tablespoons plus
2 teaspoons needed)
1 box chocolate-flavored
graham crackers
Sugar-free hot fudge

PANTRY
Powdered cocoa

HELPFUL HINT:

❷ To make serving the chocolate cheese spread easier have a small butter knife alongside.

Chocolate Cheese Spread *10 minutes*

If you like chocolate cheese (found in gourmet cheese stores) then you'll like this bitter and sweet appetizer!

Ingredients

1 (1.5-ounce) box sugar-free chocolate instant pudding mix
2/3 cup nonfat light vanilla yogurt
1 (8-ounce) package fat-free cream cheese
1 cup fat-free dessert whipped topping
2 tablespoons mini semi-sweet chocolate chips, plus 2 teaspoons
1 tablespoon cocoa powder
3 tablespoons sugar-free hot fudge
1 box chocolate-flavored graham crackers

Instructions

▸ In a large mixing bowl, blend together the pudding mix, yogurt, cream cheese, whipped topping, 2 tablespoons of the chocolate chips, and the cocoa powder with an electric mixer.
▸ Once well blended spread the mixture on a pretty serving platter. Set aside.
▸ Heat the sugar-free hot fudge topping in a small, microwave-safe bowl for 15 seconds in a carousel microwave.
▸ Using a spoon drizzle the warmed hot fudge over the plated cheese mixture.
▸ Sprinkle with the remaining 2 teaspoons of chocolate chips.
▸ Serve with chocolate-flavored graham crackers.

Yield: 18 (2-tablespoon) servings (Graham crackers not include) **Calories per serving:** 51 (12% fat); **Total fat:** 1 g; **Cholesterol:** 2 mg; **Carbohydrate:** 8 g; **Dietary Fiber:** 0 g; **Protein:** 2 g; **Sodium:** 164 mg **Diabetic Exchanges:** 1/2 carbohydrate

---

Sweet and Creamy Shrimp Spread *10 minutes*

This is ideal for parties! The sweet and creamy base complements the shrimp cocktail and tomatoes.

Ingredients

1 (8 ounce) package fat-free cream cheese
1 pound cooked and peeled large shrimp, with tails removed
1 cup grape tomatoes
1 cup shrimp cocktail sauce
1 teaspoon dried parsley
1 cup fat-free vanilla light yogurt
Butter-flavored reduced-fat crackers

Instructions

- Set the cream cheese out to soften.
- Cut the shrimp into 1/2-inch pieces and place them in a medium-size mixing bowl.
- Cut the tomatoes into thin slices.
- Stir the tomato slices and shrimp pieces together with the shrimp cocktail sauce and dried parsley. Set aside.
- In another medium-size mixing bowl, beat the cream cheese and yogurt with an electric mixer until smooth and creamy.
- Spread the cream mixture on a large dinner plate or cake plate.
- Spread the shrimp mixture over the cream cheese mixture.
- Cover and keep chilled until ready to eat.
- Serve with butter-flavored reduced-fat crackers or on slices of French or pita bread.

Yield: 16 (1/4-cup) servings (Crackers or bread not included in nutritional info)
Calories per serving: 65 (7% fat); **Total fat:** 1 g; **Cholesterol:** 58 mg; **Carbohydrate:** 6 g; **Dietary Fiber:** 1 g; **Protein:** 9 g; **Sodium:** 277 mg **Diabetic Exchanges:** 1/2 carbohydrate, 1 very lean meat

SUPPLIES LIST
2 medium-size mixing bowls
Electric mixer
Cutting board
Large dinner or cake plate

GROCERY LIST

PRODUCE
Grape tomatoes (1 cup needed)

SEAFOOD
1 pound cooked and peeled large shrimp

DAIRY
1 (8 ounce) package fat-free cream cheese
Fat-free vanilla light yogurt (1 cup needed)

PACKAGED
Butter-flavored reduced-fat crackers, French or pita bread

PANTRY
Shrimp cocktail sauce (1 cup needed)
Dried parsley

Dilly Salmon Spread *15 minutes*

Your guests will think you have been busy in the kitchen all day making this elegant and tasty spread. It's light and not fishy tasting at all.

Ingredients

1/4 cup light fat-free vanilla yogurt
1/2 cup finely chopped dill pickle
2 tablespoons fat-free sour cream
1/2 teaspoon dry dill weed
1 (7-ounce) can boneless and skinless Atlantic salmon
48 reduced-fat crackers (such as Ritz)

Instructions

▶ In a medium-size bowl, mix together the yogurt, chopped pickles, sour cream, dill weed, and salmon.

▶ To serve, place in a small serving bowl with reduced-fat crackers on the side.

Total Time: 5 minutes served in a bowl or 15 minutes spread on individual crackers. **Yield:** 16 (3 crackers with 1 teaspoon each of spread) servings **Calories per serving:** 63 (27% fat); **Total fat:** 2 g; **Cholesterol:** 11 mg; **Carbohydrate:** 7 g; **Dietary Fiber:** 0 g; **Protein:** 4 g; **Sodium:** 182 mg **Diabetic Exchanges:** 1/2 fat-free milk

---

Hawaiian Lettuce Wraps *15 minutes*

Sweet and salty Hawaiian flavors are wrapped up in crisp leaves of lettuce for a delightful appetizer.

Ingredients

1 (16-ounce) package cubed lean ham
1 small onion
1 (8-ounce) can pineapple tidbits, drained
1/2 cup Kikkoman Teriyaki Baste & Glaze
1/2 cup frozen chopped green peppers
2 large heads of iceberg lettuce

Instructions for the Hawaiian mixture (to put inside the lettuce wraps)

▸ Preheat a 12-inch or larger nonstick saucepan over high heat, and cook the cubed lean ham.
▸ Finely chop the onion to make 2/3 cup. Add the chopped onion to the cooked ham.
▸ Cook uncovered for 2 to 3 minutes until the onions are tender.
▸ Stir the drained pineapple tidbits, Teriyaki Baste & Glaze, and green peppers into the ham and onion mixture. Bring to a boil; then reduce the heat to medium and continue cooking while you prepare the lettuce. The sauce will thicken as it cooks. Stir occasionally.

Instructions to prepare the lettuce

▸ Rinse 2 large heads of iceberg lettuce.
▸ Remove the core from both heads.
▸ Separate the leaves, shake the water off of the lettuce, and place on a large platter.

Assembling the Hawaiian Lettuce Wraps

▸ Place the ham mixture in a medium bowl in the middle of the platter of lettuce.
▸ Let everyone make their own wrap by putting a 1/4 cup of the Hawaiian mixture in the middle of a leaf of lettuce and folding it up like a burrito.

Yield: 12 (1/4-cup) servings **Calories per serving:** 101 (20% fat); **Total fat:** 2 g; **Cholesterol:** 20 mg; **Carbohydrate:** 11 g; **Dietary Fiber:** 2 g; **Protein:** 10 g; **Sodium:** 739 mg **Diabetic Exchanges:** 1 vegetable, 1/2 carbohydrate, 1 lean meat

SUPPLIES LIST
12-inch or larger nonstick saucepan
Cutting board
Large platter
Medium bowl

GROCERY LIST

PRODUCE
1 small onion (to make 2/3 cup)
2 large heads of iceberg lettuce

MEATS
1 (16-ounce) package cubed lean ham

FROZEN
Frozen chopped green peppers (1/2 cup needed)

PACKAGED
1 (8-ounce) can pineapple tidbits

PANTRY
Kikkoman Teriyaki Baste & Glaze (1/2 cup needed)

HELPFUL HINT:

❷ To easily remove the core from the iceberg lettuce simply hit the head of the lettuce (with the core facing down) on the countertop. Pull the core out and discard.

Sausage Sauerkraut and Apples on Rye *15 minutes*

This unique recipe isn't too sour; it's just right. It was a hit at my holiday party!

Ingredients

1 (19.5-ounce) package sweet Italian turkey sausage links
1 (14.5-ounce) can sauerkraut
1 (20-ounce) can no-sugar-added apple pie filling
1 cup frozen chopped green pepper
1 (4-ounce) jar diced pimientos
48 rye crackers

Instructions

▸ Preheat a large nonstick skillet on high heat.
▸ While the pan is heating up cut the skin off the sausage links.
▸ Brown and crumble the sausage.
▸ Open the sauerkraut and put it into a strainer. Rinse and squeeze dry the sauerkraut and set aside.
▸ Open the can of pie filling. While the pie filling is in the can take a long knife and cut up the apples. Set aside.
▸ Once the sausage is browned, add the sauerkraut, pie filling, green peppers, and diced pimientos; stir well, cover, and continue cooking on medium-high heat for a few minutes until fully heated, stirring frequently.
▸ Serve with rye crackers.

Yield: 24 (1/4 cup with 2 crackers) servings **Calories per serving:** 122 (18% fat);
Total fat: 2 g; **Cholesterol:** 19 mg; **Carbohydrate:** 20 g; **Dietary Fiber:** 4 g; **Protein:** 5 g; **Sodium:** 333 mg **Diabetic Exchanges:** 1½ starch, ½ very lean meat

---

Cinnamon-Glazed Smoked Sausage *15 minutes*

You'll never miss the fat in these lightly sweetened reduced-fat smoke sausages.

Ingredients

1 (14-ounce) package skinless smoked sausage links
1/2 cup sugar-free butter-flavored syrup
1/2 teaspoon ground cinnamon

Instructions

▸ Preheat a large nonstick skillet over medium heat.
▸ While the pan is preheating cut the sausage links on an angle into bite-sized slices.
▸ Brown one side of sausage slices in the preheated skillet over medium heat, with the lid on.
▸ Stir together the syrup and cinnamon in a measuring cup.
▸ Once one side of the sausages is browned, reduce the heat to low and stir in the syrup mixture. Stir until the sausages are covered with the cinnamon syrup.
▸ Cover and continue cooking on medium heat until fully heated, about 3 to 4 minutes more.
▸ Turn off the heat and keep covered on the hot burner to keep warm.

Yield: 5 (3-ounce) servings **Calories per serving:** 109 (14% fat); **Total fat:** 2 g; **Cholesterol:** 28 mg; **Carbohydrate:** 21 g; **Dietary Fiber:** 1 g; **Protein:** 10 g; **Sodium:** 685 mg **Diabetic Exchanges:** 1 1/2 starch, 1 very lean meat

SUPPLIES LIST
Oven
Cutting board
Small bowl
Jelly-roll pan
Timer

GROCERY LIST

PRODUCE
1 small sweet onion

MEATS
1 (16-ounce) package baked
sliced ham

DAIRY
1 (8-ounce) package fat-free
cream cheese

PANTRY
Dried parsley

HELPFUL HINT:

> A jelly-roll pan is a baking sheet with a 1/4-inch lip around the edge.

Ham and Onion
Cheese Rollups   *30 minutes*

These are ideal for breakfast, brunch, or as an appetizer.

Ingredients

1 small sweet onion
1 (8-ounce) package fat-free cream cheese
1 teaspoon dried parsley
1 (16-ounce) package baked sliced ham

Instructions

▸ Preheat the oven to 350 degrees.
▸ Finely chop enough sweet onion to make 2 tablespoons.
▸ In a small bowl mash together with a fork the chopped onions, cream cheese, and dried parsley until well mixed.
▸ Spread 1 tablespoon cream cheese mixture down the middle of 1 slice of ham (lengthwise) and roll it up (jelly-roll-style). Place on jelly-roll pan, seam side down. Continue until all of the slices of ham are used.
▸ Bake for 12 minutes. Let rolls rest for 2 to 4 minutes before serving, since the cheese centers will be very hot.

Yield: 8 (2 rolls each) servings **Calories per serving:** 114 (27% fat); **Total fat:** 3 g;
Cholesterol: 35 mg; **Carbohydrate:** 3 g; **Dietary Fiber:** 0 g; **Protein:** 16 g;
Sodium: 885 mg **Diabetic Exchanges:** 2 1/2 very lean meat

Cherry Chutney Cocktail Spread *20 minutes*

The combination of sweet, tart, and chewy over the creamy cheese atop the buttery flavor of the crackers will make this recipe an all-time favorite. This is perfect for a cocktail or holiday party.

Ingredients

2 (8-ounce) packages fat-free cream cheese
$1/4$ cup firmly packed, dried cherries
1 (20-ounce) can no-sugar-added cherry pie filling, chilled
3 Bartlett pears, chopped into bite-size pieces to make 4 cups, chilled
$1/2$ teaspoon ground cinnamon
$1/4$ cup finely chopped green onion tops
Reduced-fat buttered flavored crackers

Instructions

▸ Set the cream cheese out to soften.
▸ Finely chop the dried cherries.
▸ In a medium-size serving bowl, stir together the cherry pie filling, chopped pears, chopped dried cherries, and cinnamon. Set aside.
▸ Spread the softened cream cheese on a large serving dish.
▸ Spread the pear and cherry mixture on top of the cream cheese.
▸ Sprinkle the green onions on top of the mixture.
▸ Serve with crackers.

Total time: 20 minutes **Yield:** 16 (2 tablespoons cream cheese and $1/4$ cup fruit topping) servings (Crackers are not included) **Calories per serving:** 72 (0% fat); **Total fat:** 0 g; **Cholesterol:** 5 mg; **Carbohydrate:** 12 g; **Dietary Fiber:** 2 g; **Protein:** 4 g; **Sodium:** 208 mg **Diabetic Exchanges:** 1 fruit, $1/2$ very lean meat

---

SUPPLIES LIST
Large serving dish
Medium-size serving bowl
Cutting board

GROCERY LIST

PRODUCE
3 Bartlett pears
2–3 green onions

DAIRY
2 (8-ounce) packages fat-free cream cheese

PACKAGED
1 (20-ounce) can no-sugar-added cherry pie filling
Dried cherries
($1/4$ cup needed)
1 box reduced-fat buttered flavored crackers

PANTRY
Ground cinnamon

SUPPLIES LIST
1- inch or larger nonstick
saucepan with lid
Strainer
Serving platter
Serving bowl

GROCERY LIST

PRODUCE
1 head iceberg lettuce

MEATS
1 (9.6-ounce) package fully
cooked turkey sausage patties
(Jimmy Dean)

FROZEN
Frozen chopped green bell
pepper

PACKAGED
1 (14.5-ounce) can sauerkraut
1 (8-ounce) can pineapple
tidbits in unsweetened juice
Sweet and sour sauce
(2/3 cup needed)

PANTRY
Garlic and ginger combination
seasoning (optional)
Cooking spray
Soy sauce (optional)

Sweet-and-Sour Lettuce Wraps *20 minutes*

Here's another great recipe for those watching their weight! Its sweet and sour tasty flavors combined with the sausage and then wrapped up in the crisp lettuce leaves are so yummy! For a quick and healthy snack or light meal, you may want to keep some of this mixture premade. My friends went nuts over it at a party I had!

Ingredients

1 (9.6-ounce) package fully cooked turkey sausage patties
1 (14.5-ounce) can sauerkraut
1 (8-ounce) can pineapple tidbits, in unsweetened juice, undrained
1/2 cup frozen chopped green bell peppers
2/3 cup sweet and sour sauce
1/2 teaspoon garlic and ginger blended seasoning (optional)
1 head iceberg lettuce, separated into leaves

Instructions

▸ Spray a 12-inch or larger nonstick saucepan with cooking spray and preheat the pan on high heat.
▸ While the pan is preheating, cut the sausage patties into tiny pieces. Add to the pan.
▸ Open the sauerkraut and drain into a strainer; rinse and squeeze dry with your hands.
▸ Add the sauerkraut, pineapple tidbits and juice, green peppers, sweet and sour sauce, and seasoning to the cooked sausage, and stir until well mixed and thoroughly heated.
▸ Turn off the heat, cover, and remove from the burner. Let the mixture rest in the pan while you prepare the lettuce leaves.
▸ Separate and remove the lettuce leaves from the head of Iceberg lettuce. Place the leaves on a serving platter.
▸ Place the sweet-and-sour mixture in a serving bowl and place next to the leaves

To assemble Sweet-and-Sour Lettuce Wraps

▸ Let guests assemble their own lettuce wraps by placing 1/4 cup of mixture on a leaf of iceberg lettuce and wrapping it up like a burrito.

▸ If desired, serve soy sauce on the side.

Yield: 14 (1/4 cup mixture and 1 leaf lettuce) servings **Calories per serving:** 75 (28% fat); **Total fat:** 2 g; **Cholesterol:** 19 mg; **Carbohydrate:** 11 g; **Dietary Fiber:** 1 g; **Protein:** 3 g; **Sodium:** 268 mg **Diabetic Exchanges:** 1/2 carbohydrate, 1/2 lean meat

HELPFUL HINTS:

❷ When the sauerkraut is drained, rinsed, and squeezed dry, it tastes more like cooked cabbage than sauerkraut in this recipe.

❷ If you can't find the garlic/ ginger seasoning at your grocery store, this recipe tastes equally good without it.

Pineapple Ham Stacks *20 minutes*

A tasty combination of sweet and slightly salty! Pair this versatile protein with pancakes or French toast for a yummy breakfast or brunch. Or cut into small portions and serve on cinnamon graham crackers. as an appetizer.

Ingredients

1 (8-ounce) can pineapple tidbits
1 (8-ounce) package fat-free cream cheese
1 tablespoon Splenda granular
8 slices from 1 (16-ounce) package 97% fat-free honey-ham
8 whole cinnamon graham crackers, if serving as an appetizer

Instructions

‣ Preheat the oven to 350 degrees.
‣ Open, drain, and discard the juice from the can of pineapple tidbits.
‣ In a medium mixing bowl, mash/mix together the drained pineapple tidbits, cream cheese, and Splenda with the back of a stiff spatula. Set aside.
‣ Place 4 slices of honey-ham on a jelly-roll pan.
‣ Spread 1/4 cup of the cream cheese mixture on each of the 4 slices of ham.
‣ Place 1 slice of ham on top of each, sandwiching the cream cheese mixture between 2 slices of ham.
‣ Bake in oven for 15 minutes.

Yield: 16 (2-piece) appetizer servings **Calories per serving:** 71 (20% fat); **Total fat:** 1 g; **Cholesterol:** 10 mg; **Carbohydrate:** 8 g; **Dietary Fiber:** 0 g; **Protein:** 5 g; **Sodium:** 315 mg **Diabetic Exchanges:** 1/2 carbohydrate, 1 very lean meat

---

SUPPLIES LIST
Oven
Medium mixing bowl
Jelly-roll pan
Timer

GROCERY LIST

MEATS
1 (16-ounce) package 97% fat-free honey-ham (8 slices needed)

DAIRY
1 (8-ounce) package fat-free cream cheese

PACKAGED
1 (8-ounce) can pineapple tidbits

PANTRY
Splenda granular
1 box cinnamon graham crackers

To serve as an appetizer:

‣ After removing the stacks from the oven, let them cool for a couple of minutes on the jelly-roll pan; then cut each ham stack into 8 rectangles.
‣ Break each whole cinnamon graham cracker into 4 small crackers.
‣ Place one Pineapple Ham Stack on each small cinnamon graham cracker.

Yield: 4 (1 Pineapple Ham Stack) side dish servings (without crackers) **Calories per serving:** 166 (18% fat); **Total fat:** 3 g; **Cholesterol:** 40 mg; **Carbohydrate:** 12 g; **Dietary Fiber:** 0 g; **Protein:** 20 g; **Sodium:** 1091 mg **Diabetic Exchanges:** 1 carbohydrate, 3 very lean meat

APPETIZERS

HELPFUL HINTS:

❷ If serving as a side dish, do not serve with crackers.

❷ To cut the Pineapple Ham Stacks into 8 appetizer pieces: cut down the center lengthwise and then cut into smaller rectangles.

❷ A jelly-roll pan is often thought of as a cookie sheet with a 1/2-inch raised edge, which prevents the juices from draining off.

Chicken and Mandarin Orange Chopped Salad (page 74)

Salads

SUPPLIES LIST
Large salad bowl
Cutting board

GROCERY LIST

PRODUCE
1 head iceberg lettuce

DAIRY
Nonfat plain yogurt
(1/2 cup needed)

PANTRY
Sugar-free French Vanilla
creamer (1/4 cup needed)
Salt

Light and Creamy
Iceberg Salad *5 minutes*

This creamy and slightly sweetened salad dressing base adapts well to a variety of seasonings. The dressing is great as a dip or as a salad dressing. When used as a salad dressing I recommend tossing the prepared salad dressing with 6 cups chopped iceberg lettuce.

Ingredients:

1/2 cup nonfat plain yogurt
1/4 cup sugar-free French Vanilla creamer
1 head iceberg lettuce
Salt, to taste

Instructions

▶ In the bottom of a large salad bowl, stir together the yogurt and creamer until well mixed.
▶ Cut lettuce into bite-size pieces to make 6 cups.
▶ Toss the prepared lettuce with salad dressing. Add salt.
▶ Serve immediately to keep the lettuce from becoming soggy.

Yield: 4 (1 1/2 cup) salads **Calories per serving:** 56 (33% fat); **Total fat:** 2 g; **Cholesterol:** 1 mg; **Carbohydrate:** 7 g; **Dietary Fiber:** 2 g; **Protein:** 3 g; **Sodium:** 37 mg **Diabetic Exchanges:** 1 vegetable, 1/2 fat

---

Light and Creamy Dilly Iceberg Salad

▸ Add $1/4$ teaspoon dry dill to the dressing mix. Toss with the lettuce.

Yield: 4 (1 1/2 cup) salads; **Calories per serving:** 56 (33% fat); **Total fat:** 2 g;
Cholesterol: 1 mg; **Carbohydrate:** 7 g; **Dietary Fiber:** 2 g; **Protein:** 3 g; **Sodium:**
37 mg **Diabetic Exchanges:** 1 vegetable, 1/2 fat

Light and Creamy Salsa Salad:

▸ Add $1/4$ cup chunky salsa and $1/4$ cup finely chopped sweet onion to the
dressing mix. Toss with iceberg lettuce.

Yield: 4 (1 1/2 cup) salads **Calories per serving:** 65 (29% fat) **Total fat:** 2 g;
Cholesterol: 1 mg; **Carbohydrate:** 9 g; **Dietary Fiber:** 2 g; **Protein:** 3 g; **Sodium:**
95 mg **Diabetic Exchanges:** 2 vegetable, 1/2 fat

SUPPLIES LIST
Medium-size bowl
Electric mixer

GROCERY LIST

PRODUCE
1¹/2 pounds red seedless
grapes

DAIRY
1 (8-ounce) package fat-free
cream cheese
(4-ounces needed)
Fat-free sour cream
(¹/4 cup needed)

PANTRY
Vanilla extract
Splenda granular

Creamy Red Grape Salad   *7 minutes*

This salad complements many dishes and is also a great snack. The creamy dressing enhances the sweet, juicy grape flavor.

Ingredients for Creamy Red Grape Salad

4 ounces fat-free cream cheese
¹/4 cup fat-free sour cream
¹/2 teaspoon vanilla extract
3 tablespoons Splenda granular
1¹/2 pounds red seedless grapes, stems removed and rinsed

Instructions

▶ In a medium-size bowl, beat together the cream cheese, sour cream, vanilla extract, and Splenda granular with an electric mixer.
▶ Place rinsed grapes in the bowl with the cream cheese mixture, and mix well with a spatula.
▶ Serve.

Yield: 6 (¹/2 cup) servings **Calories per serving:** 113 (0% fat); **Total fat:** 0 g; **Cholesterol:** 5 mg; **Carbohydrate:** 24 g; **Dietary Fiber:** 1 g; **Protein:** 4 g; **Sodium:** 146 mg **Diabetic Exchanges:** 1¹/2 fruit, ¹/2 very lean meat

---

HELPFUL HINTS:

❷ Save the other half of the cream cheese package for another recipe.

❷ Shake the grapes to help remove them from the stems.

❷ Not cutting the grapes makes this recipe quick and easy to prepare.

Southwestern Sweet Slaw *5 minutes*

Cool, creamy, and slightly sweetened, with just the right amount of zing to give it a Southwestern flair.

Ingredients

1/2 cup chunky salsa, chilled
1/2 cup fat-free sour cream
3/4 cup fat-free red French salad dressing, chilled
1 (16-ounce) bag pre-cut coleslaw mix

Instructions

▸ In a large salad bowl, stir together the salsa, sour cream, and French dressing until well mixed.
▸ Stir the coleslaw mix into the salad dressing. Serve chilled

Yield: 7 (1/2-cup) servings **Calories per serving:** 80 (0% fat); **Total fat:** 0 g; **Cholesterol:** 3 mg; **Carbohydrate:** 17 g; **Dietary Fiber:** 2 g; **Protein:** 2 g; **Sodium:** 356 mg **Diabetic Exchanges:** 1 carbohydrate

SUPPLIES LIST
Large salad serving bowl

GROCERY LIST

PRODUCE
1 (16-ounce) bag pre-cut coleslaw mix

DAIRY
Fat-free sour cream
(1/2 cup needed)

PACKAGED
Chunky salsa
(1/2 cup needed)
Fat-free red French salad dressing (1/4 cup needed)

HELPFUL HINT:

❷ Prechill the salsa and salad dressing by storing them in the refrigerator when you put away your groceries.

Celery Salad *5 minutes*

This crunchy salad is ideal for dieters.

Ingredients

1 large package of celery
1/4 cup finely chopped fresh parsley, firmly packed
3 tablespoons diced pimiento
1/3 cup fat-free Italian salad dressing

Instructions

▶ Clean the head of celery. With a large chef's knife, cut the ends off and remove and discard any bad leaves from the stalks. Cut the stalks of celery in half lengthwise.

▶ Finely chop the celery halves and place them in a large salad bowl.

▶ Add finely chopped parsley, pimiento, and fat-free Italian salad dressing to the celery.

▶ Mix all ingredients together.

▶ Serve.

Yield: 7 (3/4-cup) servings **Calories per serving:** 19 (0% fat); **Total fat:** 0 g; **Cholesterol:** 0 mg; **Carbohydrate:** 3 g; **Dietary Fiber:** 1 g; **Protein:** 1 g; **Sodium:** 211 mg **Diabetic Exchanges:** Free

---

Warm Maraschino and Mandarin Fruit Salad *10 minutes*

This warm and fruity salad fits the bill when you want something to take the chill off. It's sweet enough to satisfy your sweet tooth too!

Ingredients

2 (15-ounce) cans whole-segment mandarin oranges in light syrup
1 (6-ounce) can whole-segment mandarin oranges in light syrup
¼ teaspoon ground allspice
2 tablespoons Splenda Brown Sugar Blend
1 tablespoon butter-flavored sprinkles
15 maraschino cherries
2 tablespoons of maraschino cherry juice

Instructions:

▸ Open, drain, and discard the juice from all three cans of mandarin oranges.
▸ Place the drained oranges in a large microwave-safe bowl.
▸ Add the allspice, Splenda Brown Sugar Blend, butter-flavored sprinkles, maraschino cherries, and maraschino cherry juice to the oranges. Stir together, cover, and heat in the microwave for 2 minutes.
▸ Serve.

Yield: 6 (½-cup) servings **Calories per serving:** 135 (0% fat); **Total fat:** 0 g;
Cholesterol: 0 mg; **Carbohydrate:** 32 g; **Dietary Fiber:** 1 g; **Protein:** 1 g;
Sodium: 98 mg **Diabetic Exchanges:** 2 carbohydrate

SUPPLIES LIST
Large microwave-safe bowl
Microwave oven
Timer

GROCERY LIST

PACKAGED
2 (15-ounce) cans whole-segment mandarin oranges in light syrup
1 (6-ounce) can whole-segment mandarin oranges in light syrup
1 (6-ounce) jar maraschino cherries (15 needed)

PANTRY
Ground allspice
Splenda Brown Sugar Blend
Imitation butter-flavored sprinkles

HELPFUL HINT:

❷ Butter-flavored sprinkles come in a variety of brands, such as Molly McButter or Butter Buds. They are usually found in the spice aisle or with diet foods.

**SUPPLIES LIST FOR
SUGGESTED MEAL**
Oven
Cookie sheet
Cutting board
Large serving bowl
Timer
Blender

**GROCERY LIST FOR
SUGGESTED MEAL**
*Ingredients for the Cherry,
Bacon, and Rye Tossed Salad*

PRODUCE
*1 medium head of iceberg
lettuce

DAIRY
*Shredded fat-free mozzarella
cheese (1/2 cup needed)
Fat-free plain yogurt
(1/2 cup needed)

FROZEN
1 (16-ounce) bag frozen whole
strawberries
(no-sugar-added)

PACKAGED
*Seeded hearty rye bread
(2 slices needed)
*Low-fat Marzetti slaw
dressing (1/4 cup needed)
*Dried cherries
(1/4 cup needed)

PANTRY
*Light salt or Sea salt
(optional)
*Imitation bacon bits
(1/2 cup needed)
*Butter-flavored
cooking spray
Splenda
100% natural whey protein
powder (2 tablespoons
needed)

Cherry, Bacon, and Rye Tossed Salad *10 minutes*

This salad is ideal for a luncheon with a friend! This fabulous salad is satisfying enough for a lunch entrée. Or serve a smaller portion as a side salad with chicken or pork entrées for dinner.

Ingredients

1/4 cup firmly packed dried cherries
2 slices seeded hearty rye bread
Light salt
1 medium head of iceberg lettuce (5 cups chopped)
1/2 cup shredded fat-free mozzarella cheese
1/2 cup imitation bacon bits
1/4 cup low-fat Marzetti slaw dressing

Instructions

▶ Preheat the oven to 425 degrees.
▶ Chop the dried cherries into tiny pieces. Set aside.
▶ Spray both sides of the bread with butter-flavored cooking spray.
▶ If desired sprinkle both sides of each slice of bread with light salt.
▶ Cut the bread into small croutons and then place them on a cookie sheet. Set aside.
▶ Cut the iceberg lettuce into bite-size pieces, to make 5 cups. Place the chopped lettuce into a large serving bowl.
▶ Place the croutons on the bottom rack of the oven and bake for 3 to 4 minutes until crispy.
▶ With your hands, toss the shredded cheese, imitation bacon bits, slaw dressing, and chopped dried cherries with the chopped lettuce until well mixed.
▶ Remove the croutons from the oven and toss with the salad.
▶ Serve Immediately.

Yield: 2 (2½ cup) luncheon entrée salads **Calories per serving:** 363 (17% fat); **Total fat:** 7 g; **Cholesterol:** 20 mg; **Carbohydrate:** 55 g; **Dietary Fiber:** 7 g; **Protein:** 23 g; **Sodium:** 1272 mg **Diabetic Exchanges:** 1 starch, 1 fruit, 2 vegetable, 1 carbohydrate, 2½ lean meat

Yield: 5 (1 cup) side salads **Calories per serving:** 145 (17% fat); **Total fat:** 3 g; **Cholesterol:** 8 mg; **Carbohydrate:** 22 g; **Dietary Fiber:** 3 g; **Protein:** 9 g; **Sodium:** 509 mg **Diabetic Exchanges:** 1½ carbohydrate, 1 lean meat

Instructions to prepare the suggested meal

Set the timer for 15 minutes.

15 minutes before the meal

▸ Make Cherry, Bacon, and Rye Tossed Salad according to the directions.

5 minutes before the meal

▸ Make the Strawberry Smoothies according to the directions.

MEAL SUGGESTION: 15 MINUTES FOR TOTAL MEAL:
Strawberry Smoothie (page 283)

HELPFUL HINTS:

❷ The quickest way to slice the bread into croutons is by stacking the bread and then cutting it.

❷ Light salt has less sodium than regular salt; it is also sometimes sold as Lite Salt.

❷ You can also substitute sea salt if desired.

Chicken and Mandarin Orange Chopped Salad *10 minutes*

This salad is something you could expect to find at a chic café for at least $7.95. With this recipe you can feed six people for less than it would cost for only one entrée-sized salad dining out.

Ingredients

1 (15-ounce) can chilled mandarin oranges
1/2 cup of Marzetti low-fat slaw dressing
1/3 cup dried cranberries
1/4 cup finely crumbled feta cheese
1 medium head iceberg lettuce, chopped to make 5 cups
1 (12.5-ounce) can chunk chicken, drained

Instructions

▸ Reserve 1/4 cup of the juice from the can of mandarin oranges and discard the remaining juice. Set the mandarin oranges aside.
▸ Make the salad dressing in a small bowl; stir together the 1/4 cup reserved mandarin orange juice with the slaw dressing until well blended. Set aside.
▸ In a medium-size serving bowl, add the dried cranberries, finely crumbled feta cheese, and chopped lettuce.
▸ Add the drained chicken, oranges, and the prepared salad dressing to the lettuce, and then toss with your hands until well mixed.
▸ Serve immediately.

Yield: 3 (2²/3-cup) entrée' size servings **Calories per serving:** 384 (16% fat); **Total fat:** 7 g; **Cholesterol:** 81 mg; **Carbohydrate:** 55 g; **Dietary Fiber:** 4 g; **Protein:** 26 g; **Sodium:** 1119 mg **Diabetic Exchanges:** 2 fruit, 1 vegetable, 1 1/2 carbohydrate, 3 1/2 lean meat

---

Yield: 6 (1 1/4-cup) side salads **Calories per serving:** 192 (16% fat); **Total fat:** 4 g; **Cholesterol:** 41 mg; **Carbohydrate:** 27 g; **Dietary Fiber:** 2 g; **Protein:** 13 g; **Sodium:** 560 mg **Diabetic Exchanges:** 1 fruit, 1 carbohydrate, 2 lean meat

---

Instructions to prepare the suggested meal

Set the timer for 15 minutes.

15 minutes before the meal

▸ Begin making the Chicken and Mandarin Orange Chopped Salad. Do not toss with salad dressing until after you have made the Strawberry Smoothies.

5 minutes before the meal

▸ Make the Strawberry Smoothies.

MEAL SUGGESTION:
15 MINUTES FOR
TOTAL MEAL:
Strawberry Smoothie
(page 283)

HELPFUL HINT:

❷ Put the can of mandarin oranges in the refrigerator when you get home from the store to have them chilled and ready to use.

Chopped Italian and Rye Salad *10 minutes*

With homemade rye croutons, shredded parmesan cheese, and freshly chopped parsley this is no ordinary salad.

Ingredients

2 slices seeded rye bread
1 medium head iceberg lettuce, chopped to make 5 cups
1 cup thinly sliced cucumber (about $1/2$ cucumber)
$1/2$ cup grape tomatoes
$1/3$ cup finely chopped fresh parsley, firmly packed
$1/4$ cup fancy shredded parmesan cheese
$2/3$ cup fat-free Italian salad dressing
24 slices turkey pepperoni (for entrée salad)

Instructions

- Toast the slices of bread and set aside.
- While the bread is toasting prepare the other ingredients and place in a large salad bowl the chopped lettuce, thinly sliced cucumber, grape tomatoes, finely chopped parsley, and shredded parmesan cheese.
- Cut the toast into small squares to make croutons.
- Add the salad dressing to the salad bowl and toss well.
- Add the croutons and serve immediately.

Yield: 8 (1-cup) side salad servings **Calories per serving:** 60 (20% fat); **Total fat:** 1 g; **Cholesterol:** 2 mg; **Carbohydrate:** 9 g; **Dietary Fiber:** 2 g; **Protein:** 3 g; **Sodium:** 393 mg **Diabetic Exchanges:** 1/2 starch

---

Yield: 3 (2$2/3$-cup) entrée sized servings **Calories per serving:** 198 (24% fat); Total fat: 5 g; **Cholesterol:** 26 mg; **Carbohydrate:** 26 g; **Dietary Fiber:** 5 g; **Protein:** 12 g; **Sodium:** 1345 mg **Diabetic Exchanges:** 1 starch, 2 vegetable, 1 lean meat

---

SUPPLIES LIST FOR SUGGESTED MEAL
Electric toaster
Large salad bowl
Cutting board
Microwave-safe (4-cup glass) measuring cup or pitcher
Microwave oven
Wax paper
Timer

GROCERY LIST FOR SUGGESTED MEAL
Ingredients for the Chopped Italian and Rye Salad

PRODUCE
*1 medium head iceberg lettuce
*1 medium cucumber
*Grape tomatoes (1/2 cup needed)
*Fresh parsley (1/3 cup needed)

MEATS
1 (6 ounce) package turkey pepperoni

DAIRY
*Fancy shredded parmesan cheese (1/4 cup needed)

PACKAGED
*Seeded rye bread (2 slices needed)
1 (33.8 fl. oz) bottle of virgin Bloody Mary Mix
*Fat-free Italian dressing (2/3 cup needed)

PANTRY
Italian seasoning

Instructions to prepare the suggested meal

Set the timer for 15 minutes.

15 minutes before the meal

▶ Make the Chopped Italian and Rye Salad according to instructions.
▶ Place 2 ²/₃ cups of salad on each of 3 dinner-size plates and garnish each salad with 8 slices of turkey pepperoni. Keep chilled in the refrigerator as you make the beverages.

5 minutes before the meal

▶ Make the Warm Italian Virgin Marys.

MEAL SUGGESTION:
**15 MINUTES FOR
TOTAL MEAL:**
Warm Italian Virgin Marys
(page 282)

HELPFUL HINT:

❷ If you are making this salad ahead of time do NOT add the rye croutons or the salad dressing until just before you are ready to serve the salad; otherwise the croutons and lettuce will become soggy or wilted.

SUPPLIES LIST
Medium serving bowl
Grocery List

PRODUCE
1 fresh grapefruit

PACKAGED
2 (15-ounce) cans mandarin
oranges in light syrup

PANTRY
Splenda Brown Sugar Blend

Citrus Salad *10 minutes*

Save oodles of money making your own citrus salad that tastes twice as good as the prepackaged brands! This is equally tasty served at room temperature or chilled.

Ingredients

2 (15-ounce) cans mandarin oranges in light syrup
2 tablespoons Splenda Brown Sugar Blend
1 fresh grapefruit

Instructions

▸ Drain and reserve 1/3 cup of the juice from the mandarin oranges. Discard the remaining juice. Keep the oranges in the cans.
▸ In a medium serving bowl, stir the Splenda Brown Sugar Blend into the reserved juice until the sugar is completely dissolved.
▸ Quarter and remove the fruit segments from the grapefruit.
▸ Gently stir the mandarin orange and grapefruit segments into the sweetened juice.
▸ Serve.

Yield: 6 (1/2-cup) servings **Calories per serving:** 112 (0% fat); **Total fat:** 0 g; **Cholesterol:** 0 mg; **Carbohydrate:** 28 g; **Dietary Fiber:** 1 g; **Protein:** 1 g; **Sodium:** 7 mg **Diabetic Exchanges:** 2 fruit

---

HELPFUL HINTS:

❯ You can use regular brown sugar instead of the Splenda Brown Sugar Blend, but it will add more calories.

❯ To segment the grapefruit:

1. Cut it into quarters.

2. Run a knife between the skin and fruit to loosen the fruit from the skin.

3. Remove the fruit segments from the skins.

Cherry Berry Fruit Salad _5 minutes_

You do not need to have anything pre-chilled for this salad; the frozen berries are cold enough to chill the entire fruit salad. It is oh, so good!

Ingredients

1 (16-ounce) package frozen berry medley
1 (20-ounce) can no-sugar-added cherry pie filling
1/2 teaspoon almond extract
1 tablespoon Splenda granular
3 tablespoons fat-free whipped topping

Instructions

▸ In a medium-size serving bowl, stir together the frozen berry medley with the pie filling.
▸ Add the almond extract and Splenda.
▸ Spoon out six 1/2-cup servings of Cherry Berry Fruit Salad.
▸ Place 1/2 tablespoon of whipped topping on each serving.
▸ Serve.

Yield: 6 (1/2-cup) servings **Calories per serving:** 82 (0% fat); **Total fat:** 0 g;
Cholesterol: 0 mg; **Carbohydrate:** 19 g; **Dietary Fiber:** 3 g; **Protein:** 1 g; **Sodium:**
12 mg **Diabetic Exchanges:** 1 1/2 fruit

SUPPLIES LIST
Medium-size serving bowl

GROCERY LIST

FROZEN
1 (8-ounce) fat-free dessert whipped topping
(3 tablespoons needed)

PACKAGED
1 (16-ounce) package frozen berry medley
1 (20-ounce) can no-sugar-added cherry pie filling

PANTRY
Almond extract
Splenda granular

HELPFUL HINTS:

❷ The berries do not need to be thawed for this recipe. The benefit to using frozen berries is you don't have to pre-chill anything; the berries will chill everything nicely.

❷ The berry medley includes strawberries, blackberries, blueberries, and red raspberries.

❷ You can use regular granulated sugar but it will increase your calories.

SUPPLIES LIST
Large salad bowl
Cutting board

GROCERY LIST

PRODUCE
1 bunch fresh parsley
(1 cup chopped needed)
1 large head iceberg lettuce
1 pint grape tomatoes

PACKAGED
Fat-free Italian salad dressing
(1 cup needed)
Jar of mild pepperoncini
peppers (Vlasic)
(need 1/4 cup juice)

PANTRY
Minced garlic
Dried Italian seasoning

Tomato and Parsley Chopped Salad *10 minutes*

You're going to love the great flavor combination of Italian and Greek in this salad.

Ingredients

1 cup fat-free Italian salad dressing
1 tablespoon minced garlic (from a jar is fine)
1/2 tablespoon dried Italian seasoning
1 cup loosely packed chopped fresh parsley
1 large head of iceberg lettuce
1/4 cup juice from a jar of mild pepperoncini peppers (Vlasic)
1 pint grape tomatoes

Instructions

▶ In the bottom of a large salad bowl, stir together the salad dressing, minced garlic, dried Italian seasoning, parsley, and pepperoncini juice until well blended.
▶ Chop the lettuce to make 7 firmly packed cups.
▶ Add the lettuce to the dressing in the bottom of bowl.
▶ Add the grape tomatoes to the lettuce. Gently toss the ingredients together with your hands.
▶ Serve.

Yield: 7 (1 cup) servings **Calories per serving:** 45 (11% fat); **Total fat:** 1 g; **Cholesterol:** 1 mg; **Carbohydrate:** 9 g; **Dietary Fiber:** 2 g; **Protein:** 2 g; **Sodium:** 555 mg **Diabetic Exchanges:** 1/2 carbohydrate

---

Polynesian Fruit Salad *5 minutes*

The sweet and succulent tropical flavors of the Polynesian islands are featured in this delightful dish!

Ingredients

1 banana
10 maraschino cherries
1 (15-ounce) can tropical fruit salad, chilled and drained (reserve juice for punch on page 292)
1 (15-ounce) can whole-segment mandarin oranges, chilled and drained (reserve juice for punch on page 292)
2 tablespoons firmly packed shredded coconut

Instructions

▸ Slice the banana and place in a medium serving bowl with the maraschino cherries, fruit salad, mandarin oranges, and shredded coconut.
▸ Stir all together.

Yield: 4 (1-cup) servings **Calories per serving:** 169 (6% fat); **Total fat:** 1 g; **Cholesterol:** 0 mg; **Carbohydrate:** 40 g; **Dietary Fiber:** 2 g; **Protein:** 2 g; **Sodium:** 19 mg **Diabetic Exchanges:** 2½ fruit

---

SALADS

SUPPLIES LIST
Medium serving bowl

GROCERY LIST

PRODUCE
1 banana

PACKAGED
1 (15-ounce) can tropical fruit salad
1 (15-ounce) can whole-segment mandarin oranges
1 (6-ounce) jar maraschino cherries

PANTRY
Shredded coconut
(2 tablespoons needed)

HELPFUL HINT:

❷ Pre-chill your ingredients by placing the canned goods in the refrigerator when you arrive home with the groceries.

SUPPLIES LIST

Large salad bowl
Cutting board

GROCERY LIST

PRODUCE
1 (9-ounce) package baby
spinach

PACKAGED
Low-fat slaw dressing
(Marzetti, 1/4 cup needed)
Vanilla yogurt raisins
(21 needed)
Fat-free croutons

PANTRY
Balsamic vinegar

Sweet and Tangy Spinach Salad *5 minutes*

Don't be surprised if this becomes your new favorite spinach salad!

Ingredients

1/4 cup low-fat slaw dressing (Marzetti)
1/2 tablespoon balsamic vinegar
1 (9-ounce) package baby spinach, prewashed
1/2 cup fat-free croutons, divided
21 vanilla yogurt raisins, finely chopped

Instructions

‣ In a large salad bowl, mix together the slaw dressing with the balsamic vinegar.
‣ Combine the baby spinach leaves and croutons with the salad dressing.
‣ Toss ingredients together to coat the spinach with the dressing.
‣ Sprinkle croutons and chopped yogurt raisins on top of the salad and serve.

Yield: 4 (11/4-cup servings) **Calories per serving:** 78 (19% fat); **Total fat:** 2 g;
Cholesterol: 8 mg; **Carbohydrate:** 14 g; **Dietary Fiber:** 2 g; **Protein:** 2 g;
Sodium: 257 mg **Diabetic Exchanges:** 1 carbohydrate, 1/2 fat

---

HELPFUL HINT:

❍ A super fast way to toss ingredients together is with your hands!

Chunky Pear and Cherry Salad *15 minutes*

This salad complements pork, fish, and chicken dishes. It also makes a nutritious dessert.

Ingredients

3 Bartlett pears
1 (20-ounce) can no-sugar-added cherry pie filling, chilled
1/2 teaspoon ground cinnamon

Instructions

▶ Chop the pears into bite-size pieces to make 4 cups. Place the chopped pears in a medium-size serving bowl. Stir in the cherry pie filling and cinnamon.
▶ Serve.

Yield: 8 (1/2-cup) servings **Calories per serving:** 68 (0% fat); **Total fat:** 0 g;
Cholesterol: 0 mg; **Carbohydrate:** 17 g; **Dietary Fiber:** 3 g; **Protein:** 0 g;
Sodium: 9 mg **Diabetic Exchanges:** 1 fruit

SUPPLIES LIST
Medium-size serving bowl
Cutting board

GROCERY LIST

PRODUCE
3 Bartlett pears

PACKAGED
1 (20-ounce) can no-sugar-added cherry pie filling

PANTRY
Ground cinnamon

HELPFUL HINT:

❍ Place the can of no-sugar-added cherry pie filling in the refrigerator prior to making this recipe so it will be nice and cold when you serve it. I find this easiest to do while I am putting my groceries away as soon as I get home from the store.

Cherry-Pear Luncheon Salad *25 minutes*

This pretty salad is perfect for a ladies luncheon.

Ingredients

3 Bartlett pears, chilled
1/4 cup dried cherries
1 (20-ounce) can no-sugar-added cherry pie filling, chilled
1/2 teaspoon ground cinnamon, optional
1/2 cup light balsamic vinaigrette salad dressing, chilled
2 large heads romaine lettuce (15 cups chopped into bite-size pieces)
1 pound extra-lean Canadian bacon, sliced into thin strips
1/2 cup fat-free seasoned croutons, optional

Instructions

▸ Chop 3 pears into bite-size pieces to make 4 cups. Chop the dried cherries into tiny pieces.

▸ Place the chopped pears and dried cherries into a very large salad bowl. Stir in cherry pie filling, cinnamon, and salad dressing. Set aside.

▸ Chop the lettuce into bite-size pieces to make about 15 cups. Place in the salad bowl with the fruit mixture.

▸ Add the Canadian bacon strips to the salad.

▸ Mix all ingredients well.

▸ If desired sprinkle 1/2 cup fat-free seasoned croutons on top.

▸ Serve immediately.

Yield: 6 (2-1/2-cup) entrée size servings (croutons included) **Calories per serving:** 235 (14% fat); **Total fat:** 4 g; **Cholesterol:** 41 mg; **Carbohydrate:** 35 g; **Dietary Fiber:** 7 g; **Protein:** 16 g; **Sodium:** 1236 mg **Diabetic Exchanges:** 2 fruit, 1 vegetable, 2 lean meat

SUPPLIES LIST FOR SUGGESTED MEAL
Very large salad bowl
2-quart pitcher
Cutting board
Timer

GROCERY LIST FOR SUGGESTED MEAL
Ingredients for the Cherry-Pear Luncheon Salad

PRODUCE
*3 Bartlett pears
*2 large heads romaine lettuce
2 kiwis

MEATS
*1 pound extra-lean Canadian bacon

PACKAGED
*Dried cherries (1/4 cup needed)
*1 (20-ounce) can no-sugar-added cherry pie filling
*Light balsamic vinaigrette salad dressing (1/2 cup needed)
*Fat-free seasoned croutons (optional)
Sugar-free instant tea packets (2 quarts needed)

PANTRY
*Ground cinnamon

Instructions to prepare the suggested meal

Set the timer for 30 minutes.

30 minutes before the meal

▸ Make the Kiwi Tea and refrigerate to keep chilled.
▸ Make the salad.

MEAL SUGGESTION:
30 MINUTES FOR
TOTAL MEAL:
Kiwi Tea (page 294)

HELPFUL HINTS:

❯ You can substitute extra-lean ham for the Canadian bacon if you like.

❯ Place the can of cherry pie filling, the pears, and the salad dressing in the refrigerator as soon as you get home from the store so they are already chilled when you get ready to make the meal.

Tomato Italiano Soup (page 108)

Soups and Chowders

Beef Is Boss Chili *10 minutes*

Meat lovers especially like the chunks of roast beef in this hearty beefy chili!

Ingredients

2 (14.5-ounce) cans of diced, chili-ready peeled tomatoes
1 (15.5-ounce) hot and spicy chili beans
2 (12-ounce) cans roast beef

Instructions for entrée:

▸ Place a large Dutch oven or 4 1/2-quart saucepan on high heat.
▸ Add the tomatoes, chili beans, and roast beef to Dutch oven.
▸ Once the ingredients come to a full boil, reduce the heat to medium-low and let cook for 5 minutes.

Yield: 8 (1-cup) servings **Calories per serving:** 153 (15% fat); **Total fat:** 2 g; **Cholesterol:** 26 mg; **Carbohydrate:** 21 g; **Dietary Fiber:** 4 g; **Protein:** 13 g; **Sodium:** 1337 mg **Diabetic Exchanges:** 1 starch, 1 vegetable, 1 1/2 very lean meat

Instructions to prepare the suggested meal

Set the timer for 10 minutes.

10 minutes before the meal

▸ Prepare the Beef Is Boss Chili according to the directions.

5 minutes before the meal

▸ While the chili is cooking, prepare the the Light and Creamy Dip (dressing) according to the directions.
▸ Put celery sticks and crackers on a plate with the Light and Creamy Dip.

Chicken and White Bean Chowder *10 minutes*

Bodybuilders and fitness gurus alike will appreciate the benefits of this power-packed chowder. Not to be mistaken for white chicken chili, this chowder is full of flavor without being spicy.

Ingredients

1 (48-ounce) jar Great Northern Beans
2 (12.5-ounce) cans chunk chicken
1/4 cup diced pimiento (optional)
1 (.75-ounce) package Hidden Valley Ranch mix
1 1/3 cup fat-free sour cream
1 sweet onion

Instructions for entrée:

▸ In a Dutch oven or 4 1/2-quart saucepan over high heat, add the beans, chicken, diced pimiento, Hidden Valley Ranch mix, and sour cream. Mash with a potato masher to help break up the chicken and beans. Bring to a low boil.
▸ Reduce the heat to medium-low and cook at a low boil for a couple of minutes, stirring occasionally.
▸ Finely chop the onion to make 2/3 cup.
▸ Sprinkle 1 tablespoon finely chopped sweet onion on top of each 1 cup serving of soup and serve.

Yield: 10 (1-cup) servings **Calories per serving:** 230 (7% fat); **Total fat:** 2 g; **Cholesterol:** 35 mg; **Carbohydrate:** 26 g; **Dietary Fiber:** 8 g; **Protein:** 23 g; **Sodium:** 970 mg **Diabetic Exchanges:** 2 starch, 2 1/2 very lean meat

---

Instructions to prepare the suggested meal

Set the timer for 10 minutes.

10 minutes before the meal

▸ Prepare the Chicken and White Bean Chowder as directed.

5 minutes before the meal

▸ Slice the bell peppers and arrange on a plate with a cup of fat-free French salad dressing for dip.
▸ Finish preparing the White Bean Chowder by sprinkling 1 tablespoon of finely chopped sweet onion on top of each 1-cup serving of chowder.

SUPPLIES LIST FOR SUGGESTED MEAL
Dutch oven or 4 1/2-quart saucepan
Potato masher
Cutting board
Timer

GROCERY LIST FOR SUGGESTED MEAL
Ingredients for the Chicken and White Bean Chowder

PRODUCE
*1 sweet onion (2/3 cup chopped needed)
3 to 4 bell peppers (to slice as a side with dip)

DAIRY
*Fat-free sour cream (1 1/3 cups needed)

PACKAGED
*1 (48-ounce) jar Great Northern Beans
*2 (12.5-ounce) cans chunk chicken
*Diced pimiento (optional)
*1 (.75-ounce) package Hidden Valley Ranch mix
Fat-free French salad dressing (for pepper dip)

MENU SUGGESTION: 10 MINUTES FOR TOTAL MEAL:
Sliced bell peppers with fat-free French salad dressing for dip

HELPFUL HINTS:

❷ To save time you can buy a pre-sliced vegetable tray, but it will be more expensive.

❷ The liquid from the cans of chicken are used to enhance the flavor of this chowder.

89

SUPPLIES LIST FOR
SUGGESTED MEAL
Dutch oven or 4¹/2-quart
saucepan
Potato masher
Timer
Large salad bowl
Cutting board

GROCERY LIST FOR
SUGGESTED MEAL
*Ingredients for the Hawaiian
Sweet Potato Soup

PRODUCE
1 head iceberg lettuce
*1 onion (¹/2 cup finely
chopped needed)

MEATS
*1 (8-ounce) package diced ham

DAIRY
Nonfat plain yogurt
(¹/2 cup needed)

PACKAGED
*1 (40-ounce) can sweet
potatoes in syrup
*1 (8-ounce) can pineapple
tidbits in unsweetened juice

PANTRY
*Chicken broth (2 cups needed)
*Ground red pepper
Sugar-free French Vanilla
creamer (¹/4 cup needed)
Salt
Dry dill

MEAL SUGGESTION:
10 MINUTES FOR
TOTAL MEAL:
Light and Creamy Dilly Iceberg
Salad (page 67)

HELPFUL HINT:

❯ You can make the broth by
using bouillon, but it will add
sodium to the soup.

Hawaiian Sweet Potato Soup *10 minutes*

My nineteen-year-old daughter loves this soup, even though she's not usually a fan of sweet potatoes. This unique recipe really does satisfy us on those days when we crave something sweet and salty.

Ingredients

1 (8-ounce) package diced ham
1 small sweet onion
2 cups chicken broth
1 (40-ounce) can sweet potatoes in syrup
1 (8-ounce) can pineapple tidbits in unsweetened juice
¹/4 teaspoon ground red pepper

Instructions for entrée:

▸ In a Dutch oven or 4¹/2-quart saucepan, cook the diced ham on high heat.
▸ While the ham is cooking, finely chop the onion to make ¹/2 cup.
▸ Add the onions to the cooked ham.
▸ Add the chicken broth, sweet potatoes in syrup, pineapples in unsweetened juice, and ground red pepper to the ham mixture.
▸ With a potato masher, break up the sweet potatoes, and mix the ingredients until the potatoes are well mashed and the broth thickens.
▸ Bring to a boil.
▸ Reduce the heat to medium-low and let simmer.

Yield: 8 (1-cup) servings **Calories per serving:** 172 (11% fat); **Total fat:** 2 g; **Cholesterol:** 15 mg; **Carbohydrate:** 32 g; **Dietary Fiber:** 2 g; **Protein:** 7 g; **Sodium:** 621 mg **Diabetic Exchanges:** 1 starch, 1 carbohydrate, ¹/2 lean meat

Instructions to prepare the suggested meal

Set the timer for 10 minutes.

10 minutes before the meal

▸ Prepare the Hawaiian Sweet Potato Soup according to the directions.

5 minutes before the meal

▸ Prepare the Light and Creamy Dilly Iceberg Salad as directed.

Egg Drop Soup *10 minutes*

If you had known egg drop soup was so super simple to make, I bet you would have started making it years ago!

Ingredients

1 (48-ounce) can light and fat-free chicken broth
1/4 cup cornstarch
2 eggs
1/2 teaspoon light salt

Instructions for entrée:

▸ Reserve 1/2 cup chicken broth and place into a 1-cup measuring cup.
▸ Pour the remaining chicken broth into a 4-quart nonstick saucepan over high heat.
▸ Stir together the reserved chicken broth and cornstarch until the cornstarch is dissolved. Set aside.
▸ In a small bowl, with a whisk or fork beat the eggs and set aside.
▸ When the broth comes to a boil, stir in the cornstarch mixture. The broth will begin to thicken.
▸ After the soup comes to a boil again, slowly whisk in the beaten egg.
▸ Stir in the light salt.
▸ Reduce the heat to low and keep warm until ready to eat.
▸ Pepper to taste, if desired.

Yield: 6 (1-cup) servings **Calories per serving:** 49 (32% fat); **Total fat:** 2 g; **Cholesterol:** 71 mg; **Carbohydrate:** 5 g; **Dietary Fiber:** 0 g; **Protein:** 3 g; **Sodium:** 566 mg **Diabetic Exchanges:** 1/2 starch, 1/2 fat

---

Instructions to prepare the suggested meal

Set the timer for 20 minutes.

20 minutes before the meal

▸ Make the the Egg Drop soup, and then reduce the heat to low to keep warm.

11 minutes before the meal

▸ Make the Mushroom Parmesan Muffin Toppers.

SOUPS AND CHOWDERS

SUPPLIES LIST FOR SUGGESTED MEAL
1-cup measuring cup
4-quart nonstick saucepan
Small bowl
Whisk
Oven
Baking sheet
Cutting board
Timer

GROCERY LIST FOR SUGGESTED MEAL
Ingredients for the Egg Drop Soup

PRODUCE
4 ounces fresh mushrooms

DAIRY
*Eggs (2 needed)
1/4 cup finely shredded parmesan cheese

PACKAGED
4 English muffins

PANTRY
*1 (48-ounce) can light and fat-free chicken broth
*Cornstarch (1/4 cup needed)
*Light salt
Garlic salt
Nonfat butter-flavored cooking spray

MEAL SUGGESTION: 20 MINUTES FOR TOTAL MEAL:
Mushroom Parmesan Muffin Toppers (page 237)

HELPFUL HINTS:

❯ Use a 1-cup measuring cup to measure the 1/2 cup of broth, and then stir the cornstarch in the measuring cup to save cleaning another bowl.

❯ Sea salt can be substituted for light salt.

**SUPPLIES LIST FOR
SUGGESTED MEAL**
Large nonstick Dutch oven
Cutting board
Whisk
2 cookie sheets or jelly-roll pans
Timer

**GROCERY LIST FOR
SUGGESTED MEAL**
*Ingredients for the
Southwestern Chicken
Enchilada Soup*

PACKAGED
*1 (27-ounce) package
6-inch corn tortillas
(21 tortillas needed)
*1 (15.5-ounce) jar mild
chunky salsa
*1 (15-ounce) can
no-salt-added golden sweet
whole kernel corn

MEAT
*2 (12.5-ounce) cans chunk
chicken breast

PANTRY
*8 cups chicken broth made
from bouillon
Light salt
Taco seasoning
Nonstick cooking spray

**MEAL SUGGESTION:
20 MINUTES FOR
TOTAL MEAL:**
Salt and Pepper Baked Corn
Tortilla Chips (page 235) or
Southwestern Corn Tortilla
Chips (page 236)

Southwestern Chicken Enchilada Soup *15 minutes*

Every generation will enjoy the flavors of this mildly spicy soup.

Ingredients

8 cups chicken broth made from bouillon
1 (15.5-ounce) jar mild chunky salsa
1 (15-ounce) can no-salt-added golden sweet whole kernel corn
2 (12.5-ounce) cans chunk chicken breast
12 (6-inch) corn tortillas

Instructions

▸ In a large nonstick Dutch oven or soup pan over high heat, add the chicken broth.
▸ Add salsa, corn, and chicken breasts to the broth.
▸ Stir and bring to a boil.
▸ Cut the corn tortillas into 1-inch squares. Set aside.
▸ Once the soup comes to a full boil, add the cut-up tortillas. Reduce the heat to medium low and continue cooking for 1 additional minute.
▸ Stir the soup with a whisk to break the corn tortillas into tiny pieces.
▸ Turn off the heat and let sit for a few minutes before serving.

Yield: 15 (1-cup) servings **Calories per serving:** 104 (12% fat); **Total fat:** 1 g; **Cholesterol:** 20 mg; **Carbohydrate:** 12 g; **Dietary Fiber:** 1 g; **Protein:** 10 g; **Sodium:** 516 mg **Diabetic Exchanges:** 1 starch, 1 1/2 very lean meat

---

Instructions to prepare the suggested meal

Set the timer for 20 minutes.

20 minutes before the meal

▸ Make the Southwestern Chicken Pot Pie Soup according to the directions.

10 minutes before the meal

▸ Make the Southwestern Corn Tortilla Chips or Salt and Pepper Baked Corn Tortilla Chips according to the directions.

Vegetarian Southwestern Tomato Soup *15 minutes*

The secret ingredients in this soup take ordinary tomato soup to a whole new level. This extraordinary thick and spicy tomato soup is anything but ordinary.

Ingredients

2 (14.5-ounce) cans of Mexican-style stewed tomatoes
1 (28-ounce) can enchilada sauce (mild)
2 (15.25-ounce) cans whole kernel corn
1 (31-ounce) can of refried beans
1 (46 fluid ounce) can tomato juice

Instructions for entrée:

▸ In a large Dutch oven or soup pan, stir together over high heat the tomatoes, enchilada sauce, corn, and refried beans until well mixed.
▸ Stir frequently until the soup begins to boil. Let it cook at a low boil for a couple minutes; then serve.

Yield: 19 (1-cup) servings **Calories per serving:** 114 (0% fat); **Total fat:** 0 g; **Cholesterol:** 0 mg; **Carbohydrate:** 21 g; **Dietary Fiber:** 5 g; **Protein:** 5 g; **Sodium:** 1067 mg **Diabetic Exchanges:** 1 starch, 1 vegetable

---

Instructions to prepare the suggested meal

Set the timer for 15 minutes.

15 minutes before the meal

▸ Prepare the Vegetarian Southwestern Tomato Soup as directed.

10 minutes before the meal

▸ Make the Southwestern Corn Tortilla Chips.

5 minutes before the meal

▸ Reduce the heat under the soup to low to keep warm while the Southwestern Corn Tortilla Chips bake.

SUPPLIES LIST FOR SUGGESTED MEAL
Large nonstick Dutch oven or soup pan
Oven
2 cookie sheets or jelly-roll pans
Timer

GROCERY LIST FOR SUGGESTED MEAL
Ingredients for the Vegetarian Southwestern Tomato Soup

PACKAGED
*2 (14.5-ounce) cans of Mexican-style stewed tomatoes
*1 (28-ounce) can enchilada sauce (mild)
*2 (15.25-ounce) cans whole kernel corn
*1 (31-ounce) can of refried beans
*1 (46 fluid ounce) can tomato juice
9 (6-inch) corn tortillas

PANTRY
Light salt
Taco seasoning
Nonstick cooking spray

MEAL SUGGESTION: 10 MINUTES FOR TOTAL MEAL:
Southwestern Corn Tortilla Chips (page 236)

Salmon Chowder   *15 minutes*

The fats in this creamy chowder are the healthy kind that help fight heart disease and cancer. They are also known to help ease the discomfort of arthritis.

Ingredients

2 (15-ounce) cans diced potatoes
1 (14.75-ounce) can salmon
2 cups 1% low-fat milk
1 1/4 teaspoon Old Bay Seasoning
1 1/4 teaspoon lemon pepper seasoning salt
1/2 teaspoon dried dill weed

Instructions *for entrée:*

▸ In a nonstick Dutch oven or 4 1/2-quart saucepan over medium heat, mash the diced potatoes with a potato masher.
▸ While the potatoes are heating, pour the salmon into a separate bowl. Using your hands break up the salmon and remove any bones you may see or feel. Add the salmon to the potatoes.
▸ Add the milk, Old Bay Seasoning, lemon pepper seasoning salt, and dry dill weed to the Dutch oven or pan.
▸ While the chowder is cooking, mash the potato mixture. There will still be chunks of potato, but the mashed potatoes will act as a thickening agent. Stir occasionally until fully heated, and then serve.

Yield: 7 1/2 (1-cup) servings **Calories per serving:** 173 (18% fat); **Total fat:** 4 g; **Cholesterol:** 50 mg; **Carbohydrate:** 19 g; **Dietary Fiber:** 3 g; **Protein:** 17 g; **Sodium:** 667 mg **Diabetic Exchanges:** 1 1/2 starch, 2 lean meat

Instructions to prepare the suggested meal

Set the timer for 15 minutes.

15 minutes before the meal

▸ Prepare the Salmon Chowder as directed.

5 minutes before the meal

▸ As the Salmon Chowder is cooking, prepare the Light and Creamy Salsa Salad according to the directions.

MEAL SUGGESTION:
15 MINUTES FOR
TOTAL MEAL:
Light and Creamy Salsa
Salad (page 67)
Oyster Crackers

HELPFUL HINTS:

❷ The liquid in the can of salmon is used to enrich the flavor of this chowder.

❷ To lower the fat content, replace the low-fat milk with skim milk. Use salmon packed in water instead of oil.

❷ To make a prettier presentation when serving, place a sprig of fresh dill on top of the soup.

❷ Old Bay Seasoning is found in the spice aisle.

SUPPLIES LIST FOR
SUGGESTED MEAL
Large nonstick Dutch oven or
4 1/2-quart saucepan
Potato masher
Large salad bowl
Cutting board
Timer

GROCERY LIST FOR
SUGGESTED MEAL
*Ingredients for the Corny
Clam Chowder

PRODUCE
1 head iceberg lettuce
Sweet onion

DAIRY
Nonfat plain yogurt
(1/2 cup needed)

PACKAGED
*3 (6 1/2-ounce) cans
minced clams
*1 (8-ounce) bottle of
clam juice
*2 (10 3/4-ounce) cans Healthy
Request cream of celery soup
*1 (15-ounce) can diced
potatoes
*1 (15-ounce) can whole
kernel corn
*Oyster crackers (optional)

PANTRY
*Old Bay Seasoning
Sugar-free French vanilla
creamer (1/4 cup needed)
Salt
Dry dill

Corny Clam Chowder   *15 minutes*

Why spend the big bucks at a fancy restaurant when you can make this quick and easy chowder at home for a fraction of the cost and calories?

Ingredients

3 (6 1/2-ounce) cans minced clams
1 (8-ounce) bottle of clam juice, well shaken
2 (10 3/4-ounce) cans Healthy Request cream of celery soup
1 (15-ounce) can diced potatoes
1 (15-ounce) can whole kernel corn
1 teaspoon of Old Bay Seasoning

Instructions *for entrée:*

▸ Place a large nonstick Dutch oven or 4 1/2-quart saucepan on medium heat.
▸ Add the minced clams, clam juice, cream of celery soup, potatoes, corn, and Old Bay Seasoning to the pan. Use a potato masher to mash together the ingredients while cooking. This will help the potatoes break down and thicken the chowder.
▸ Once the chowder is fully heated, serve.

Yield: 8 (1-cup) servings **Calories per serving:** 144 (14% fat); **Total fat:** 2 g; **Cholesterol:** 15 mg; **Carbohydrate:** 23 g; **Dietary Fiber:** 3 g; **Protein:** 7 g; **Sodium:** 1056 mg **Diabetic Exchanges:** 1 1/2 starch, 1 very lean meat

---

Instructions to prepare the suggested meal

Set the timer for 15 minutes.

15 minutes before the meal

▸ Prepare the Corny Clam Chowder according to the directions.

5 minutes before the meal

▸ While the Corny Clam Chowder is cooking, make the Light and Creamy Dilly Iceberg Salad according to the directions.

MEAL SUGGESTION:
**15 MINUTES FOR
TOTAL MEAL:**
Light and Creamy Dilly
Iceberg Salad (page 67,
variation)
Oyster Crackers

HELPFUL HINT:

❷ The liquid from the cans of minced clams is used to to enrich the flavor of this chowder.

❷ Healthy Request Soup is 98% fat-free and is reduced in sodium.

SUPPLIES LIST FOR
SUGGESTED MEAL
4 1/2-quart saucepan or
Dutch oven
Oven
Cookie sheet
Timer

GROCERY LIST FOR
SUGGESTED MEAL
*Ingredients for the Ham,
Green Bean, and Potato Soup

MEAT
*1 pound package diced
lean ham

DAIRY
Shredded fat-free mozzarella
cheese (1 cup needed)
Shredded parmesan cheese
(1/4 cup needed)
Fat-free feta cheese
crumbles (1/4 cup needed)

PACKAGED
*2 (15-ounce) cans sliced new
potatoes
*2 (14.5-ounce) cans
French-style green beans
*Fat-free Italian salad
dressing
(1/2 cup needed)
Fat-free multi-grain
whole-wheat bread
(7 slices needed)

*Grocery list continued
on next page*

Ham, Green Bean, and Potato Soup *15 minutes*

This is one of my all-time favorite soups! Light and filling at the same time.

Ingredients

1 pound package diced lean ham
2 (15-ounce) cans sliced new potatoes
2 (14.5-ounce) cans French-style green beans
4 cups chicken broth (or chicken bouillon broth)
1/2 cup fat-free Italian salad dressing
1 tablespoon dried parsley
1 tablespoon butter-flavored sprinkles

Instructions *for entrée:*

- In a 4 1/2-quart saucepan or Dutch oven, cook the ham on high heat.
- While the meat is cooking, drain the potatoes and green beans.
- Add the potatoes, green beans, chicken broth, salad dressing, dried parsley, and butter-flavored sprinkles to the ham. Stir to mix well.
- Once the soup comes to a boil, reduce the heat to medium-low.
- Cook with the lid off until the rest of the meal is completed.

Yield: 9 (1-cup) servings **Calories per serving:** 170 (21% fat); **Total fat:** 4 g; **Cholesterol:** 27 mg; **Carbohydrate:** 19 g; **Dietary Fiber:** 4 g; **Protein:** 14 g; **Sodium:** 1748 mg **Diabetic Exchanges**: 2 1/2 carbohydrate, 2 lean meat

---

Instructions to prepare the suggested meal

Set the timer for 20 minutes.

20 minutes before the meal

- ▶ Preheat the oven to 450 degrees.
- ▶ Prepare the Cheesy Triangles recipe and set aside. *Do not bake yet.*
- ▶ Make the Ham, Green Bean, and Potato Soup recipe.
- ▶ Once the soup comes to a boil, reduce the heat to medium-low to simmer.

5 minutes before the meal

- ▶ While the soup is simmering bake the Cheesy Triangles.

PANTRY
*Dried parsley
*Butter-flavored sprinkles
(Butter Buds)
*4 cups chicken broth
Nonfat butter-flavored
cooking spray

**MEAL SUGGESTION:
20 MINUTES FOR
TOTAL MEAL:**
Cheesy Triangles (page 230)

HELPFUL HINTS:

❯ If you'd like to use fresh parsley, substitute the dried parsley for 2 tablespoons of fresh, chopped parsley.

❯ Chicken broth is lower in sodium than chicken bouillon broth; however, chicken bouillon broth is usually less expensive. Chicken bouillon broth is easily made by simply stirring bouillon into water until it dissolves. Follow the directions on the bouillon package.

❯ Butter-flavored sprinkles are found in the spice aisle and are known as Molly McButter and Butter Buds.

SUPPLIES LIST FOR
SUGGESTED MEAL
Oven
Medium-sized (4 1/2-quart)
saucepan
2-3 oven-safe bowls
Toaster
Jelly-roll pan
Cutting board
Serving plate
Small bowl
Timer

GROCERY LIST FOR
SUGGESTED MEAL
*Ingredients for the Potato
Reuben Chowder

PRODUCE
2 large tomatoes

MEATS
*2 (2-ounce) packages lean
sliced corned beef

DAIRY
*3 slices natural Swiss cheese

PACKAGED
*2 (15-ounce) cans
diced potatoes
*2 (10 3/4-ounce) 98% fat-
free cream of celery soup
*Sauerkraut
(1/2 cup needed)
*Hearty rye bread
(3 slices needed)
Light Miracle Whip
(2 tablespoons needed)
Fat-free Miracle Whip
(1 tablespoon needed)

PANTRY
*Beef broth (2 cups needed)
Ketchup
Sweet relish
Dried parsley (optional)

Potato Reuben Chowder *20 minutes*

Do you like Reuben sandwiches made with rye bread, Swiss cheese, and sauerkraut? How about cream of potato soup? If you like them both, then you'll be delighted with this hearty chowder! Mm! Mm!

Ingredients

2 (2-ounce) packages lean sliced corned beef
2 (15-ounce) cans diced potatoes
2 (10 3/4-ounce) 98% fat-free cream of celery soup
2 cups beef broth
1/2 cup of sauerkraut
3 slices hearty rye bread
3 slices natural Swiss cheese

Instructions for entrée:

▸ Place the oven rack on the top shelf. Preheat the oven to 500 degrees.
▸ Preheat a 4 1/2-quart saucepan on medium heat.
▸ Cut the corned beef into thin strips. Place in the saucepan and heat over medium heat.
▸ Add the diced potatoes, cream of celery soup, and beef broth to the saucepan. Stir together and continue to cook on medium heat.
▸ Drain, rinse, and squeeze sauerkraut dry. Add to the soup. (Save the remaining sauerkraut for use in another recipe.)
▸ Toast the bread in toaster.
▸ While the bread is toasting, cut 3 slices of natural Swiss cheese into thin strips. Set aside.
▸ Cut the toasted bread into cubes to make croutons. Set aside.
▸ Place the oven-safe bowls on a jelly-roll pan. Place 1 cup of soup into each soup bowl.
▸ Divide croutons evenly and place on top of the soup; then divide the cheese strips evenly and place on top of the croutons.
▸ Place the jelly-roll pan in the oven on the top shelf, and bake 1 to 2 minutes, or until the cheese is melted.
▸ Transfer the bowls onto serving plates using pot holders (so you don't burn your hands).
▸ Repeat the final two steps until all of the soup is used.
▸ Serve immediately.

Yield: 8 (1-cup) servings **Calories per serving:** 190 (28% fat); **Total fat:** 6 g; **Cholesterol:** 19 mg; **Carbohydrate:** 26 g; **Dietary Fiber:** 4 g; **Protein:** 9 g; **Sodium:** 1297 mg **Diabetic Exchanges:** 2 starch, 1 lean meat

Instructions to prepare the suggested meal

30 minutes before the meal

- ▸ Begin making the soup according to the directions.
- ▸ Make the Tomato Slices with Homemade Thousand Island Dressing according to the directions.
- ▸ When the soup is fully heated, assemble the soups with rye croutons and Swiss cheese; then bake for 1 1/2 to 2 minutes on the top rack of the oven or until the cheese is melted.
- ▸ Place the crackers in a basket and serve with the meal.

SOUPS AND CHOWDERS

**MEAL SUGGESTION:
30 MINUTES FOR
TOTAL MEAL:**
Tomato Slices with
Homemade Thousand Island
Dressing page (213)
Rye Crackers

HELPFUL HINTS:

❷ For a more elegant presentation, serve the soup in hollowed-out rye bread rolls.

❷ Do not place the croutons and cheese on the soup until right before you bake the soup. Otherwise, the croutons will get soggy.

SUPPLIES LIST FOR
SUGGESTED MEAL
Large nonstick Dutch oven or
soup pan
Small bowl
Whisk
Oven
Large mixing bowl
Baking sheet
Medium-size bowl
Timer

GROCERY LIST FOR
SUGGESTED MEAL
*Ingredients for the Crabby
Corn Soup

DAIRY
* Eggs (2 needed)
Light fat-free vanilla yogurt
(1 cup needed)

FROZEN
1 (16-ounce) bag whole frozen
strawberries
2 (8-ounce) fFat-free dessert
whipped topping (2¹/2 cups
needed)

PACKAGED
*2 (14.75-ounce) cans
cream-style corn
*2 (12-ounce) packages leg-
style imitation crab meat
Heart Smart Bisquick
reduced-fat baking mix
(2 cups needed)

PANTRY
*1 (48-ounce) can light and
fat-free chicken broth
*Cornstarch
(¹/4 cup needed)
*Light salt
Granulated sugar
Splenda granular
Butter-flavored cooking
spray

Crabby Corn Soup   *20 minutes*

I got this idea from a local Chinese restaurant. They use shrimp in their recipe, but I prefer the imitation crab meat. The cost to make this entire meal is less than the cost of one bowl of this soup at the restaurant.

Ingredients

1 (48-ounce) can light and fat-free chicken broth
¹/4 cup cornstarch
2 eggs
2 (14.75-ounce) cans cream-style corn
2 (12-ounce) packages leg-style imitation crab meat
¹/2 teaspoon light salt

Instructions *for entrée:*

▸ Set aside ¹/2 cup chicken broth.
▸ Pour the remaining chicken broth into a large nonstick Dutch oven or soup pan. Cook over high heat.
▸ In a small bowl stir together with a whisk or a fork the reserved ¹/2 cup chicken broth and the cornstarch until the cornstarch is dissolved. Set aside.
▸ In a small bowl, with a whisk or fork, beat the eggs and set aside.
▸ When the chicken broth comes to a boil, slowly stir in the cornstarch mixture. The broth will thicken.
▸ Once the broth comes to a boil again, slowly stir the beaten egg into the boiling broth with either a whisk or a slotted spoon
▸ Reduce the heat to medium-low. Stir in the cream-style corn.
▸ Cut the imitation crab meat into bite-size pieces and add to the soup.
▸ Stir in the salt.
▸ Stir the soup occasionally, until heated through.

Yield: 11 (1-cup) servings **Calories per serving:** 153 (11% fat); **Total fat:** 2 g; **Cholesterol:** 69 mg; **Carbohydrate:** 23 g; **Dietary Fiber:** 1 g; **Protein:** 11 g; **Sodium:** 565 mg **Diabetic Exchanges:** 1¹/2 starch, 1 very lean meat

Instructions to prepare the suggested meal

Set the timer for 30 minutes.

30 minutes before the meal

- ▸ Make the Crabby Corn Soup.

15 minutes before the meal

- ▸ Make the Easiest Strawberry Shortcakes.

MEAL SUGGESTION:
30 MINUTES FOR
TOTAL MEAL:
Easiest Strawberry Shortcake
(page 260)

HELPFUL HINT:

❯ The consistency of this broth is like egg drop soup.

SUPPLIES LIST FOR
SUGGESTED MEAL
Large Dutch oven or soup pan
Medium mixing bowl
Cutting board
2 baking sheets
Timer

GROCERY LIST FOR
SUGGEST MEAL
*Ingredients for the
Chicken Pot Pie Soup

PACKAGED
*2 (14.5-ounce) cans
vegetable medley
*1 package (8-inch) flour
tortillas (8 tortillas needed)

POULTRY
*2 (12.5-ounce) cans chunk
chicken breast in water

PANTRY
*Chicken broth
(8 cups needed, made
from bouillon is fine)
*Cornstarch
(1/4 cup needed)
* Minced garlic
(2 tablespoons needed)
Garlic salt
Dried parsley
Paprika
Butter-flavored
cooking spray

Chicken Pot Pie Soup *20 minutes*

Rose Hall inspired this recipe. She used to make the best homemade chicken pot pie soup! She spent a lot of time preparing her homemade pot pie squares from scratch using flour and water. My super-simple method of using flour tortillas is every bit as tasty and a lot easier!

Ingredients

8 cups chicken broth (made from bouillon is fine)
2 (14.5-ounce) cans vegetable medley
2 (12.5-ounce) cans chunk chicken breast in water
1/4 cup cornstarch
2 tablespoons minced garlic (from a jar is fine)
1 1/2 teaspoon garlic salt
4 (8-inch) flour tortillas

Instructions for entrée:

▸ In a large Dutch oven or soup pan over high heat, add the chicken broth.
▸ Drain and reserve the liquid from the vegetable medley; add the vegetables to the broth. Place the reserved liquid from the vegetables into a medium bowl. Set aside.
▸ Add the chicken breast to the broth.
▸ Stir cornstarch into the reserved liquid from the vegetables until the cornstarch is dissolved. Stir into the soup.
▸ Add the minced garlic and garlic salt to the soup and stir.
▸ Cut the tortillas into 1-inch squares. Set aside.
▸ Once the soup comes to a full boil, stir in the tortilla squares and reduce the heat to medium.
▸ Cook for 2 additional minutes at a low boil.

Yield: 14 (1-cup) servings **Calories per serving:** 119 (9% fat); **Total fat:** 1 g; **Cholesterol:** 22 mg; **Carbohydrate:** 14 g; **Dietary Fiber:** 2 g; **Protein:** 11 g; **Sodium:** 776 mg **Diabetic Exchanges:** 1 starch, 1 1/2 very lean meat

---

Instructions to prepare the suggested meal

Set the timer for minutes 25 minutes.

25 minutes before the meal
- ▸ Preheat the oven to 450 degrees.
- ▸ Prepare the Chicken Pot Pie Soup according to the directions.

10 minutes before the meal
- ▸ Prepare the Homemade Seasoned Crackers according to the directions.

**MEAL SUGGESTION:
25 MINUTES FOR
TOTAL MEAL:**
Homemade Seasoned
Crackers (page 232)

HELPFUL HINTS:

❯ The easiest way to cut the tortillas into squares is to stack them into one pile and cut all of them at the same time.

❯ You can substitute reduced-sodium chicken broth but it will cost more than using bouillon.

SUPPLIES LIST FOR
SUGGESTED MEAL
Nonstick Dutch oven
or soup pan
Cutting board
Timer
Small serving plate
Basket for crackers

GROCERY LIST FOR
SUGGESTED MEAL
*Ingredients for the
Southwestern Pork Chowder

PRODUCE
Fresh celery sticks

MEATS
*2¹/2 pounds of boneless
pork loin

PACKAGED
*2 (14.5-ounce) cans of
Mexican-style stewed
tomatoes
*1 (28-ounce) can enchilada
sauce (mild)
*2 (15.25-ounce) cans
whole kernel corn
*1 (31-ounce) can of fat-free
refried beans
*1 (46 fluid ounce) can
tomato juice
*Whole-grain instant brown
rice (1¹/4 cups needed)
Fat-free ranch salad dressing
Whole-grain saltine crackers

Southwestern Pork Chowder *30 minutes*

This hearty chowder would be perfect for a men's event. For extra fun have different tasty toppers. Some suggestions: fat-free shredded cheddar cheese, reduced-fat Mexican-style shredded cheese, fat-free sour cream, or diced jalapeño peppers.

Ingredients

2 (14.5-ounce) cans of Mexican style stewed tomatoes
1 (28-ounce) can enchilada sauce (mild)
2 (15.25-ounce) cans whole kernel corn
1 (31-ounce) can of fat-free refried beans
1 (46 fluid ounce) can tomato juice
2¹/2 pounds of boneless pork loin
1¹/4 cups whole-grain instant brown rice

Instructions for entrée:

▸ In a large Dutch oven or soup pan, stir together over high heat the tomatoes, enchilada sauce, corn, refried beans, and tomato juice until well mixed.
▸ Stir frequently until the chowder comes to a full boil. While you wait for the chowder to boil, remove and discard all visible fat from the boneless pork loin and cut into ¹/2-inch cubes.
▸ Add the pork to the boiling chowder and stir.
▸ When the chowder returns to a full boil, add the whole-grain instant brown rice and stir until well mixed.
▸ Bring back to a full boil and allow to boil for 5 minutes, stirring frequently.
▸ Reduce the heat to low and simmer. The chowder will thicken as it sits.

Yield: 20 (1-cup) servings **Calories per serving:** 187 (16% fat); **Total fat:** 3 g; **Cholesterol:** 22 mg; **Carbohydrate:** 25 g; **Dietary Fiber:** 5 g; **Protein:** 13 g; **Sodium:** 1031 mg **Diabetic Exchanges:** 1 starch, 2 vegetable, 1 lean meat

Instructions to prepare the suggested meal

Set the timer for 30 minutes.

30 minutes before the meal

> Prepare the Southwestern Pork Chowder according to the directions.

5 minutes before the meal

> Place celery sticks on a plate with fat-free ranch salad dressing.
> Arrange crackers in a basket to serve on the side.

MEAL SUGGESTION:
30 MINUTES FOR
TOTAL MEAL:
Fresh celery sticks with
fat-free ranch salad dressing
for dipping
Whole-grain saltine crackers

HELPFUL HINT:

❷ After the fat has been removed from the pork, you should have approximately 1 3/4 pounds of lean meat.

❷ To save time and work you could purchase pre-cut pork stir-fry; however, that is more expensive.

Tomato Italiano Soup *30 minutes*

Joe, my seventh-grade neighbor, was pleasantly surprised at how much he liked this soup. He said, "This tastes like something you'd get at a fine Italian restaurant!"

Ingredients

1 (19.2-ounce) package Italian-style ground turkey
1 small bunch fresh kale (2 cups chopped)
1 (28-ounce) can petite diced tomatoes
1 (1-pound 10-ounce) jar Prego Three Cheese spaghetti sauce
1 (1-pound 9.75-ounce) jar Chunky Garden Prego spaghetti sauce
4 cups water
2 tablespoons Italian seasoning
3 tablespoons Splenda granular

Instructions for entrée:

▸ In a nonstick Dutch oven or soup pan brown the ground turkey on medium-high heat. Stir occasionally with a pancake turner.
▸ While the turkey is browning, rinse the kale, cut and discard the stems, and finely chop. Firmly press the kale into a measuring cup to make 2 cups. Set aside.
▸ Stir in the tomatoes, spaghetti sauce, water, Italian seasoning, chopped kale, and Splenda.
▸ Stir well to mix.
▸ Increase the heat to high to bring to a boil, stirring occasionally.
▸ Once the soup is at a full boil, reduce the heat to medium and let simmer for 15 minutes at a low boil, stirring occasionally.

Yield: 12 (1-cup) servings **Calories per serving:** 185 (33% fat); **Total fat:** 7 g; **Cholesterol:** 41 mg; **Carbohydrate:** 21 g; **Dietary Fiber:** 4 g; **Protein:** 9 g; **Sodium:** 890 mg **Diabetic Exchanges:** 1 vegetable, 1 carbohydrate, 1 lean meat, 1 fat

---

SUPPLIES LIST FOR
SUGGESTED MEAL
Nonstick Dutch oven
or soup pan
Oven
Baking sheet
Cutting board
Timer

GROCERY LIST FOR
SUGGESTED MEAL
*Ingredients for the
Tomato Italiano Soup

PRODUCE
*1 small bunch fresh kale
4 ounces fresh mushrooms

POULTRY
*1 (19.2-ounce) package Italian
style ground turkey

DAIRY
Finely shredded parmesan
cheese (1/4 cup needed)

PACKAGED
*1 (28-ounce) can petite
diced tomatoes
*1 (1-pound 10-ounce) jar
spaghetti sauce
(Prego Three Cheese)
*1 (1-pound 9.75-ounce) jar
spaghetti sauce
(Chunky Garden Prego)
4 English muffins

PANTRY
*Splenda granular
(3 tablespoons needed)
Garlic salt
Italian seasoning
(2 tablespoons needed)
Nonfat butter-flavored
cooking spray

Instructions to prepare the suggested meal

Set the timer for 30 minutes.

30 minutes before the meal

- Preheat the oven to 450 degrees.
- Prepare the Tomato Italiano Soup according to the directions.

15 minutes before the meal

- Prepare the Mushroom Parmesan Muffin Toppers according to the directions.

**MEAL SUGGESTION:
30 MINUTES FOR
TOTAL MEAL:**
Mushroom Parmesan Muffin
Toppers (page 237)

HELPFUL HINTS:

❷ Using a pancake turner to stir the browning turkey is easier and quicker than using a spoon.

❷ If using sweet Italian sausage links, remove the casing before browning. This is easily done by running scissors through the casing and then removing the sausage. Discard the skins.

Chicken Florentine Soup *30 minutes*

Many years ago there was a popular recipe for a low-carb soup that promoted weight loss. It had a lot of ingredients in it and took a lot of time to make. This soup is inspired by that recipe; however, there are a lot fewer ingredients, so you can make it quickly.

Ingredients

6 cups chicken broth
1 pound parsnips
1 medium turnip
2 (12.5-ounce) cans chunk chicken
1 pound frozen chopped spinach
1 tablespoon Splenda granular
2 tablespoon minced garlic

Instructions for entrée:

▸ Pour the chicken broth into a large Dutch oven or 4-quart saucepan. Bring to a boil over high heat.
▸ While the broth is coming to a boil, peel and slice the parsnips. Place into boiling broth.
▸ Peel and finely chop the turnip to make 1 cup. Place in the broth.
▸ Let the soup boil on high heat for 5 minutes.
▸ Add the chunk chicken to the boiling soup. Stir to break up the chicken.
▸ Bring the soup back to a boil and add the frozen chopped spinach, Splenda, and minced garlic.
▸ Reduce the heat to medium-low and let simmer, stirring occasionally.

Yield: 8 (1-cup) servings **Calories per serving:** 178 (18% fat); **Total fat:** 4 g; **Cholesterol:** 38 mg; **Carbohydrate:** 15 g; **Dietary Fiber:** 5 g; **Protein:** 21 g; **Sodium:** 1146 mg **Diabetic Exchanges:** 1 starch, 2 1/2 very lean meat

Instructions to prepare the suggested meal

Set the timer for 30 minutes.

30 minutes before the meal

- Preheat the oven to 450 degrees
- Prepare the Chicken Florentine Soup according to the directions.

10 minutes before the meal

- While the soup is cooking, make the Cheesy Triangles according to the directions.

MEAL SUGGESTION:
30 MINUTES FOR
TOTAL MEAL:
Cheesy Triangles (page 230)

HELPFUL HINTS:

❷ Parsnips are a root vegetable, shaped like a carrot, but white in color. They are low in carbs and have a sweet flavor.

❷ To save time you could use a food processor to cut the vegetables.

❷ Cut the thick ends of the parsnips into smaller pieces.

❷ Turnips have the consistency of potatoes and taste like a very mild radish.

SUPPLIES LIST FOR
SUGGESTED MEAL
Large soup pan or Dutch oven
Oven
Large mixing bowl
Whisk
Large baking sheet
Timer

GROCERY LIST FOR
SUGGESTED MEAL
*Ingredients for the
Minestrone Soup

MEATS
*1 (36-ounce) package
extra-lean ground beef

DAIRY
Fat-free sour cream (1 cup
plus 2 tablespoons needed)
Eggs (6 needed)

PACKAGED
*1 (64-ounce) jar
vegetable juice
*1 (26-ounce) jar Italian
Garden combination
chunky pasta sauce
1 cup elbow macaroni
*2 (15-ounce) cans
mixed vegetables
*1 (15.5-ounce) can great
northern beans
Heart Smart Bisquick
reduced-fat baking mix
(3 cups needed)

PANTRY
*Dried Italian seasoning
Dried minced onion
Garlic salt
Olive oil cooking spray

Minestrone Soup *25 minutes*

This is so hearty and filling that even a big man with a big appetite (who thinks soup alone doesn't make a meal) will request this soup for dinner!

Ingredients

1 (36-ounce) package extra-lean ground beef
1 (64-ounce) jar vegetable juice
1 (26-ounce) jar Italian Garden combination chunky pasta sauce
1½ tablespoons Italian seasoning
1 cup elbow macaroni
2 (15-ounce) cans mixed vegetables
1 (15.5-ounce) can great northern beans

Instructions for entrée:

▸ In a large soup pan or Dutch oven, cook and crumble the ground beef over high heat.
▸ Once the meat begins to crumble, stir in the vegetable juice, pasta sauce, and Italian seasoning. Stir well and bring to a boil.
▸ After the soup comes to a full boil, stir in the elbow macaroni, and continue cooking at a full boil. Stir occasionally.
▸ Boil for 10 to 12 minutes or until the pasta is tender. Once the pasta is fully cooked, stir in the mixed vegetables and beans. Cook for a couple more minutes until the vegetables and beans are fully heated.

Yield: 18 (1-cup) servings **Calories per serving:** 193 (19% fat); **Total fat:** 4 g;
Cholesterol: 31 mg; **Carbohydrate:** 22 g; **Dietary Fiber:** 4 g; **Protein:** 17 g;
Sodium: 686 mg **Diabetic Exchanges:** 1 starch, 1 vegetable, 2 lean meat

---

Instructions to prepare the suggested meal

Set the timer for 25 minutes.

25 minutes before the meal

▶ Make the Minestrone Soup according to the directions.

15 minutes before the meal

▶ Make the Italian Seasoned Scones according to the directions and bake.

MEAL SUGGESTION:
25 MINUTES FOR
TOTAL MEAL:
Italian Seasoned Scones
(page 245)

HELPFUL HINT:

❯ After this is fully cooked you can place it in a crockpot on low heat until ready to serve.

SUPPLIES LIST FOR
SUGGESTED MEAL
Large nonstick Dutch oven
or soup pan
Cutting board
Medium bowl
Potato masher
Oven
Baking sheet
Timer

GROCERY LIST FOR
SUGGESTED MEAL
*Ingredients for the German
Potato Soup

PRODUCE
*1 medium sweet onion

MEATS
*2 (16-ounce) packages 96%
fat-free lean ham, cubed

DAIRY
Fancy shredded parmesan
cheese blend
(1/3 cup needed)

PACKAGED
*1 (8.25-ounce) can
sliced carrots
*3 (15-ounce) cans
diced potatoes
Seeded hearty rye bread
(6 slices needed)

PANTRY
*Chicken flavored granules
instant bouillon (1/4 cup or
12 chicken bouillon cubes)
*Garlic salt
Butter-flavored cooking spray
*Cornstarch
(1/2 cup needed)
*Dried parsley (optional)
*Black pepper (optional)
*Salt (optional)

German Potato Soup *30 minutes*

This soup is sure to make people feel warm and cozy; it's just that kind of down-home goodness!

Ingredients

13 cups water, divided
1/4 cup chicken-flavored granules instant bouillon
    (or 12 chicken bouillon cubes)
2 (16-ounce) packages 96% fat-free lean ham, cubed
1 medium sweet onion
1/2 cup cornstarch
1 (8.25-ounce) can sliced carrots
3 (15-ounce) cans diced potatoes

Optional: Salt and pepper to taste OR add 1 1/2 tablespoons garlic salt,
    1/4 teaspoon ground black pepper, and 1 tablespoon dried parsley

Instructions for entrée:

▸ In a large nonstick Dutch oven or soup pan bring 12 cups hot water, chicken-flavored granules, and cubed ham to a boil.

▸ While the broth is coming to a boil, chop the sweet onion and add it to the broth.

▸ In a medium bowl stir together the cornstarch and the remaining 1 cup of water until the cornstarch is dissolved. Stir the cornstarch mixture into the boiling broth to thicken. Let it boil while you do the next step.

▸ In a medium bowl, using a potato masher combine the sliced carrots with one of the cans of diced potatoes, until the vegetables are well mashed. Stir into the boiling broth along with the remaining 2 cans of diced potatoes. Return to a boil. Once the soup comes to a boil, reduce the heat to medium and let simmer until the potatoes are fully heated.

▸ If desired you can season with the optional seasonings, or you can let each person season to taste with salt and pepper.

Yield: 21 (1-cup) servings **Calories per serving:** 108 (22% fat); **Total fat:** 3 g;
Cholesterol: 23 mg; **Carbohydrate:** 11 g; **Dietary Fiber:** 1 g; **Protein:** 10 g;
Sodium: 891 mg **Diabetic Exchanges:** 1/2 starch, 1 1/2 very lean meat

---

Instructions to prepare the suggested meal

Set the timer for 30 minutes.

30 minutes before the meal

▸ Make the German Potato Soup.

10 minutes before the meal

▸ Make the Garlic and Parmesan Rye Toast.

**MEAL SUGGESTION:
30 MINUTES FOR
TOTAL MEAL:**
Garlic and Parmesan Rye
Toast (page 231)

HELPFUL HINTS:

❷ Chicken broth can be substituted for the bouillon, but unless it is on sale, the broth will be more expensive than the water and bouillon.

❷ Low-sodium chicken broth can be substituted as well, which will lower the sodium count for those on lower-sodium diets.

❷ If the 96% fat-free packages of lean cubed ham are not in stock, you can purchase lean ham and cut it into cubes yourself.

SUPPLIES LIST FOR
SUGGESTED MEAL
Large nonstick Dutch oven
or soup pan
Cutting board
Oven
2 baking sheets
Timer

GROCERY LIST FOR
SUGGESTED MEAL
*Ingredients for the Creamy
Chicken and Noodle Soup

PRODUCE
*Celery (6 stalks needed)

PACKAGED
*1 (12-ounce) package
fettuccine
*1 (14.5-ounce) can
sliced carrots
*2 (12.5-ounce) cans chunk
chicken breast in water
Fat-free flour tortillas
(4 tortillas needed)

PANTRY
*Chicken broth made from
bouillon (13 cups needed)
*Minced garlic
(2 tablespoons needed)
*Cornstarch
(1/2 cup needed)
Garlic salt
Dried parsley
Paprika
Butter-flavored
cooking spray

Creamy Chicken and Noodle Soup *30 minutes*

This is my best chicken noodle soup recipe yet! Grandma would be so proud.

Ingredients

13 cups chicken broth made from bouillon, divided
6 stalks celery
2 tablespoons minced garlic (from a jar)
1 (12-ounce) package fettuccine
1/2 cup cornstarch
1 (14.5-ounce) can sliced carrots
2 (12.5-ounce) cans chunk chicken breast in water

Instructions for entrée:

▸ In a large nonstick Dutch oven or soup pan, bring 12 cups of chicken broth to a boil.
▸ Finely chop the celery with the leaves to make 2 cups. Add to the broth.
▸ Add the minced garlic to the broth and stir well.
▸ Bring the soup to a full boil.
▸ Break the fettuccine in half and add to the boiling broth.
▸ Cook the soup at a full boil for 12 to 14 minutes or until the fettuccine is tender, stirring occasionally.
▸ Once the pasta is tender, dissolve the cornstarch into the remaining 1 cup of chicken broth and pour into the soup. The broth will thicken.
▸ Add the sliced carrots and chicken to the soup. Break up the big chunks of chicken before adding.
▸ Stir until everything is heated through.

Yield: 16 (1-cup) servings **Calories per serving:** 153 (9% fat); **Total fat:** 1 g; **Cholesterol:** 19 mg; **Carbohydrate:** 22 g; **Dietary Fiber:** 1 g; **Protein:** 12 g; **Sodium:** 541 mg **Diabetic Exchanges:** 1 1/2 starch, 1 very lean meat

Instructions to prepare the suggested meal

Set the timer for 30 minutes.

30 minutes before the meal

▸ Make the Creamy Chicken Noodle Soup according to the directions. After you put the pasta into the boiling broth, make the Homemade Seasoned Crackers.

10 minutes before the meal

▸ Begin making the Homemade Seasoned Crackers according to the directions.

5 minutes before the meal

▸ Place the seasoned crackers in the oven. Bake until crispy, 3 to 4 minutes.
▸ Finish making the soup.

MEAL SUGGESTION:
**30 MINUTES FOR
TOTAL MEAL:**
Homemade Seasoned
Crackers (page 232)

HELPFUL HINT:

❯ To make the broth: Add 1/4 cup chicken granules instant bouillon to 12 cups of water, stirring until dissolved. Make an additional cup of broth to dissolve the cornstarch in by stirring 1 teaspoon chicken granules to the 1 cup water and stir until dissolved.

SUPPLIES LIST FOR
SUGGESTED MEAL
2 baking sheets
Large Dutch oven
or soup pan with lid
Cutting board
Timer

GROCERY LIST FOR
SUGGESTED MEAL
*Ingredients for the Beef and
Mushroom Noodle Soup

PRODUCE
*2 medium sweet onions
*1 (16-ounce) package sliced
fresh mushrooms

PACKAGED
*1 (12-ounce) package
fettuccine
*2 (12-ounce) cans roast beef
and gravy (Hormel)
Flour tortillas (6 needed)

PANTRY
*Beef broth made from
bouillon (13 cups total
needed)
*Cornstarch
(1/2 cup needed)
*Ground black pepper
Butter-flavored sprinkles
Butter-flavored cooking spray

Beef and Mushroom Noodle Soup *30 minutes*

This is so hearty that I hate to call it a soup, but it has too much rich and creamy broth to be just beef and noodles!

Ingredients

13 cups beef broth made from bouillon, divided
2 medium sweet onions
1 (12-ounce) package fettuccine
1/2 cup cornstarch
2 (12-ounce) cans roast beef and gravy
1 (16-ounce) package sliced fresh mushrooms
1/2 teaspoon ground black pepper

Instructions *for entrée:*

▸ In a large Dutch oven or soup pan, bring 12 cups of beef broth to a boil over high heat.
▸ Chop the onions to make 2 cups, and add to the the broth.
▸ Once the broth comes to a boil, break the fettuccine in half and stir into the broth.
▸ Bring back to a full boil. Let the soup boil until the fettuccine becomes tender, about 10 minutes.
▸ Dissolve the cornstarch in the remaining cup of beef broth.
▸ Reduce the heat to medium, and stir the dissolved cornstarch liquid along with the beef and gravy, sliced mushrooms, and ground black pepper. Stir well to mix all ingredients.
▸ Cover and let cook, stirring occasionally, until the mushrooms are tender.

Yield: 15 (1-cup) servings **Calories per serving:** 174 (12% fat); **Total fat:** 2 g; **Cholesterol:** 21 mg; **Carbohydrate:** 23 g; **Dietary Fiber:** 1 g; **Protein:** 15 g; **Sodium:** 1023 mg **Diabetic Exchanges:** 1 1/2 starch, 1 1/2 very lean meat

Instructions to prepare the suggested meal

Set the timer for 30 minutes.

30 minutes before the meal

- ▸ Begin making the soup according to the directions.

20 minutes before the meal

- ▸ Preheat the oven to 450 degrees.
- ▸ Break the fettuccine in half and add to the boiling broth.
- ▸ Begin making the Homemade Butter-flavored Crackers, but do not bake. Set aside.

10 minutes before the meal

- ▸ Add the dissolved cornstarch to the boiling soup along with the beef and gravy, mushrooms, and ground black pepper.

5 minutes before the meal

- ▸ Bake the crackers for 3 to 4 minutes.

SOUPS AND CHOWDERS

MEAL SUGGESTION: 30 MINUTES FOR TOTAL MEAL: Homemade Butter-flavored Crackers (page 233)

HELPFUL HINTS:

❷ You can use real beef broth, but it will be more expensive than making beef broth from bouillon.

❷ Hormel makes canned roast beef.

**SUPPLIES LIST FOR
SUGGESTED MEAL**
Nonstick Dutch oven
or soup pan
2 baking sheets or cookie
sheets
Cutting board
Oven
Timer

**GROCERY LIST FOR
SUGGESTED MEAL**
*Ingredients for the Broccoli
and Cauliflower Chowder*

MEAT SUBSTITUTE
*2 (1-pound) packages
vegetarian ground sausage

DAIRY
Shredded cheddar cheese
(1/2 cup needed)

FROZEN
*1 (32-ounce) bag frozen
hash browns
*2 (1-pound) packages frozen
broccoli and cauliflower

PACKAGED
4 whole-wheat bagels

PANTRY
*Chicken broth made from
bouillon (8 cups needed)
*Steak seasoning salt
*Dried chopped chives
(2 tablespoons needed,
plus 2 teaspoons for the
bagel crisps)
Garlic salt
Butter-flavored
cooking spray

Broccoli and Cauliflower Chowder *25 minutes*

This vegetarian chowder is chock-full of hearty flavor. Don't let the title fool you!

Ingredients

8 cups chicken broth made from bouillon
1 (32-ounce) bag frozen hash browns
2 (1-pound) packages vegetarian ground sausage
2 (1-pound) packages frozen broccoli and cauliflower
1 tablespoon steak seasoning salt
2 tablespoon dried chives

Instructions for entrée:

▸ In a large soup pan or nonstick Dutch oven, add the chicken broth, hash browns, and sausage. Using your hands, break up the ground sausage in the broth.
▸ Cover and cook over high heat, stirring occasionally.
▸ Once the soup comes to a boil, stir in the frozen broccoli and cauliflower, steak seasoning salt, and dried chives.
▸ Reduce the heat to medium, and cook until the broccoli and cauliflower are fully heated and tender.

Yield: 15 (1-cup) servings **Calories per serving:** 168 (19% fat); **Total fat:** 3 g; **Cholesterol:** 0 mg; **Carbohydrate:** 19 g; **Dietary Fiber:** 4 g; **Protein:** 14 g; **Sodium:** 770 mg **Diabetic Exchanges:** 1 1/2 starch, 1 1/2 very lean meat

Instructions to prepare the suggested meal

Set the timer for 25 minutes.

25 minutes before the meal

▶ Begin making the Broccoli and Cauliflower Chowder.

15 minutes before the meal

▶ Preheat the oven to 450 degrees.
▶ Begin making the bagel crisps, but do NOT put into the oven.

10 minutes before the meal

▶ Continue making the soup by stirring the broccoli and cauliflower, steak seasoning, and dried chives into the soup.
▶ Cover, reduce the heat to medium, and continue cooking until the broccoli and cauliflower are fully heated and tender.

5 minutes before the meal

▶ Put the bagel crisps into the oven for 4 to 5 minutes or until crispy.

**MEAL SUGGESTION:
25 MINUTES FOR
TOTAL MEAL:**
Cheddar Chive Bagel Crisps
(page 234)

HELPFUL HINT:

❯ I used Tone's steak seasoning salt. It has salt, dehydrated garlic, black pepper, dehydrated onion, spices, and red pepper in it.

Sweet-and-Spicy Pork (page 150)

Main Meals

MINI INDEX

(continued on page 124)

Baked Beans with Smoked Sausage *10 minutes*

For a fun entrée serve in a pie plate, with gingham handkerchiefs as napkins.

Ingredients

1 (14-ounce) package lean smoked sausage
1 small sweet onioin
1 (15-ounce) can butter beans, drained
2 (16-ounce) cans fat-free baked beans
3/4 cup thick-and-spicy, brown-sugar-flavored barbecue sauce
    (your favorite brand)
1/4 cup Splenda Brown Sugar Blend

Instructions for entrée

▸ Slice the sausage into bite-size pieces and chop the onion to make 1/2 cup. Set aside. Spray a large nonstick saucepan with nonfat cooking spray.
▸ Over medium high heat, cook the sausage with the onion.
▸ Stir the butter beans, baked beans, barbecue sauce, and Splenda Brown Sugar Blend into the sausage and onion mixture until well mixed.
▸ Cover and cook on medium heat for 5 minutes or until fully heated.

Yield: 8 (1-cup) servings **Calories per serving:** 301 (7% fat); **Total fat:** 2 g; **Cholesterol:** 18 mg; **Carbohydrate:** 55 g; **Dietary Fiber:** 8 g; **Protein:** 15 g; **Sodium:** 1251 mg **Diabetic Exchanges:** 31/2 starch, 1 very lean meat

---

Instructions to prepare the suggested meal

Set the timer for 15 minutes.

15 minutes before the meal

▸ Make the Baked Beans with Smoked Sausage according to the directions. After cooking, turn the heat down to the lowest temperature to keep warm, and cover.

5 minutes before the meal

▸ Make the Southwestern Sweet Slaw according to instructions.

SUPPLIES LIST FOR SUGGESTED MEAL
Large salad serving bowl
Large nonstick saucepan with lid
Cutting board
Timer

GROCERY LIST FOR SUGGESTED MEAL
Ingredients for the Baked Beans with Smoked Sausage

PRODUCE
1 (16-ounce) bag pre-cut cole slaw mix
*1 small sweet onion

MEATS
*1 (14-ounce) package lean smoked sausage

DAIRY
Fat-free sour cream
(1/2 cup needed)

PACKAGED
*1 (15-ounce) can butter beans
*2 (16-ounce) cans baked beans
*Thick-and-spicy, brown-sugar-flavored barbecue sauce (your favorite brand)
(3/4 cup needed)
Chunky salsa (1/2 cup needed)
Fat-free red French salad dressing
(3/4 cup needed)

PANTRY
*Splenda Brown Sugar Blend
*Nonstick cooking spray

MENU SUGGESTION: 15 MINUTES FOR TOTAL MEAL:
Southwestern Sweet Slaw (page 69)

**SUPPLY LIST FOR
SUGGESTED MEAL**
Medium-sized bowl
Cutting board
Serving platter
Microwave oven
Microwave-safe bowl
Wax paper
Timer

**GROCERY LIST FOR
SUGGESTED MEAL**
*Ingredients for the Ham
with Honeydew Chutney

PRODUCE
*¹/₂ small honeydew melon
(*Fresh parsley
*1 small sweet onion

MEATS
*1 pound package sliced lean
ham steaks (approx. 7 per
package)

DAIRY
Fat-free shredded mozzarella
cheese (1 cup needed)
Shredded parmesan cheese
(¹/₄ cup needed)

PACKAGED
2 (14.5-ounce) cans
green beans
1 (15-ounce) can
diced potatoes
*Fat-free zesty Italian
salad dressing
Fat-free multi-grain whole-
wheat bread (7 slices needed)

PANTRY
*Splenda granular
Diced pimentos
Butter-flavored sprinkles
Real bacon bits
Butter-flavored cooking spray

Ham with Honeydew Chutney *10 minutes*

This was a huge hit at a birthday party brunch that I had for my neighbor! Everyone loved it! The cool, sweet melon chutney served on top of the warm, salty ham is a wonderful flavor combination!

Ingredients

¹/₂ of a small honeydew melon
1 tablespoon fresh parsley, packed
1 rounded tablespoon chopped sweet onion
2 tablespoons fat-free zesty Italian salad dressing
1 tablespoon Splenda granular
1 pound package sliced lean ham steaks (approx. 7 per package)

Instructions for entrée:

▸ Cut the melon half into bite-size pieces and place in a medium bowl.
▸ Finely chop the parsley to make 1 packed tablespoon, and part of a sweet onion to make 1 rounded tablespoon.
▸ Stir the cubed melon, chopped parsley, onions, salad dressing, and Splenda together until well mixed. Set aside.
▸ Place the ham steaks on a serving platter. Cover and cook in a carousel microwave for 2 to 3 minutes or until fully heated.
▸ Serve the chutney on the side, or spoon it over the cooked ham steaks.

Yield: 7 (¹/₄ cup chutney on top of a 2¹/₂-ounce lean ham steak) servings **Calories per serving:** 124 (27% fat); **Total fat:** 4 g; **Cholesterol:** 36 mg; **Carbohydrate:** 5 g; **Dietary Fiber:** 1 g; **Protein:** 17 g; **Sodium:** 930 mg **Diabetic Exchanges:** ¹/₂ fruit, 2¹/₂ lean meat

---

Instructions to prepare the suggested meal

Set the timer for 20 minutes.

20 minutes before the meal

▸ Make the Cheesy Triangles according to the directions, but do not bake. Set aside.

15 minutes before the meal

▸ Make the Ham with Honeydew Chutney according to the directions; do not cook the ham.

10 minutes before the meal

▸ Make the Green Beans and Potatoes according to the directions.

5 minutes before the meal

▸ Bake the Cheesy Triangles.

3 minutes before the meal

▸ Remove the Green Beans and Potatoes from the microwave; cover to keep warm.
▸ Cook the ham in the microwave for 2 to 3 minutes, until fully heated, and then spoon the honeydew chutney over the ham and serve.
▸ Remove the Cheesy Triangles from the oven and serve.
▸ Serve the Green Beans and Potatoes.

MAIN MEALS

MEAL SUGGESTION: 20 MINUTES FOR TOTAL MEAL:
Green Beans and Potatoes (page 198)
Cheesy Triangles (page 230)

HELPFUL HINTS:

❷ 1/2 tablespoon of dried parsley can be substituted for the fresh chopped parsley if desired.

❷ Ideally this chutney tastes best if the melon and salad dressing are chilled; however, eaten at room temperature is completely fine as well.

❷ Sugar can be substituted for the Splenda granular, but it will add more calories.

❷ Chutney is any combination of fruits, vegetables, and seasonings mixed together. It is usually served as a topping or a side dish to complement an entrée. Chutneys can be served either hot, cold or at room temperature. I prefer this dish chilled, but it is also good at room temperature.

Maple-Glazed Ham Steaks *5 minutes*

These are ideal for breakfast or brunch, but they are also good as a dinner entrée with vegetable side dishes.

Ingredients

4 (3-ounce) extra-lean ham steaks
1¹/₂ tablespoons sugar-free maple flavored syrup
Paprika (optional)

Instructions *for entrée:*

▸ Place the ham steaks in a 12-inch nonstick skillet over medium-high heat. Cook for one to two minutes or until the bottom is browned. Turn the ham steaks over.
▸ Reduce the heat to medium; evenly drizzle the sugar-free maple-flavored syrup over the center of the ham steaks.
▸ Using a fork pierce multiple holes in the ham steaks to allow the syrup to get inside the steaks.
▸ Lightly sprinkle paprika over the ham steaks for color, if desired.
▸ Remove from heat and serve.

Yield: 4 (3-ounce) ham steaks **Calories per serving:** 139 (32% fat); **Total fat:** 5 g; **Cholesterol:** 47 mg; **Carbohydrate:** 1 g; **Dietary Fiber:** 0 g; **Protein:** 21 g; **Sodium:** 1146 mg **Diabetic Exchanges:** 3 lean meat

---

SUPPLIES LIST FOR SUGGESTED MEAL
12-inch nonstick skillet
Medium nonstick saucepan with lid
Cutting board
Medium (2-quart) microwavable-safe bowl
Electric mixer
Wax paper
Microwave oven
Timer

GROCERY LIST FOR SUGGESTED MEAL
Ingredients for the Maple-Glazed Ham Steaks

PRODUCE
1 medium onion

MEATS
*4 (3-ounce) extra-lean ham steaks

DAIRY
2 slices thinly sliced Swiss cheese
Eggs (6 needed)

FROZEN
1 (2-pound) package frozen broccoli

PACKAGED
1 (6-ounce) can tomato paste
Light potato bread (6 slices needed)

Grocery list continued on next page

128

Instructions to prepare the suggested meal

Set the timer for 25 minutes.

25 minutes before the meal
- Start making the Broccoli and Onions with Swiss Cheese recipe according to the directions.

20 minutes before the meal
- Make the Tomato Pudding according to the directions.

10 minutes before the meal
- Cook the Tomato Pudding.
- Cook the ham.

5 minutes before the meal
- Finish the Broccoli and Onions with Swiss Cheese recipe.

PANTRY
*Sugar-free maple flavored syrup
*Paprika (optional)
Onion salt
Celery salt
Splenda Brown Sugar Blend

MEAL SUGGESTION:
25 MINUTES FOR
TOTAL MEAL:
Broccoli and Onions with Swiss Cheese (page 227)
Tomato Pudding (page 214)

HELPFUL HINT:

❯ Using pre-sliced ham steaks makes this super easy, but you can also used left over ham from the holidays as well.

Pork Stew
(Quick-Fix Pork Stew) *15 minutes*

This is definitely a comfort-food meal. Who would have ever thought that something this satisfying could be made in only fifteen minutes? This would have taken my grandmother hours.

Ingredients

2 pounds pork loin
1 large onion
2 (15-ounce) cans sliced new potatoes
2 (7-ounce) cans mushrooms (pieces and stems)
1 (8.5-ounce) can peas and carrots
1 (12-ounce) jar home-style pork gravy
1/2 teaspoon rubbed thyme

Instructions for entrée:

▸ Preheat a 12-inch nonstick saucepan on high.
▸ Remove and discard all visible fat from the pork loin. (You will end up with 1 1/2 pounds of meat.)
▸ Cut the pork into 1-inch chunks.
▸ Brown the meat in the preheated nonstick saucepan. Cover.
▸ While the meat is cooking, chop the onion to make 1 1/2 cups.
▸ Stir onions into the meat. (Note: The meat is not fully cooked yet) Cover, and continue to cook on high.
▸ Open and drain the sliced new potatoes, mushrooms, and peas and carrots. Set aside.
▸ Reduce the heat to medium.
▸ Stir in the gravy, thyme, sliced new potatoes, mushrooms, and peas and carrots.
▸ Continue cooking and stirring until fully heated and well mixed.

Yields: 7 (1-cup) servings **Calories per serving:** 292 (29% fat); **Total fat:** 9 g;
Cholesterol: 59 mg; **Carbohydrate:** 26 g; **Dietary Fiber:** 5 g; **Protein:** 25 g;
Sodium: 862 mg **Diabetic Exchanges:** 1 1/2 starch, 1 vegetable, 3 lean meat

---

Instructions to prepare the suggested meal

Set the timer for 30 minutes.

30 minutes before the meal

▸ Prepare the Chunky Pear and Cherry Salad according to recipe directions.

15 minutes before the meal

▸ Prepare the Pork Stew according to the recipe directions.

**MEAL SUGGESTION:
30 MINUTES FOR
TOTAL MEAL:**
Chunky Pear and Cherry
Salad (page 83)

HELPFUL HINT:

❯ To make this recipe even faster, you can purchase stir-fry pork, but this will make the recipe more expensive.

SUPPLIES LIST FOR SUGGESTED MEAL
12-inch nonstick saucepan
Medium-sized serving bowl
Cutting board
Timer

GROCERY LIST FOR SUGGESTED MEAL
Ingredients for the Ham, Green Beans, and Potatoes (One-Pan Meal)

MEATS
*1-pound package diced lean ham

PACKAGED
*2 (15- ounce) cans sliced new potatoes
*2 (14.5-ounce) cans French-style green beans
*Fat-free Italian salad dressing (1/3 cup needed)
1 (20-ounce) can no-sugar-added apple pie filling
1 (25-ounce) jar unsweetened applesauce
Dried mixed berries (1/2 cup needed)

PANTRY
*Dried parsley
*French-fried onions (1/3 cup needed)
Allspice
Splenda granular

Ham, Green Beans, and Potatoes (One-Pan Meal) *15 minutes*

I am not a fan of one-pan meals, but this flavor combination goes together so well that it seems like they were meant to be together. Kind of like peanut butter and jelly sandwiches. . . . but a LOT healthier!

Ingredients for Ham, Green Beans, and Potatoes

1-pound package diced lean ham
2 (15-ounce) cans sliced new potatoes
2 (14.5-ounce) cans French-style green beans
1/3 cup fat-free Italian salad dressing
1/2 tablespoon dried parsley
1/4 cup French-fried onions, crushed

Instructions for entrée:

▸ In a 12-inch nonstick saucepan, cook ham on high heat.
▸ While the meat is cooking, drain the potatoes and green beans.
▸ Add the potatoes, green beans, salad dressing, and dried parsley to the cooked ham. Stir until well mixed.
▸ Once it comes to a boil, reduce the heat to medium-low and continue to let it simmer for 5 more minutes to heat thoroughly, and to infuse the seasonings and flavors.
▸ Just before serving sprinkle the top with French-fried onions.

Yield: 5 1/2 (1-cup) servings **Calories per serving:** 264 (22% fat); **Total fat:** 6 g; **Cholesterol:** 44 mg; **Carbohydrate:** 29 g; **Dietary Fiber:** 5 g; **Protein:** 21 g; **Sodium:** 2056 mg **Diabetic Exchanges:** 1 1/2 starch, 1 vegetable, 2 1/2 lean meat

---

Instructions to prepare the suggested meal

Set the timer for 15 minutes.

15 minutes before the meal

> ▸ Place the ingredients for the Very Berry Spiced Applesauce in the refrigerator to chill.
> ▸ Prepare the Ham, Green Beans, and Potatoes according to the directions.

5 minutes before the meal

> ▸ Prepare the Very Berry Spiced Applesauce.

MENU SUGGESTION:
15 MINUTES FOR
TOTAL MEAL:
Very Berry Spiced Applesauce
(199)

HELPFUL HINT:

❷ If you'd like to use fresh parsley, substitute 1 tablespoon fresh for the 1/2 tablespoon of dried.

SUPPLIES LIST FOR
SUGGESTED MEAL
Cutting board
12-inch nonstick
saucepan with lid
Large microwave-safe bowl
Microwave oven
Wax paper
2 1/2-quart saucepan
Small bowl
Timer

GROCERY LIST FOR
SUGGESTED MEAL
*Ingredients for the Ham and
Yam Stove-Top Casserole

PRODUCE
*1 medium sweet onion

MEATS
*1 pound of lean, sliced
honey ham lunch meat

PACKAGED
*1 (40-ounce) can
sweet potatoes
*Honey barbecue sauce
(1/4 cup needed)
1 (14-ounce) can turnip greens
2 (14-ounce) cans
mustard greens
1 (29-ounce) can no-sugar-
added yellow cling peaches
Cinnamon-flavored candies
(red hots) (1/3 cup needed)

Grocery list continued
on next page

Ham and Yam Stove-Top Casserole *15 minutes*

I enjoyed the flavor of this so much that it was hard to limit myself to just one serving.

Ingredients

1 pound of lean honey ham sliced lunch meat
1 medium sweet onion
1 (40-ounce) can sweet potatoes
1/4 cup honey barbecue sauce

Instructions for entrée:

▸ Cut the lunch meat into bite-size pieces. Set aside.

▸ Chop the onion to make 1 cup.

▸ Spray a 12-inch nonstick saucepan with butter-flavored cooking spray.

▸ Over medium-high heat cook the ham and chopped onions. Stir well, cover, and let cook until the onions are tender.

▸ Drain and discard the juice from the sweet potatoes. With a large knife cut the sweet potatoes into smaller pieces while still in the can.

▸ Gently stir the sweet potatoes and honey barbecue sauce, being careful not to break up the sweet potatoes.

▸ Cook uncovered on medium-high until heated through.

Yield: 6 (1-cup) servings **Calories per serving:** 309 (13% fat); **Total fat:** 5 g; **Cholesterol:** 40 mg; **Carbohydrate:** 48 g; **Dietary Fiber:** 4 g; **Protein:** 19 g; **Sodium:** 1134 mg **Diabetic Exchanges:** 3 starch, 2 very lean meat

---

Instructions to prepare the suggested meal

Set the timer for 30 minutes.

30 minutes before the meal

- Prepare the Ham and Yam Stove-Top Casserole according to the directions up to 5 minutes before the meal.

20 minutes before the meal

- While the ham and onions are cooking, begin making the Hot Spiced Peaches up to the point at which you add the cornstarch paste to the peaches.

10 minutes before the meal

- Make the Mixed Greens according to the directions.

5 minutes before the meal

- Stir the sweet potatoes in gently with the honey barbecue sauce, and then turn off the burner, cover, and let sit on the warm burner to keep warm.
- Add the cornstarch paste to the Hot Spiced Peaches and let sit according to the directions.

PANTRY
*Butter-flavored
cooking spray
Onion salt
Butter-flavored sprinkles
(Butter Buds)
Liquid smoke
Splenda granular
Honey
Cornstarch

**MEAL SUGGESTION:
30 MINUTES FOR
TOTAL MEAL:**
Hot Spiced Peaches
(page 258)
Mixed Greens (page 203)

Open–Faced Cranberry Beef and Feta Sandwiches on Toasted Rye *15 minutes*

Tyler, a finicky eater who proclaims he doesn't like beef, gobbled this recipe up and even requested seconds! The cocoa takes the edge off the beefy flavor. This is a unique flavor combination of sweet and slightly salty.

Ingredients

1/3 cup dried cranberries
1 pound extra-lean ground beef
1 teaspoon cocoa
1/2 teaspoon garlic salt (plus more for sprinkling on bread-optional)
6 slices seeded rye bread
1/2 cup fat-free shredded mozzarella cheese
2 tablespoons reduced-fat feta cheese crumbles
1/3 cup dried cranberries

Instructions for entrée:

▶ Preheat the oven to 400 degrees.
▶ Chop the dried cranberries and set aside to use later.
▶ In a medium nonstick skillet, cook and crumble ground beef with the cocoa and garlic salt over high heat until fully cooked.
▶ Spray one side of each slice of rye bread with butter-flavored cooking spray. If desired sprinkle the buttered side lightly with garlic salt. Place the butter side down on a baking sheet.
▶ Evenly divide the cooked beef mixture over the 6 slices of bread.
▶ Sprinkle the beef with the mozzarella cheese, feta cheese, and cranberries. Then spray the tops with butter-flavored cooking spray.
▶ Bake for 5 minutes or until the bottoms are crispy and golden.

Yield: 6 **Calories per serving:** 225 (21% fat); **Total fat:** 5 g; **Cholesterol:** 44 mg; **Carbohydrate:** 22 g; **Dietary Fiber:** 3 g; **Protein:** 23 g; **Sodium:** 498 mg
Diabetic Exchanges: 1 starch, 1/2 carbohydrate, 3 lean meat

SUPPLIES LIST FOR SUGGESTED MEAL
Medium-sized nonstick skillet
Baking sheet
Oven
Medium-sized serving bowl
Cutting board
Timer

GROCERY LIST FOR SUGGESTED MEAL
Ingredients for the Open-Faced Cranberry Beef and Feta Sandwiches on Toasted Rye

PRODUCE
1 1/2 pounds fresh broccoli
(to be used as a side with dip)

MEATS
*1 pound extra-lean ground beef

DAIRY
*Fat-free shredded mozzarella cheese (1/2 cup needed)
*Reduced-fat feta cheese crumbles
(2 tablespoons needed)

Grocery list continued on next page

Instructions to prepare the suggested meal

Set the timer for 30 minutes.

30 minutes before the meal

> ▸ Make the Very Berry Spiced Applesauce.

20 minutes before the meal

> ▸ Make the Open-Faced Cranberry Beef and Feta Sandwiches on Toasted Rye.

5 minutes before the meal

> ▸ Clean and cut fresh broccoli into bite-size pieces to serve with fat-free ranch salad dressing as the dip, if desired.

PACKAGED
*Seeded rye bread
(6 slices needed)
*Dried cranberries
(1/3 cup needed)
Fat-free ranch dressing (for dipping broccoli if desired)
1 (20-ounce) can no-sugar-added apple pie filling
1 (25-ounce) jar unsweetened applesauce
Dried mixed berries
(1/2 cup needed)

PANTRY
*Cocoa
*Garlic salt
*Butter-flavored cooking spray
Allspice
Splenda granular

**MEAL SUGGESTION:
30 MINUTES FOR
TOTAL MEAL:**
Very Berry Spiced Applesauce (page 199)
Fresh broccoli with fat-free salad dressing for dip (if desired)

**SUPPLIES LIST FOR
SUGGESTED MEAL**
Medium-sized nonstick skillet
Baking sheet
Oven
Medium-sized mixing bowl
Timer

**GROCERY LIST FOR
SUGGESTED MEAL**
*Ingredients for the Little
Italy Open-Faced Sandwiches*

PRODUCE
Fresh bell peppers
(to slice and serve
with dip on the side)

MEATS/POULTRY
*1 pound extra-lean
ground beef
*18 slices turkey pepperoni

DAIRY
*Fat-free shredded
mozzarella cheese
(6 tablespoons needed)
*Grated parmesan cheese
(6 teaspoons needed)

PACKAGED
*French bread
(6 slices needed)
*Spaghetti sauce
(18 tablespoons needed)
Fat-free ranch salad dressing
(to serve with sliced peppers,
if desired)
1 (20-ounce) can no-sugar-
added cherry pie filling
1 (25-ounce) jar unsweetened
applesauce

PANTRY
*Cocoa
*Butter-flavored
cooking spray
Almond extract
Splenda granular
*Garlic salt (optional)

Little Italy Open-Faced Sandwiches *15 minutes*

Special thanks to my neighbor Tyler Frendt, who helped me create this specialty!

Ingredients

1 pound extra-lean ground beef
1 teaspoon cocoa
1/2 teaspoon garlic salt, optional
6 slices French bread
18 tablespoons spaghetti sauce
6 tablespoons fat-free shredded mozzarella cheese
6 teaspoons grated parmesan cheese
18 slices turkey pepperoni

Instructions for entrée:

▸ Preheat the oven to 400 degrees.
▸ In a medium nonstick skillet, cook and crumble extra-lean ground beef with the cocoa and garlic salt over high heat until fully cooked.
▸ Spray one side of each slice of French bread with butter-flavored cooking spray. Place the butter side down on a baking sheet.
▸ Evenly divide the cooked beef mixture over the bread slices.
▸ Put 3 tablespoons of your favorite spaghetti sauce over the cooked beef on each piece of French bread.
▸ Sprinkle each with 1 tablespoon of fat-free mozzarella cheese and 1 teaspoon of grated parmesan cheese. Spray the tops of the cheeses with butter-flavored cooking spray.
▸ Place 3 slices of turkey pepperoni on each.
▸ Bake for 5 minutes or until the bottoms are crispy and golden.

Yield: 6 **Calories per serving:** 242 (24% fat); **Total fat:** 6 g; **Cholesterol:** 52 mg; **Carbohydrate:** 21 g; **Dietary Fiber:** 1 g; **Protein:** 25 g; **Sodium:** 622 mg **Diabetic Exchanges:** 1 1/2 starch, 3 lean meat

Instructions to prepare the suggested meal

Set the timer for 25 minutes.

25 minutes before the meal

 ▸ Make the Tart Cherry Applesauce.

20 minutes before the meal

 ▸ Wash and cut fresh bell peppers into strips to serve with fat-free ranch salad dressing as a dip, if desired.

15 minutes before the meal

 ▸ Make the Little Italy Open-Faced Sandwiches.

**MEAL SUGGESTION:
30 MINUTES FOR
TOTAL MEAL:**
Tart Cherry Applesauce
(page 202)
Bell pepper strips with fat-free ranch salad dressing

HELPFUL HINT:

❷ If desired sprinkle the buttered side lightly with garlic salt before placing on the baking sheet, for added Italian flavor.

**SUPPLY LIST FOR
SUGGESTED MEAL**
Oven
8 x 8-inch baking dish
Aluminum foil
12-inch nonstick saucepan
and lid
Cutting board
Timer

**GROCERY LIST FOR
SUGGESTED MEAL**
*Ingredients for the Spiced
Ham Steaks

PRODUCE
8 ounces pre-sliced fresh
mushrooms

MEATS
*8 (2-ounce) slices cooked,
lean ham

PACKAGED
*Cherry cola (1/2 cup
needed)
2 (14.5-ounce) cans Italian
cut green beans
1 (15-ounce) can diced
potatoes
Fat-free Italian dressing
Whole-grain rolls
Diced pimientos

PANTRY
*Splenda Brown Sugar Blend
*Allspice
*Butter-flavored
cooking spray
Butter-flavored sprinkles
(Butter Buds)
Real Bacon bits

Spiced Ham Steaks *15 minutes*

Now you can enjoy the flavors of the holidays all year long with this quick and easy mini version of holiday ham.

Ingredients

1/2 cup cherry cola
1 tablespoon Splenda Brown Sugar Blend
1 teaspoon allspice
8 (2-ounce) slices cooked, lean ham

Instructions *for entrée:*

▸ Place the oven rack in the middle of the oven and preheat to 350 degrees.
▸ Generously spray an 8 x 8-inch baking dish with butter-flavored cooking spray. Set aside.
▸ Add the cherry cola, Splenda Brown Sugar Blend, and allspice to the baking dish. Stir together until the sugar is dissolved.
▸ Place the sliced ham in the juice in the pan.
▸ Cover with foil and place in the oven.
▸ Bake for 15 minutes, or until warmed through.
▸ Serve the sauce from the ham on the side, to pour over the ham slices.

Yield: 8 (2-ounce) slices **Calories per serving:** 97 (30% fat); **Total fat:** 3 g; **Cholesterol:** 31 mg; **Carbohydrate:** 2 g; **Dietary Fiber:** 0 g; **Protein:** 14 g; **Sodium:** 753 mg **Diabetic Exchanges:** 2 lean meat

---

Instructions to prepare the suggested meal

Set the timer for 20 minutes.

20 minutes before the meal

- Preheat the oven to 350 degrees.
- Make the Spiced Ham Steaks according to the directions, and bake for 15 minutes.

10 minutes before the meal

- Make the Green Beans and Potatoes according to the directions.
- Put whole-grain rolls in the bread basket.

1 minute before meal

- Remove the ham from the oven and pour the sauce into a gravy boat to serve on the side.

MEAL SUGGESTION:
**20 MINUTES FOR
TOTAL MEAL:**
Green Beans and Potatoes
(page 198)
Whole-Grain Rolls

HELPFUL HINTS:

❯ Sliced ham lunch meat from the deli (1/4-inch-thick slices) works well in this recipe.

❯ This can also easily and quickly be cooked in the microwave instead of the oven. Simply cook, covered, for 3 minutes or until fully heated.

SUPPLIES LIST FOR
SUGGESTED MEAL
Large 12-inch nonstick
saucepan
Cutting board
Toaster
Medium-sized serving bowl
Whisk

GROCERY LIST FOR
SUGGESTED MEAL
*Ingredients for the Chipped
Beef Gravy over Toast Points

DAIRY
*Fat-free skim milk
(2 1/2 cups needed)

MEAT
*4 (2-ounce) packages
cooked, chopped, pressed
corned beef (Buddig Brand)

FROZEN
1 (8-ounce) container Fat-free
dessert whipped topping
(1 cup needed)

PACKAGED
2 (20-ounce) cans
crushed pineapple
1 (1.34-ounce) packet of
sugar-free French
vanilla pudding mix
Chopped walnuts
(3 tablespoons needed)

Grocery list continued
on next page

Chipped Beef Gravy over Toast Points *15 minutes*

During my childhood, this was one of my all-time favorites! As I matured, my hips and thighs could not handle the high-fat and high-calorie version my mom made. Now, I am happy to say, we can enjoy this dish guilt free and inexpensively!

Ingredients

1/2 cup cornstarch
2 1/2 cups fat-free skim milk
1/4 teaspoon ground black pepper
1 tablespoon butter-flavored sprinkles (Butter Buds)
1 (8.5-ounce) can sweet peas
4 (2-ounce) packages chopped, pressed corned beef (Buddig brand)
9 slices light five-grain bread

Instructions for entrée:

- In a 12-inch nonstick saucepan over medium heat, dissolve the cornstarch in the milk.
- Add the black pepper and Butter Buds to the milk mixture. Whisk all together over medium heat.
- Once the cornstarch is completely dissolved, drain and discard the liquid from the sweet peas, and then add them and stir well.
- Place all 4 packages of the corned beef in a stack on the cutting board and slice into 1/2-inch-wide thin strips.
- Add the beef strips to the pan and stir to mix all together.
- Let cook until it makes a thick gravy, stirring frequently.
- While the gravy is cooking, toast the bread. Cut the slices of toast in half diagonally.
- For each serving: place 1 1/2 slices of toast on a plate and cover with 1/2 cup of the chipped beef gravy.
- Salt to taste, if desired.

Yield: 6 (2/3 cups beef gravy over 1 1/2 slices bread) servings **Calories per serving:** 221 (13% fat); **Total fat:** 3 g; **Cholesterol:** 29 mg; **Carbohydrate:** 34 g; **Dietary Fiber:** 2 g; **Protein:** 15 g; **Sodium:** 899 mg **Diabetic Exchanges:** 2 starch, 1/2 fat-free milk, 1 very lean meat

---

Instructions to prepare the suggested meal

Set the timer for 20 minutes.

20 minutes before the meal

‣ Make the chipped beef according to the directions

10 minutes before the meal

‣ Make the pineapple pudding according to the directions. Place in the refrigerator until the Chipped Beef Gravy is ready to serve.

Tuna á la King *15 minutes*

Even people who are not big fans of Charlie the Tuna like this!

Ingredients

3 tablespoons cornstarch
2¹/2 cups nonfat skim milk
3 (5-ounce) cans tuna in water
1 (8.5-ounce) can peas and carrots
1¹/2 teaspoons lemon pepper seasoning salt
1 (7.5-ounce) can buttermilk biscuits

Instructions

▸ Preheat the oven to 400 degrees.
▸ Mix together the cornstarch and milk until the cornstarch is dissolved.
▸ Add the cornstarch mixture to a 12-inch nonstick saucepan and cook over medium heat.
▸ Add the tuna, peas and carrots, and lemon pepper seasoning salt to the cornstartch mixture. Stir occasionally, bringing it to a low boil.
▸ Make the buttermilk biscuits according to the package directions.
▸ Once the sauce has come to a low boil, turn off the heat. The sauce will thicken as it sits.
▸ Remove the biscuits from the oven.
▸ Place 2¹/4 biscuits on each plate, pour 1 cup of tuna mixture over the biscuits, and serve.

Yield: 4 (1 cup Tuna á La King over 2¹/4 biscuits) servings **Calories per serving:** 337 (22% fat); **Total fat:** 8 g; **Cholesterol:** 33 mg; **Carbohydrate:** 32 g; **Dietary Fiber:** 2 g; **Protein:** 33 g; **Sodium:** 1217 mg **Diabetic Exchanges:** 2 starch, 3¹/2 lean meat

SUPPLIES LIST FOR SUGGESTED MEAL
Oven
12-inch nonstick saucepan
Large salad bowl
Cutting board
Medium-sized serving bowl
Timer

GROCERY LIST FOR SUGGESTED MEAL
Ingredients for the Tuna á la King

PRODUCE
1 (9-ounce) package baby spinach
1 pound fresh strawberries
3 fresh kiwis

DAIRY
*Nonfat skim milk (2¹/2 cups needed)
*1 (7.5-ounce) can buttermilk biscuits

SEAFOOD
*3 (5-ounce) cans tuna in water

Grocery list continued on next page

Instructions to prepare the suggested meal

Set the timer for 30 minutes.

30 minutes before the meal
- Preheat the oven to 400 degrees.
- Make the Strawberry and Kiwi Chutney according to the directions.

20 minutes before the meal
- Make the Tuna á La King according to the directions.

10 minutes before the meal
- Make the spinach salad according to the directions

2 minutes before the meal
- Plate the meal and serve.

PACKAGED
*1 (8.5-ounce) can peas and carrots
Low-fat slaw dressing
(Marzetti) (1/4 cup needed)
Vanilla yogurt raisins
(21 needed)
Fat-free croutons
Fat-free Italian salad
dressing (1/3 cup needed)

PANTRY
*Cornstarch
(2 tablespoons needed)
*Lemon pepper
seasoning salt
Balsamic vinegar
Splenda

**MEAL SUGGESTION:
30 MINUTES FOR
TOTAL MEAL:**
Strawberry and Kiwi Chutney
(page 221)
Sweet and Tangy Spinach
Salad (page 82)

**SUPPLIES LIST FOR
SUGGESTED MEAL**
Large indoor electric
nonstick grill
Small bowl
Medium-sized serving bowl
Microwave-safe bowl

**GROCERY LIST FOR
SUGGESTED MEAL**
*Ingredients for the Savory
Boneless Pork Sirloin Chops*

PRODUCE
3 Bartlett pears

MEATS
*6 extra-lean pork sirloin
boneless chops (2 pounds)

PACKAGED
1 (20-ounce) can no-sugar-
added cherry pie filling
2 (14.5-ounce) cans
green beans
1 (15-ounce) can
diced potatoes
Real bacon bits
(2 tablespoons needed)
Fat-free Italian salad dressing,
(2 tablespoons needed)

PANTRY
*Ground sage
(1/2 teaspoon needed)
*Steak seasoning (I use
Grill Mates Montreal Steak)
(2 teaspoons needed)
*Dried parsley flakes
(1 teaspoon needed)
Ground cinnamon
(1/4 teaspoon needed)
Diced pimentos
(2 tablespoons needed)
Butter-flavored sprinkles
(Butter Buds)
(3 tablespoons needed)

Savory Boneless Pork Sirloin Chops   *15 minutes*

If you've never cooked with sage and you have to buy it for the first time to make this recipe, it will be worth it. The flavor combinations of these seasonings are just that good.

Ingredients

1/2 teaspoon ground sage
2 teaspoons steak seasoning (Grill Mates Montreal Steak)
1 teaspoon dried parsley flakes
6 extra-lean boneless pork sirloin chops (2 pounds)

Instructions for entrée:

▸ Preheat the large indoor electric nonstick grill.
▸ In a small bowl stir together the sage, steak seasoning, and dried parsley flakes.
▸ Place the pork chops on the grill.
▸ Sprinkle the seasoning mixture evenly on top of the pork chops.
▸ Close and firmly press the lid down. Cook the pork chops until the juices run clear and there is no visible pink.

Yield: 8 (4-ounce) servings **Calories per serving:** 140 (35% fat); **Total fat:** 5 g; **Cholesterol:** 65 mg; **Carbohydrate:** 0 g; **Dietary Fiber:** 0 g; **Protein:** 22 g; **Sodium:** 207 mg **Diabetic Exchanges:** 3 lean meat

---

Instructions to prepare the suggested meal

Set the timer for 30 minutes.

30 minutes before the meal
- Make the Chunky Pear and Cherry Salad.

15 minutes before the meal
- Plug in the indoor electric grill, and make the Green Beans and Potatoes.

7 minutes before the meal
- Make the pork sirloin chops.

2 minutes before the meal
- Reheat the green beans in the microwave if needed.

MEAL SUGGESTION:
30 MINUTES FOR TOTAL MEAL:
Chunky Pear and Cherry Salad (page 83)
Green Beans and Potatoes (page 198)

HELPFUL HINTS:

> If you do not have a large indoor electric nonstick grill, you can pan-fry these pork chops, but it will take twice as long, since you need to turn them over to cook both sides.

SUPPLIES LIST FOR SUGGESTED MEAL
Large indoor nonstick electric grill
2½-quart nonstick saucepan
12-inch nonstick skillet
Serving bowl

GROCERY LIST FOR SUGGESTED MEAL
Ingredients for the Cajun-Inspired Smoked Pork Chops

PRODUCE
1 large head cauliflower
1 (8-ounce) package fresh, sliced mushrooms

MEATS
*1 (19-ounce) package fully cooked smoked pork chops (5 chops)

DAIRY
Fat-free light vanilla yogurt (⅓ cup needed)

PACKAGED
1 (25-ounce) jar unsweetened applesauce
Cinnamon-flavored candies (Red Hots) (½ cup needed)
Fat-free ranch salad dressing (½ cup needed)
French-fried onions (¼ cup needed)

PANTRY
Cajun seasoning (McCormick brand) (1 teaspoon needed)
Chicken-flavored bouillon cube (1 needed)

Cajun-Inspired Smoked Pork Chops *15 minutes*

A slight hint of Cajun spices is united with the mellow sweetness of vanilla, making these smoky pork chops a family favorite.

Ingredients

1 (19-ounce) package fully cooked smoked pork chops (5 chops)
⅓ cup fat-free light vanilla yogurt
1 teaspoon Cajun seasoning (McCormick brand)

Instructions for entrée:

▸ Plug in a large indoor electric grill and preheat for at least 5 minutes.
▸ Place the pork chops on the preheated grill.
▸ Spread 1 tablespoon fat-free light vanilla yogurt on each pork chop and sprinkle 1 teaspoon Cajun seasoning evenly on all of the pork chops.
▸ Close the lid and cook until heated through.
▸ Take the drippings from the drip pan and drizzle over the meat.

Yield: 5 (slightly less than 3¾-ounce) servings **Calories per serving:** 137 (35% fat); **Total fat:** 5 g; **Cholesterol:** 58 mg; **Carbohydrate:** 2 g; **Dietary Fiber:** 0 g; **Protein:** 20 g; **Sodium:** 1362 mg **Diabetic Exchanges:** 3 lean meat

Instructions to prepare the suggested meal

Set the timer for 25 minutes.

25 minutes before the meal

- ▸ Plug in a large indoor electric grill.
- ▸ Begin making the Mushroom and Cauliflower in a Creamy Sauce to the point where you let it sit on the burner, covered without heat.

15 minutes before the meal

- ▸ Make the Candied Applesauce according to the directions. Remember to stir occasionally while waiting for the Cajun-Inspired Smoked Pork Chops to cook.

10 minutes before the meal

- ▸ Begin making the Cajun-Inspired Smoked Pork Chops according to the directions.

5 minutes before the meal

- ▸ While the pork is grilling, finish the mushroom and cauliflower dish.
- ▸ Place the pork chops on a serving platter.
- ▸ Dish up the Candied Applesauce, and serve the entire meal.

MAIN MEALS

MEAL SUGGESTION: 25 MINUTES FOR TOTAL MEAL:
Candied Applesauce (page 223)
Mushrooms and Cauliflower in Creamy Sauce (page 224)

SUPPLIES LIST FOR SUGGESTED MEAL
12-inch nonstick saucepan with lid
4-quart saucepan with lid
Cutting board
Knife

GROCERY LIST FOR SUGGESTED MEAL
Ingredients for the Sweet-and-Spicy Pork

PRODUCE
*2 medium onions

MEAT
*2¹/2 pounds pork loin

PACKAGE
*2 (14.5-ounce) cans green beans

PANTRY
*Cajun seasoning
*Sugar-free butter-flavored syrup (¹/3 cup needed)
*Honey (2 tablespoons needed)
*Ground black pepper
Instant whole-grain brown rice OR whole-grain brown rice

Sweet-and-Spicy Pork *20 minutes*

Unlike traditional fat-laden sweet-and-spicy pork dishes, this one is every bit as delicious with a fraction of the calories!

Ingredients

2¹/2 pounds pork loin
2 medium onions
2 (14.5-ounce) cans green beans
2 teaspoons Cajun seasoning
¹/3 cup sugar-free butter-flavored syrup
2 tablespoons honey
¹/4 teaspoon ground black pepper

Instructions for entrée:

▸ Preheat a 12-inch nonstick saucepan on high heat.
▸ While the pan is preheating, trim and remove all visible fat from the pork loin. (After the fat is removed, it will yield approximately 1 3/4 pounds of meat.)
▸ Cut the pork loin into 1-inch chunks.
▸ Place the pork into the preheated pan and brown on high heat.
▸ Cover and continue cooking on high, stirring occasionally.
▸ While the meat is cooking, cut the onions in half, and then cut the halves into thin slices. (While cutting the onions, remember to occasionally stir the meat.)
▸ Drain the green beans.
▸ Reduce the heat to medium.
▸ Stir the sliced onions, Cajun seasoning, syrup, and green beans into the cooked meat.
▸ Cover and continue cooking.
▸ Remove from heat and stir in the honey and ground black pepper.

Total time: 20 minutes **Yield:** 6 (1-cup) servings **Calories per serving:** 267 (31% fat); **Total fat:** 9 g; **Cholesterol:** 75 mg; **Carbohydrate:** 17 g; **Dietary Fiber:** 2 g; **Protein:** 28 g; **Sodium:** 713 mg **Diabetic Exchanges:** 2 vegetable, ¹/2 carbohydrate, 3¹/2 lean meat

---

Instructions to prepare the suggested meal

25 minutes before the meal

▸ Begin making the instant whole-grain brown rice as directed on the box. When the rice has finished cooking, keep it covered and turn off the heat. Let it sit on a warm burner. This will keep the rice warm until dinner.

20 minutes before the meal

▸ Begin cooking the main entrée according to the directions.

MEAL SUGGESTION: 25 MINUTES FOR TOTAL MEAL:
Instant whole-grain brown rice

HELPFUL HINTS:

❷ To save time you can purchase pre-cut pork stir-fry, but remember it will be more expensive.

❷ To save even more money, cook whole-grain rice instead of instant whole-grain rice.

❷ There is enough natural fat in this lean pork that it will brown itself without adding extra oil.

German Bratwurst with Honey Mustard Potatoes *20 minutes*

I love being able to eat bratwurst that isn't laden with fat! Mmm . . . Mmm . . .

Ingredients

4 links from a (19.5-ounce) package turkey bratwurst
1 (20-ounce) bag of frozend diced potatoes with onions and green peppers
1 (4-ounce) jar of pimientos
1 (14.5-ounce) can of sauerkraut
$1/2$ cup fat-free honey mustard salad dressing

Instructions for entrée:

▸ Preheat a 12-inch nonstick saucepan on high heat.
▸ While the saucepan is heating, cut the bratwurst links into $1/2$-inch slices and place in the pan.
▸ Cover and cook, stirring occasionally.
▸ While the bratwurst is cooking, cut the top off of one bag of frozen diced potatoes, and microwave on high heat for 3 minutes.
▸ While the potatoes are cooking, drain the pimientos and set aside. Drain, rinse, and squeeze the sauerkraut dry. Set aside.
▸ Stir the potatoes into the bratwurst.
▸ Once the liquid evaporates, reduce the heat to medium-low. Gently stir in the pimiento and sauerkraut until well mixed.
▸ Stir in the honey mustard salad dressing.
▸ Turn the heat off and cover. Let sit for five minutes before serving.

Yield: 6 (1-cup) servings **Calories per serving:** 272 (28% fat); **Total fat:** 8 g; **Cholesterol:** 49 mg; **Carbohydrate:** 32 g; **Dietary Fiber:** 5 g; **Protein:** 16 g; **Sodium:** 1465 mg **Diabetic Exchanges:** 1 starch, 1 carbohydrate, 2 lean meat

---

SUPPLIES LIST FOR SUGGESTED MEAL
12-inch nonstick saucepan
Cutting board
Medium-sized serving bowl

GROCERY LIST FOR SUGGESTED MEAL
*Ingredients for the German Bratwurst with Honey Mustard Potatoes

PRODUCE
3 fresh pears

MEAT
*1 (19.5 ounce) package turkey bratwurst (4 links used)

DAIRY
Nonfat vanilla yogurt ($1/2$ cup needed)
Reduced-fat feta cheese finely crumbled (2 tablespoons needed)

FROZEN
*1 (20-ounce) bag of diced potatoes with onion and green peppers

PACKAGED
*1 (4-ounce) jar of pimientos
*1 (14.5-ounce) can of sauerkraut
*Fat-free honey mustard salad dressing ($1/2$ cup needed)
Light balsamic vinaigrette salad dressing (2 teaspoons needed)

PANTRY
Light salt or sea salt
Raisins ($1/4$ cup needed)
Finely chopped pecans

Instructions to prepare the suggested meal

Set the timer for 30 minutes.

30 minutes before the meal

> ▸ Make the Pear Chutney and put it in the refrigerator so it will be nicely chilled.

20 minutes before the meal

> ▸ Make the German Bratwurst with Honey Mustard Potatoes.

MEAL SUGGESTION:
30 MINUTES FOR TOTAL MEAL:
Pear Chutney (page 201)

HELPFUL HINT:

❯ Turkey bratwurst is easier to cut when it is slightly frozen.

SUPPLIES LIST FOR
SUGGESTED MEAL
12-inch nonstick saucepan
with lid
Large salad bowl

GROCERY LIST FOR
SUGGESTED MEAL
*Ingredients for the
Tuna Casserole Delight

PRODUCE
1 head iceberg lettuce
(6 cups chopped)

SEAFOOD
*3 (5-ounce) cans tuna
in water

DAIRY
*99% fat-free lemon
flavored yogurt
Nonfat plain yogurt
(1/2 cup needed)
Sugar-free French vanilla
creamer (1/4 cup needed)

PACKAGED
*1 (16-ounce) box
small shells pasta
*1 (8.5-ounce) can peas
and carrots

PANTRY
*Chicken broth
(3 cups needed)
*Lemon pepper
seasoning salt
*Dry dill weed
Salt

Tuna Casserole Delight *20 minutes*

This unique blend of ingredients complements the tuna to perfection.

Ingredients

3 cups chicken broth
1 teaspoon lemon pepper seasoning salt
1 (16-ounce) box of small shells pasta
1 (8.5-ounce) can peas and carrots
3 (5-ounce) cans tuna in water
1 (6-ounce) 99% fat-free lemon flavored yogurt
1 teaspoon dry dill weed, divided

Instructions *for entrée:*

- Preheat a 12-inch nonstick saucepan on high heat.
- Add 3 cups of chicken broth to the pan. Bring to a boil.
- Once the broth comes to full boil, stir in the lemon pepper seasoning salt and the pasta.
- When the contents of the pan return to a full boil, cover, reduce the heat to medium and cook at a low boil. Stir occasionally.
- Drain the peas and carrots and the tuna. Set aside.
- Once the pasta shells are tender, drain the pasta and return to the pan. Reduce the heat to medium low. Stir in the drained peas and carrots, tuna, lemon-flavored yogurt, and 3/4 teaspoon dry dill weed into the pasta shells.
- Once finished sprinkle the remaining 1/4 teaspoon dry dill weed on top.
- Cover and let sit on medium-low heat until ready to eat.

Yield: 9 (1-cup) servings **Calories per serving:** 280 (6% fat); **Total fat:** 2 g;
Cholesterol: 14 mg; **Carbohydrate:** 44 g; **Dietary Fiber:** 2 g; **Protein:** 21 g;
Sodium: 617 mg **Diabetic Exchanges:** 3 starch, 2 very lean meat

---

Instructions to prepare the suggested meal

Set the timer for 20 minutes.

20 minutes before the meal

> Prepare the Tuna Casserole Delight as directed up to the point after you add the pasta shells.

10 minutes before the meal

> Prepare the Light and Creamy Iceberg Salad according to the directions.
> Finish preparing the Tuna Casserole Delight.

MEAL SUGGESTION:
20 MINUTES FOR
TOTAL MEAL:
Light and Creamy Iceberg
Salad (page 66)

HELPFUL HINT:

❷ Chicken broth is lower in sodium than chicken bouillon broth; however, chicken bouillon broth is usually less expensive. Chicken bouillon broth is easily made by simply stirring bouillon into water until it dissolves. Follow the directions on the bouillon package.

SUPPLIES LIST FOR SUGGESTED MEAL
Oven
12-inch or larger
nonstick skillet
Microwave oven
Microwave-safe bowl
9 x 13-inch baking dish
Timer
Large salad serving bowl

GROCERY LIST FOR SUGGESTED MEAL
*Ingredients for the Sausage
and Bean Enchiladas

PRODUCE
1 (16-ounce) bag precut
cole slaw mix

POULTRY
*1 (14-ounce) package lean
turkey breakfast sausage
(7 links needed)

DAIRY
Fat-free sour cream
(1/2 cup needed)
*Fancy Shredded Fiesta
Blend Cheese
(1/3 cup needed)

PACKAGED
*1 (16-ounce) can fat-free
refried beans
*1 (13.5-ounce) package
fat-free tortillas
(10 tortillas per package)
*1 (10-ounjce) can
enchilada sauce
*Chunky salsa
(1 1/2 cups total needed)
Fat-free red French
salad dressing
(1/4 cup needed)
*Nonfat cooking spray

Sausage and Bean Enchiladas *20 minutes*

We like the texture and flavor the browned sausage gives these enchiladas. Who'd ever think sausage and refried beans could be in a low-fat meal?

Ingredients

7 lean turkey breakfast sausage links (1/2 of a 14-ounce package)
1 (16-ounce) can fat-free refried beans
1 cup salsa
1 (13.5-ounce) package fat-free tortillas
1 (10-ounce) can enchilada sauce
1/3 cup Fancy Shredded Fiesta Blend Cheese**

Instructions *for entrée:*

▸ Place the oven rack on the top shelf.
▸ Preheat the oven to 400 degrees.
▸ Spray a 12-inch or larger nonstick skillet with nonfat cooking spray. Preheat the skillet over high heat.
▸ Remove and discard the skins from the sausage links.
▸ Brown and crumble the sausage over high heat.
▸ Once the meat is browned, stir in the refried beans and salsa. Reduce the heat to medium.
▸ ***Open the package of tortillas and cook the tortillas inside the package in the microwave for 1 minute 30 seconds or until fully heated.
▸ Pour the enchilada sauce in a microwave-safe bowl, cover, and cook in the microwave for 1 minute 30 seconds or until heated through.
▸ Generously spray a 9 x 13-inch baking dish.
▸ Spread 1/4 cup cooked bean and sausage mixture into a heated tortilla, roll, and place in the prepared baking dish. Repeat with the remaining 9 tortilla rolls. Place the tortilla rolls snugly together in the dish.
▸ Pour the enchilada sauce over the tortilla rolls.
▸ Sprinkle the cheese over the tortilla rolls.
▸ Place in the oven on the top rack and bake for 5 minutes.

Yield: 5 (2 sausage and bean tortilla) servings **Calories per serving:** 412 (24% fat); **Total fat:** 11 g; **Cholesterol:** 70 mg; **Carbohydrate:** 58 g; **Dietary Fiber:** 8 g; **Protein:** 19 g; **Sodium:** 1662 mg **Diabetic Exchanges:** 4 starch, 1 1/2 medium-fat meat

---

Instructions to prepare the suggested meal

Set the timer for 20 minutes.

20 minutes before the meal

- ▸ Prepare the enchiladas according to these instructions.
- ▸ While the enchiladas are in the oven, prepare the Southwestern Slaw.

5 minutes before the meal

- ▸ Place the Sausage and Bean Enchiladas in the oven on the top rack and bake for 5 minutes.

MEAL SUGGESTION:
20 MINUTES FOR
TOTAL MEAL:
Southwestern Sweet Slaw
(page 69)

HELPFUL HINTS:

❍ Turkey breakfast sausage links come in a 14-ounce package. For this recipe you will only use half. Save the other half for another recipe.

** Fancy Shredded Fiesta Blend Cheese is a blend of shredded cheeses used in Mexican recipes.

*** Opening the packaging prevents the packaging from exploding in the microwave as the tortillas cook. Heating the tortillas inside the packaging saves having to clean another plate.

**SUPPLIES LIST FOR
SUGGESTED MEAL**
12-inch or larger nonstick
saucepan with lid
2 cutting boards
Medium-sized mixing bowl
Timer

**GROCERY LIST FOR
SUGGESTED MEAL**
*Ingredients for the Chicken
and Stuffing Skillet Dinner*

PRODUCE
1 1/2 pounds fresh baby carrots
(as a side)
*3 stalks celery with leaves
*1 (8-ounce) package sliced
mushrooms

POULTRY
*2 pounds boneless, skinless
chicken breast

PACKAGED
*1 (10 3/4-ounce) can 98% fat-
free cream of chicken soup
*1 (6-ounce) box of chicken-
flavored stuffing mix
1 (20-ounce) can no-sugar-
added cherry pie filling
1 (25-ounce) jar unsweetened
applesauce

PANTRY
Almond extract
Splenda
*Nonstick cooking spray

Chicken and Stuffing Skillet Dinner *20 minutes*

This is the epitome of comfort food. Special thanks to Kristie Jaegly of Oregon, Ohio, for this meal. Her recipe originally took an hour to make.

Ingredients for Chicken and Stuffing Skillet Meal

2 pounds boneless, skinless chicken breast
3 stalks celery with leaves, washed
1 (8-ounce) package sliced mushrooms
1 (10 3/4-ounce) can 98% fat-free cream of chicken soup
1 (6-ounce) box of chicken flavored stuffing mix
1 cup water

Instructions for entrée:

‣ Generously spray a 12-inch or larger nonstick saucepan with fat-free cooking spray. Place over high heat.
‣ Remove and discard the fat from the chicken breasts and cut the chicken into bite-size pieces. Place in the preheated pan and cook over high heat to brown, with the lid on, stirring occasionally.
‣ Chop the celery and leaves into small pieces to make approximately 1 1/2 cups.
‣ Stir the celery and sliced mushrooms into the chicken. Reduce the heat to medium, cover, and continue cooking until the celery is tender.
‣ Stir the soup, stuffing mix, and water into the saucepan until well mixed.
‣ Cover and let simmer over medium-low heat until completely heated.
‣ To prevent illness, make sure to thoroughly wash the cutting board with hot, soapy water after cutting the chicken before using it to cut anything else.

Yield: 6 (slightly under 1 cup) servings **Calories per serving:** 314 (12% fat); **Total fat**: 4 g; **Cholesterol:** 93 mg; **Carbohydrate:** 27 g; **Dietary Fiber:** 2 g; **Protein:** 41 g; **Sodium:** 875 mg **Diabetic Exchanges:** 2 starch, 5 very lean meat

---

Instructions to prepare the suggested meal

Set the timer for 20 minutes.

20 minutes before the meal

- Prepare the Chicken and Stuffing Skillet Dinner according to the directions.

5 minutes before the meal

- Prepare the Tart Cherry Applesauce according to the directions, and set aside.
- Place the fresh baby carrots in serving dish.

**MEAL SUGGESTION:
20 MINUTES FOR
TOTAL MEAL:**
Tart Cherry Applesauce
(page 202)
Fresh baby carrots

HELPFUL HINT:

❍ If using frozen chicken breasts, defrost partially in the microwave so that the meat will be easier to cut.

SUPPLIES LIST FOR
SUGGESTED MEAL
12-inch or larger nonstick
saucepan with lid
Medium microwave-safe
serving bowl
Microwave oven
Timer

GROCERY LIST FOR
SUGGESTED MEAL
*Ingredients for the Beefy
Green Beans and Potatoes

PRODUCE
Cherry tomatoes, for garnish

PACKAGED
*1 (7-ounce) can sliced
mushrooms stems and pieces
*Diced pimento (optional)
*2 (15-ounce) cans sliced
new potatoes
*2 (14.5-ounce) cans
whole green beans
*2 (12-ounce) cans roast beef
1 (29-ounce) can pumpkin
(not pie mix)

PANTRY
*Steak seasoning
(I used McCormick Montreal)
Light butter
*Butter-flavored
cooking spray
Butter-flavored sprinkles
*Minced garlic
Salt and pepper

Beefy Green Beans and Potatoes *20 minutes*

Bob Evans restaurant inspired this meal. The flavor of the green beans and potatoes in the beef gravy exemplifies down-home cooking. This is a lot like a stew, but we substitute low-calorie green beans for the starchy carrots and peas.

Ingredients

2 (14.5-ounce) cans whole green beans
2 (15-ounce) cans sliced new potatoes
1 (7-ounce) can sliced mushrooms, stems and pieces
1 1/2 tablespoons minced garlic
2 (12-ounce) cans roast beef
2 tablespoon diced pimiento (optional)
1 teaspoon steak seasoning**

Instructions for entrée:

▸ Drain and discard the liquid from the green beans, potatoes and mushrooms. Set aside.
▸ Spray a 12-inch or larger nonstick saucepan with butter-flavored cooking spray.
▸ Add the minced garlic and roast beef to pan. Break up one can of the meat with your hands, and leave the other can whole chunks. Bring to a boil over high heat.
▸ Reduce the heat to medium and add the diced pimiento (optional), potatoes, steak seasoning, and mushrooms.
▸ Cover and let cook over medium heat until heated through, stirring occasionally.
▸ Salt and pepper to taste, if desired

Yield: 5 (1 1/2-cup) servings **Calories per serving:** 268 (12% fat); **Total fat:** 4 g; **Cholesterol:** 41 mg; **Carbohydrate:** 40 g; **Dietary Fiber:** 6 g; **Protein:** 20 g; **Sodium:** 2157 mg **Diabetic Exchanges:** 2 1/2 starch, 1 vegetable, 2 very lean meat

Instructions to prepare the suggested meal

Set the timer for 20 minutes.

20 minutes before the meal

▸ Begin making the Beefy Green Beans and Potatoes recipe.

7 minutes before the meal

▸ Make the Mashed Pumpkins recipe according to the directions.

**MEAL SUGGESTION:
20 MINUTES FOR
TOTAL MEAL:**
Mashed Pumpkin
(page 205)
Rye bread
Cherry tomatoes for garnish

HELPFUL HINT:

❯ I used McCormick Grill Mates Montreal Steak Seasoning

SUPPLIES LIST FOR SUGGESTED MEAL
12-inch nonstick saucepan
Cutting board
Knife

GROCERY LIST FOR SUGGESTED MEAL
Ingredients for the Pork Stroganoff

PRODUCE
*1 medium sweet yellow onion
*1 (8-ounce) package sliced fresh mushrooms

PACKAGED
*1 (12-ounce) package extra wide egg noodles (egg-free pasta can be substituted for a lower cholesterol meal.) (4 cups needed)

MEATS
*2 pounds pork loin

DAIRY
*Fat-free sour cream (1 cup needed)
Light butter (2 tablespoons needed)

FROZEN
1 (2-pound) package frozen broccoli, cauliflower, and carrots blend

PANTRY
*Minced garlic
*Beef broth (3 cups needed)
Butter-flavored sprinkles (Butter Buds) (6 tablespoons needed)
Honey (2 tablespoons needed)

Pork Stroganoff *30 minutes*

Tender and succulent chunks of pork complement this creamy mushroom sauce. It's sure to satisfy your loved ones.

Ingredients

2 pounds pork loin
1 medium sweet yellow onion
3 cups beef broth (or beef bouillon broth)
2 teaspoons minced garlic
4 cups extra wide egg noodles
1 (8-ounce) package of sliced fresh mushrooms
1 cup fat-free sour cream

Instructions for entrée:

▸ Preheat a 12-inch nonstick saucepan on high heat.
▸ Cut and discard all visible fat from the pork loin.
  (This will yield approximately $1\frac{1}{2}$ pounds of lean meat.)
▸ Cut the meat into half-inch bite-size pieces.
▸ Place the meat into the preheated pan.
▸ While the meat is cooking cut the onion into small pieces to make 1 cup.
  (Remember to stir the meat occasionally while cutting the onion.)
▸ Add the onion to meat and stir. Continue cooking on high.
▸ Stir in the beef broth and minced garlic. Once the liquid comes to a full boil, add the noodles to the pan and press them into the broth using the back of a spatula.
▸ Once the noodles are submerged in the broth, arrange (do not stir) fresh mushrooms on top of the noodles.
▸ Cover and cook at a medium-low boil for 4 minutes.
▸ Remove the lid, stir, and continue cooking on medium-low heat. Stir occasionally as the broth reduces**.
▸ After the broth has reduced and the pasta is tender, stir in the sour cream.

Yield: 7 (1-cup) servings- Nutritional info figured using broth, not bouillon.
Calories per serving: 280 (26% fat); **Total fat:** 8 g; **Cholesterol:** 81 mg;
Carbohydrate: 24 g; **Dietary Fiber:** 1 g; **Protein:** 27 g; **Sodium:** 456 mg
Diabetic Exchanges: 1 1/2 starch, 3 lean meat

Instructions to prepare the suggested meal

Set the timer for 30 minutes.

30 minutes before the meal

- ▶ Prepare the Pork Stroganoff recipe up to the point of covering and cooking for 4 minutes.

10 minutes before the meal

- ▶ Make the Broccoli, Cauliflower, and Carrots according to recipe directions.

6 minutes before the meal

- ▶ Complete the Pork Stroganoff recipe.

**MEAL SUGGESTION:
30 MINUTES FOR
TOTAL MEAL:**
Broccoli, Cauliflower, and
Carrots (lightly sweetened)
(page 222)

HELPFUL HINTS:

❯ Beef broth is lower in sodium than beef bouillon broth; however, bouillon broth is usually less expensive. Beef bouillon broth is easily made by stirring bouillon into water until it dissolves. Follow the directions on the bouillon package.

** To "reduce the broth" means that the broth has thickened.

SUPPLIES LIST FOR
SUGGESTED MEAL
12-inch nonstick saucepan
Cutting board
Small bowl

GROCERY LIST FOR
SUGGESTED MEAL
*Ingredients for the Turkey
Asparagus Casserole in
Dill Cream Sauce*

POULTRY
*1¹/2 lbs boneless,
skinless turkey breast

DAIRY
Fat-free sour cream
(1 cup needed)
Plain nonfat yogurt
(¹/2 cup needed)

PACKAGED
*1 (12-ounce) package
extra-wide egg noodles
(4 cups needed)
*2 (14.5- ounce) cans
asparagus cuts and tips
1 (20-ounce) can
crushed pineapple
1 (10-ounce) jar
maraschino cherries
Miniature marshmallows
(2 cups needed)

PANTRY
Chicken broth
(or chicken bouillon broth)
(3 cups needed)
*Minced garlic
*Dry dill weed
Splenda granular
Chopped pecans
(¹/2 cup needed)

Turkey Asparagus Casserole in Dill Cream Sauce *30 minutes*

Don't be surprised if this creamy home-style comfort food becomes a favorite recipe for your family.

Ingredients

3 cups of chicken broth (or chicken bouillon broth)**
1¹/2 pounds boneless, skinless turkey breast
2 teaspoons dry dill weed, divided
2 teaspoons of minced garlic
4 cups extra wide egg noodles***
2 (14.5-ounce) cans asparagus cuts and tips
1 cup fat-free sour cream

Instructions for entrée:

‣ Preheat a 12-inch nonstick saucepan on high heat.
‣ Add the chicken broth to the preheated pan. (You can make your own broth by dissolving 3 chicken bouillon cubes in 3 cups water.)
‣ Cut the turkey into bite-size pieces.
‣ Add the turkey to the boiling broth.
‣ Stir occasionally.
‣ Stir in 1teaspoon dry dill weed and the minced garlic.
‣ Add the noodles and press them into the broth using the back of a spatula.
‣ Cover and cook at a medium-low boil for 5 minutes.
‣ Open and drain the asparagus; set aside.
‣ Remove the lid from the broth, gently stir in the drained asparagus, and continue cooking on medium-low heat with the lid off. Gently stir as the broth reduces. (You need to stir gently so that you don't break up the asparagus.)
‣ In a small bowl stir together the remaining 1 teaspoon dill weed and the sour cream. Add to the pan and gently stir until well mixed.

Yield: 6 (1⅓-cups) servings Nutritional info figured using broth, not bouillon. (Larger serving size due to vegetable in dish) **Calories per serving:** 310 (14% fat); **Total fat:** 5 g; **Cholesterol:** 99 mg; **Carbohydrate:** 29 g; **Dietary Fiber:** 3 g; **Protein:** 37 g; **Sodium:** 1004 mg **Diabetic Exchanges:** 2 starch, 3 very lean meat

Instruction to prepare the suggested meal:

Set the timer for 30 minutes.

30 minutes before the meal

- ▸ Prepare the Turkey Asparagus Casserole in Dill Cream Sauce up to the point of opening and draining the asparagus and setting it aside.

10 minutes before the meal

- ▸ Make the Pineapple Cherry Delight and set aside.
- ▸ Finish the Turkey Asparagus Casserole in Dill Cream Sauce.

MEAL SUGGESTION:
30 MINUTES FOR TOTAL MEAL:
Pineapple Cherry Delight (page 249)

HELPFUL HINTS:

** Chicken broth is lower in sodium than chicken bouillon broth; however, bouillon is usually less expensive. To make chicken bouillon broth, simply stir bouillon into water until dissolved. Follow the directions on the bouillon package.

*** Egg-free wide pasta can be substituted for the extra wide egg noodles to reduce cholesterol.

**SUPPLIES LIST FOR
SUGGESTED MEAL**
Nonstick Dutch oven or
4¹/2-quart saucepan
Large salad bowl

**GROCERY LIST FOR
SUGGESTED MEAL**
*Ingredients for the Beef
Is Boss Chili Mac*

PRODUCE
1 head iceberg lettuce
(6 cups chopped)

DAIRY
Nonfat plain yogurt
(¹/2 cup needed)
Sugar-free French
vanilla creamer (¹/4 cup
needed)*Fat-free shredded
cheddar cheese (optional to
top chili)

PACKAGED
*2 (14.5-ounce) cans diced
chili-ready, peeled tomatoes
*1 (15.5-ounce) can hot and
spicy chili beans
*2 (12-ounce) cans roast beef
(Hormel)
*1 (8-ounce) box thin
spaghetti

PANTRY
Salt (dash needed)
*Nonstick cooking spray
(optional)

Beef Is Boss Chili Mac *25 minutes*

This meal is for the kids and adults alike. It's hearty and satisfying.

Ingredients

2 (14.5-ounce) cans of diced, chili-ready, peeled tomatoes
1 (15.5-ounce) can hot and spicy chili beans
2 (12-ounce) cans (Hormel) roast beef
2 cups water
1 (8-ounce) box thin spaghetti

Instructions for entrée:

▸ Place a large Dutch oven or 4¹/2-quart saucepan on high heat.
▸ Add the tomatoes, beans, and roast beef.
▸ Add the water and bring to boil.
▸ Once the water is boiling, break the spaghetti into the boiling broth.
▸ Make sure the spaghetti is submerged in the broth.
▸ Reduce the heat to medium and cook at a low boil, stirring occasionally, until the spaghetti is tender.

Yield: 9 (1-cup) servings **Calories per serving:** 229 (10% fat); **Total fat:** 3 g; **Cholesterol:** 23 mg; **Carbohydrate:** 37 g; **Dietary Fiber:** 4 g; **Protein:** 14 g; **Sodium:** 1190 mg **Diabetic Exchanges:** 2 starch, 1 vegetable, 1¹/2 very lean meat

Instructions to prepare the suggested meal

Set the timer for 25 minutes.

25 minutes before the meal

> ‣ Prepare Beef Is Boss Chili Mac according to the directions.

14 minutes before the meal

> ‣ While waiting for the spaghetti to get tender, make the Light and Creamy Iceberg Salad.

MEAL SUGGESTION: 25 MINUTES FOR TOTAL MEAL:
Light and Creamy Iceberg Salad (page 66)

HELPFUL HINTS:

❍ For a tasty topping add shredded fat-free cheddar cheese to the top of the Chili Mac. Spray nonstick cooking spray on top of the cheese, cover, and let the cheese melt.

❍ The easiest way to break the spaghetti in pieces is to pour it out of the box and make it into a log with one hand at each end and bend it till it breaks in half like a twig.

**SUPPLIES LIST FOR
SUGGESTED MEAL**
Large electric indoor grill
Large mixing bowl
1/2 cup-size measuring cup
(for measuring patty size)
Hamburger press (optional)
9x13 baking dish
Wax paper or aluminum foil
12-inch nonstick
saucepan and lid
Cutting board
Timer

**GROCERY LIST FOR
SUGGESTED MEAL**
*Ingredients for the Italian
Mini Meat Loaves*

PRODUCE
8 ounces pre-sliced fresh
mushrooms
2 pounds fresh grapes

MEATS/POULTRY
*2 (19.2-ounce) packages
Italian-flavored ground turkey
20 slices of turkey pepperoni

DAIRY
*2 eggs

PACKAGED
*1 (14.5-ounce) can Italian
diced tomatoes
* Italian-flavored bread
crumbs (2 cups needed)
*1 (14-ounce) jar pizza sauce
2 (14.5-ounce) Italian cut
green beans
2 (15-ounce) cans sliced
potatoes

PANTRY
Butter-flavored sprinkles
(Butter Buds)
Italian seasoning

Italian Mini Meat Loaves *30 minutes*

This is a wonderful dish that can stay in the oven until everyone is ready to come to the table.

Ingredients

2 egg whites
1 (14.5-ounce) can Italian diced tomatoes
2 (19.2-ounce) packages Italian-flavored ground turkey
2 cups Italian-flavored bread crumbs
1 (14-ounce) jar pizza sauce

Instructions for entrée:

▸ Preheat a large indoor electric grill.
▸ In a large mixing bowl, add the egg whites, tomatoes, ground turkey, and bread crumbs. Mix together well with your hands.
▸ Form 6 ($1/2$-cup serving) meat loaf patties, place the patties on wax paper or aluminum foil, set aside.
▸ Place the meat loaf patties on the preheated grill and close the lid to cook.
▸ While patties are cooking, make another 6 meat loaf patties and set aside.
▸ When the first patties are fully cooked, place them in a 9 x 13-inch baking dish and pour half of the jar of pizza sauce over the patties. Place in the oven to keep warm.
▸ Place the second batch of patties on the grill to cook.
▸ Remove the baking dish from the oven and place the remaining cooked meat loaf patties on top of those already in the pan and pour remaining pizza sauce on top and return to the oven.
▸ Bake for an additional 5 minutes.

Yield: 12 (1-patty) servings **Calories per serving:** 214 (26% fat); **Total fat:** 6 g; **Cholesterol:** 52 mg; **Carbohydrate:** 17 g; **Dietary Fiber:** 2 g; **Protein:** 22 g; **Sodium:** 532 mg **Diabetic Exchanges:** 1 starch, 3 lean meat

Instructions to prepare the suggested meal

Set the timer for 30 minutes.

30 minutes before the meal

- ▶ Preheat the oven to 350 degrees.
- ▶ Preheat the electric indoor grill.
- ▶ Make the Italian Mini Meat Loaves according to the directions.

10 minutes before the meal

- ▶ Prepare the Italian Green Beans and Potatoes according to the directions.

**MEAL SUGGESTION:
30 MINUTES FOR
TOTAL MEAL**
Italian Green Beans and
Sliced Potatoes (page 197)
Grapes

HELPFUL HINT:

❯ I use a Tupperware hamburger press to make the patties quickly and easily.

**SUPPLIES LIST FOR
SUGGESTED MEAL**
12-inch nonstick saucepan
with lid
Cutting board
Medium-sized bowl
Microwave oven
Microwave-safe bowl
Wax paper
Timer

**GROCERY LIST FOR
SUGGESTED MEAL**
*Ingredients for the Onion
and Mushroom-Smothered
Burgers*

PRODUCE
*2 medium sweet onions
*1 (8-ounce) package sliced
fresh mushrooms
Cluster of grapes or orange
slices as a side

MEATS
*1 (16-ounce) package lean
ground beef (8% fat)

PACKAGED
2 (14.5-ounce) cans green
beans
1 (15-ounce) can diced
potatoes
Fat-free Italian salad
dressing
Diced pimentos

PANTRY
*Garlic salt
*Liquid smoke
*Worcestershire sauce
Butter-flavored sprinkles
Real bacon bits
*Nonfat butter-flavored
cooking spray

Onion and Mushroom–Smothered Burgers *25 minutes*

This is one of my all-time favorite ways to eat burgers.

Ingredients

2 medium sweet onions
1 (8-ounce) package sliced fresh mushrooms
1 teaspoon garlic salt, divided
1 (16-ounce) package lean ground beef (8% fat)
1/2 teaspoon liquid smoke
1/2 teaspoon Worcestershire sauce

Instructions for entrée:

▸ Preheat a 12-inch nonstick saucepan on medium-high heat.
▸ Thinly slice the onions. Separate the slices.
▸ Spray the preheated saucepan with cooking spray. Add the onions, mushrooms, and 1/2 teaspoon garlic salt. Stir, cover, and cook, stirring occasionally.
▸ In a medium-size bowl, mix together the ground beef, liquid smoke, the remaining 1/2 teaspoon garlic salt, and the worcestershire sauce, using your hands.
▸ Make 4 (4-ounce) hamburger patties. Set aside.
▸ Move the cooked vegetables to one side of the saucepan. Place the hamburgers on the other side of the saucepan.
▸ Cover and cook on high heat until the patties are brown on the bottom.
▸ Turn the hamburgers over and reduce the heat to medium.
▸ Stir the mushrooms and onions over the bottom of the pan to absorb the juices from the pan bottom.
▸ Cook the meat to desired doneness.

Yield: 4 servings **Calories per serving:** 184 (28% fat); **Total fat:** 6 g; **Cholesterol:** 62 mg; **Carbohydrate:** 8 g; **Dietary Fiber:** 2 g; **Protein:** 27 g; **Sodium:** 339 mg **Diabetic Exchanges:** 2 vegetable, 3 lean meat

---

Instructions to prepare the suggested meal

Set the timer for 25 minutes.

25 minutes before the meal

> ‣ Prepare the Onion and Mushroom-Smothered Burgers according to the directions.

10 minutes before the meal

> ‣ Prepare the Green Beans and Potatoes.
> ‣ Continue making the burgers.

5 minutes before the meal

> ‣ Wash the grapes or oranges and put on the serving plate.
> ‣ Finish cooking the Onion and Mushroom-Smothered Burgers.

MENU SUGGESTION:
25 MINUTES FOR
TOTAL MEAL:
Green Beans and Potatoes
(page 198)
Cluster of grapes or
orange slices

SUPPLIES LIST FOR
SUGGESTED MEAL
Cutting board
Large Dutch oven or soup
pan
Strainer
Large serving bowl
Medium serving bowl
Muffin tins
Medium-sized microwave-
safe serving bowls
Microwave oven
Oven
Timer

GROCERY LIST FOR
SUGGESTED MEAL
*Ingredients for the Penne in
Creamy Italian Sauce

MEATS/POULTRY
1 package sliced turkey
pepperoni (15 slices needed)

DAIRY
Light butter
100% grated parmesan
cheese
*Fat-free sour cream
(1 cup needed)
*Low-fat ricotta cheese
(1/2 cup needed)

PACKAGED
*1 (16-ounce) box penne pasta
*1 can pitted ripe olives
(aka: black olives)
*1 (14-ounce) jar pizza sauce
*1 (14.5-ounce) can Italian
diced tomatoes
1 (7.5-ounce) can
home-style biscuits
3 (14.5-ounce) cans Italian
cut green beans
1 (6.5-ounce) can mushrooms,
stems and pieces
Italian salad dressing
(1/4 cup needed)

*Grocery list continued
on next page*

Penne in Creamy Italian Sauce *30 minutes*

Isn't it nice to know that we can enjoy creamy pasta without all of the fats usually associated with cream sauces?

Ingredients

1 (16-ounce) box penne pasta
1 can pitted ripe olives**
1 cup fat-free sour cream
1 (14-ounce) jar pizza sauce
1 (14.5-ounce) can Italian diced tomatoes
1/2 cup low-fat ricotta cheese
1 teaspoon garlic salt

Instructions for entrée:

▸ Add 3 quarts of water to a large Dutch oven or soup pan, and bring to a boil over high heat.
▸ Once the water is boiling, add the pasta. Return to a boil and stir occasionally.
▸ Open, drain, and discard the liquid from the can of olives. Place the drained olives in a microwave-safe bowl and heat for 1 minute; set aside.
▸ Once the pasta is cooked, drain and return to the pan.
▸ Stir in the sour cream, pizza sauce, tomatoes, ricotta cheese, garlic salt, and the heated olives. Return the pan to medium heat and cook until all ingredients are fully heated.

Yield: 9 (1-cup) servings **Calories per serving:** 272 (11% fat); **Total fat:** 3 g; **Cholesterol:** 8 mg; **Carbohydrate:** 48 g; **Dietary Fiber:** 3 g; **Protein:** 11 g; **Sodium:** 530 mg **Diabetic Exchanges:** 3 starch

---

Instructions to prepare the suggested meal

Set the timer for 30 minutes

30 minutes before the meal
- Preheat the oven to 425 degrees.
- Add 3 quarts of water to a large Dutch oven or soup pan over high heat. Bring to a boil.

25 minutes before the meal
- Begin making the Italian Pull-Apart Muffins according to the directions.

20 minutes before the meal
- Stir the penne pasta into the boiling water.

10 minutes before the meal
- Place the muffins into the preheated oven.
- Make the Pepperoni and Green Beans according to the directions.

5 minutes before the meal
- Drain the pasta and place back into the pan.
- Continue following the directions for the penne pasta.

1 minute before meal
- Remove muffins from the oven.
- Serve the meal.

PANTRY
Italian seasoning
*Garlic salt
Olive oil cooking spray

**MEAL SUGGESTION:
30 MINUTES FOR
TOTAL MEAL:**
Italian Pull-Apart Muffins
(page 238)
Pepperoni and Mushroom
Green Beans (page 206)

HELPFUL HINT:

** Ripe olives are also known as black olives.

SUPPLIES LIST FOR SUGGESTED MEAL
Oven
Cookie sheet
12-inch or larger nonstick saucepan
Small bowl
Cutting board
Large salad bowl
Large microwave-safe bowl
Microwave oven
Timer

GROCERY LIST FOR SUGGESTED MEAL
*Ingredients for the Beef Gravy over Biscuits

PRODUCE
1 large package celery
1 bunch fresh parsley
(1/4 cup needed)

MEATS
*1 (16-ounce) package extra-lean ground beef

DAIRY
*Skim milk
(3 cups needed)
*1 (7.5-ounce) can home-style biscuits

PACKAGED
*1 (8.5-ounce) can peas and carrots
Diced pimento
(3 tablespoons needed)
Fat-free Italian salad dressing
(1/3 cup needed)
2 (15-ounce) cans whole segment mandarin oranges in light syrup
1 (6-ounce) can whole segment mandarin oranges in light syrup
1 (6-ounce) jar maraschino cherries

Grocery list continued on next page

Beef Gravy over Biscuits *30 minutes*

This is every bit as good as I remember my Mom's beef gravy, but with a lot fewer calories.

Ingredients

1 (7.5-ounce) can home-style biscuits
1 (16-ounce) package extra-lean ground beef
1 1/2 teaspoon steak seasoning* (McCormick Montreal)
1 (8.5-ounce) can peas and carrots
2 tablespoons cornstarch
3 cups skim milk

Instructions for entrée:

- Place the oven rack in the middle of the oven. Preheat the oven to 400 degrees.
- Place the biscuits on an ungreased cookie sheet; set aside.
- Spray a 12-inch or larger nonstick saucepan with cooking spray. Brown and crumble the ground beef with the steak seasoning over high heat.
- Drain the liquid from the peas and carrots into a small bowl. Set the peas and carrots aside.
- Add the cornstarch to the liquid from the peas and carrots, and mix until dissolved. Set aside.
- Once the meat is fully browned, reduce the heat to medium.
- Stir the milk and the dissolved cornstarch into the browned meat. Gently stir in the peas and carrots. Cook over medium heat, bringing to a slow boil, stirring occasionally.
- Let the meat and vegetable mixture cook at a slow boil for 10 minutes.
- Place the biscuits in the oven and bake for 10 minutes.
- Turn off the heat. As the mixture sits, the gravy will thicken.
- Serve the beef gravy over the biscuits.

Yield: 5 (3/4 cup beef gravy with 2 biscuits) servings **Calories per serving:** 300 (18% fat); **Total fat:** 6 g; **Cholesterol:** 53 mg; **Carbohydrate:** 33 g; **Dietary Fiber:** 2 g; **Protein:** 29 g; **Sodium:** 823 mg **Diabetic Exchanges:** 1 1/2 starch, 1/2 fat-free milk, 3 lean meat

Instructions to prepare the suggested meal

Set the timer for 30 minutes.

30 minutes before the meal

- Place the rack in the middle of the oven. Preheat the oven to 400 degrees.
- Make the Beef Gravy over Biscuits recipe, but do not bake the biscuits at this time.

20 minutes before the meal

- Make the Celery Salad according to the directions. Place in the refrigerator .until ready to serve.
- Check the Beef Gravy. Do not let it come to a full boil.

10 minutes before the meal

- Stir the gravy occasionally.
- Place the biscuits in the oven and bake for 10 minutes.
- Make the Warm Maraschino and Mandarin Fruit Salad according to the directions.

3 minutes before the meal

- Turn the heat off of the meat gravy, stir, and let the gravy thicken.
- When the biscuits are done, remove from the oven.
- Serve the meal.

PANTRY
* Steak seasoning (I used McCormick Montreal brand.)
*Cornstarch
(2 tablespoons needed)
Ground allspice
Splenda Brown Sugar Blend
Butter-flavored sprinkles
*Nonstick cooking spray

MEAL SUGGESTION:
30 MINUTES FOR
TOTAL MEAL:
Celery Salad (page 70)
Warm Maraschino and
Mandarin Fruit Salad (page 71)

HELPFUL HINT:

> Make sure to rinse the pan out as soon as it is empty to make cleaning easier.

Grocery list continued
on next page

Pasta Ribbons in Creamy Tomato Sauce *25 minutes*

If you are a weight watcher like me, you will be so satisfied with the portion of this pasta that you won't even miss the meat.

Ingredients

1 (12-ounce) package egg-free wide pasta ribbons
1 cup low-fat ricotta cheese
1/2 cup light fat-free vanilla yogurt
1 (26-ounce) jar spaghetti sauce
1/2 teaspoon onion salt
1 (14.5-ounce) can Italian diced tomatoes, drained
3 tablespoons fancy shredded parmesan cheese blend

Instructions for entrée:

▸ Fill a Dutch oven or soup pan with 3 quarts of hot water and bring to a boil over high heat.
▸ Add the pasta to the boiling water. Spray the top of the water with nonstick cooking spray to prevent it from boiling over. Cook the pasta until tender, about 8 to 10 minutes.
▸ Drain the cooked pasta and return it to the pan. Place the pan back on the burner.
▸ Reduce the heat to medium-low and stir in the ricotta cheese, yogurt, spaghetti sauce, onion salt, and tomatoes. Stir together and heat through.
▸ Sprinkle the parmesan cheese blend on top of the pasta and serve.

Yield: 9 (1-cup) servings **Calories per serving:** 210 (7% fat); **Total fat:** 1 g; **Cholesterol:** 7 mg; **Carbohydrate:** 38 g; **Dietary Fiber:** 3 g; **Protein:** 9 g; **Sodium:** 513 mg **Diabetic Exchanges:** 2 starch, 2 vegetable

---

Instructions to prepare the suggested meal

Set the timer for 30 minutes.

30 minutes before the meal

- Place the oven rack in the middle of the oven.
- Preheat the oven to 350 degrees.
- Fill a Dutch oven or soup pan with 3 quarts of hot water and bring to a boil over high heat.
- Start making the crescent rolls according to the directions.

20 minutes before the meal

- Add the pasta to the boiling water. Spray the top of the water with nonstick cooking spray to prevent it from boiling over.
- If more time is needed, continue making the crescent rolls. Set aside. Do not place in the oven at this time.

15 minutes before the meal

- Make the green beans according to recipe.

10 minutes before the meal

- Put the crescent rolls into the oven. Bake 8-10 minutes or until golden brown.
- Take a break from making the green beans long enough to finish making the pasta dish.

5 minutes before the meal

- Finish making the green beans.

1 minute before meal

- Remove the crescent rolls from the oven..

PANTRY
Worcestershire sauce
Dried minced onions
Dried Italian seasoning
Minced garlic
Garlic salt
Butter-flavored cooking spray
*Onion salt
*Nonstick cooking spray

**MEAL SUGGESTION:
30 MINUTES FOR
TOTAL MEAL:**
Italian Cream Cheese
Crescents (page 239)
Italian Green Beans with Black
Olives and Mushrooms
(page 217)

Linguine with Creamy Sausage, Mushroom, and Asparagus Sauce *30 minutes*

Why spend the big bucks for fancy gourmet meals when you can enjoy fine cuisine like this in only minutes within the comfort of your own home (and at a fraction of the price)?!

Ingredients

1 (16-ounce) package lean turkey breakfast sausage
¹/₄ teaspoon of dried thyme
1 (8-ounce) package sliced fresh mushrooms
2¹/₂ cups fat-free milk
2 tablespoons cornstarch
1 (16-ounce) box linguine
2 (14.5-ounce) cans asparagus cuts and tips, drained

Instructions for entrée:

▸ Fill a large soup pan or Dutch oven with 4 quarts of water. Spray the top of the water with nonstick cooking spray and bring to a boil over high heat.
▸ In a 12-inch nonstick saucepan, brown and crumble the sausage over high heat until fully cooked.
▸ Add the thyme and sliced mushrooms.
▸ In a small bowl combine the milk and cornstarch. Stir with a fork until the cornstarch is completely dissolved.
▸ Reduce the sausage mixture to medium heat, and pour in the milk and cornstarch. Stir until mixed well.
▸ Add the linguine to the boiling water. Return to a full boil and cook for 10 to 12 minutes or until the pasta is tender.
▸ Add the asparagus to the sauce and stir gently, being careful not to break up the asparagus. Reduce the heat to medium-low and cook at a low simmer until heated through.
▸ Drain the linguine and pour into a large pasta bowl.
▸ Pour the sauce over the linguine and serve.

Yield: 8 (3/4 cup sauce and 1 cup firmly packed linguine) servings **Calories per serving:** 360 (18% fat); **Total fat:** 7 g; **Cholesterol:** 49 mg; **Carbohydrate:** 51 g; **Dietary Fiber:** 3 g; **Protein:** 21 g; **Sodium:** 735 mg **Diabetic Exchanges:** 3 starch, 1 vegetable, 1 1/2 lean meat

Instructions to prepare the suggested meal

Set the timer for 30 minutes.

30 minutes before the meal

- ▸ Begin making the Linguine with Creamy Sausage, Mushroom, and Asparagus Sauce according to the directions.

15 minutes before the meal

- ▸ Add the pasta to the water. Cook according to package directions.
- ▸ Begin making the Very Berry Spiced Applesauce according to the recipe directions.

3 minutes before the meal

- ▸ Drain the linguine.
- ▸ Place the drained linguine in a large pasta bowl, and pour the sauce over the linguine.
- ▸ Serve the linguine and applesauce.

MEAL SUGGESTION: 30 MINUTES FOR TOTAL MEAL:
Very Berry Spiced Applesauce (page 199)

HELPFUL HINTS:

❷ Spraying the top of the pasta water with cooking spray helps the water not to boil over.

❷ To save time and cleaning, stir the cornstarch and milk together in a 4-cup measuring cup instead of using a measuring cup to measure the milk and then dirtying another bowl to dissolve the cornstarch in.

❷ Optional: For added pizzazz top the linguine with grated fat-free parmesan cheese.

❷ If you can afford baby portabella mushrooms, I would recommend them over the sliced button mushrooms. Do not substitute canned mushrooms in this recipe.

SUPPLIES LIST FOR SUGGESTED MEAL
Oven
Cutting board
12-inch nonstick saucepan
Large bowl
Microwave oven
Potato masher
Electric mixer
Timer

GROCERY LIST FOR SUGGESTED MEAL
*Ingredients for the Shepherd's Pie One-Pan Dinner

PRODUCE
*1 medium sweet onion

MEATS
*2¼ pounds extra-lean ground beef

DAIRY
*Fat-free sour cream (½ cup needed)

PACKAGED
*2 (15-ounce) cans of mixed vegetables
*1 (0.87-ounce) package brown gravy mix
*2 (14.5-ounce) cans diced potatoes

PANTRY
*Butter-flavored sprinkles (Butter Buds, 2 tablespoons needed)

Shepherd's Pie One-Pan Dinner *30 minutes*

This meal captures the essence of good old fashioned homestyle comfort food!

Ingredients

2¼ pounds extra-lean ground beef
1 medium sweet onion
2 (15-ounce) cans of mixed vegetables
1 (0.87-ounce) package brown gravy mix
2 (14.5-ounce) cans diced potatoes
½ cup fat-free sour cream
2 tablespoons butter-flavored sprinkles (Butter Buds)

Instructions *for entrée:*

- Place the oven rack on the top shelf of the oven and preheat the oven to 450 degrees.
- In a large nonstick saucepan over high heat, brown and crumble the ground beef.
- While the meat is browning, chop the onion to make 1 cup. Add the onions to the browning meat.
- Open the mixed vegetables, but do not drain. Set aside.
- Once the meat is completely browned, add the undrained mixed vegetables and the brown gravy mix to the meat; stir until well mixed.
- Reduce the heat to medium-low and cook at a low boil.
- Open and drain the potatoes. Place the drained potatoes in a microwave-safe bowl, cover, and cook in the microwave for 2 to 3 minutes or until completely heated and soft.
- Add sour cream and Butter Buds to the cooked potatoes. Begin mashing the potatoes by hand with a potato masher; then finish mashing with an electric mixer until creamy. The potatoes will be slightly chunky.
- Stir 1 cup of the mashed potatoes into the cooked beef and vegetables until well mixed.
- Spread the remaining mashed potatoes on top of the beef and vegetables.
- Put the pan in the oven on the top shelf and bake for 7 minutes.
- Take the pan out of the oven and let stand for a few minutes before serving, to let the gravy thicken.

Yield: 7 (1½-cups) servings **Calories per serving:** 361 (20% fat); **Total fat:** 8 g; **Cholesterol:** 83 mg; **Carbohydrate:** 36 g; **Dietary Fiber:** 5 g; **Protein:** 37 g; **Sodium:** 1167 mg **Diabetic Exchanges:** 1½ starch, 2 vegetables, 4 lean meats

Instructions to prepare the suggested meal

▸ While this meal is baking in the oven, place bread and butter on the table.

**SUPPLIES LIST FOR
SUGGESTED MEAL**
Oven
12-inch nonstick oven-safe
saucepan
4-quart nonstick saucepan
Timer

**GROCERY LIST FOR
SUGGESTED MEAL**
*Ingredients for the Cheese
Is King Macaroni and Cheese*

MEATS
4 slices 97% fat-free
honey ham

DAIRY
*2 (8-ounce) packages
shredded fat-free cheddar
cheese (only sold in 8-oz)

PACKAGED
*3 cups elbow macaroni
*1 box Three Cheese
Flavored Baked Crisp Snacks
Crackers
(24 crackers needed)
3 (14.5-ounce) cans no salt
added French-style green
beans
Low-fat slaw dressing
(1/4 cup needed (I used
Marzetti)

PANTRY
*Chicken broth (4 cups
needed)
Soy sauce
Minced garlic
Ground black pepper
*Butter-flavored cooking
spray

Cheese Is King Macaroni and Cheese *25 minutes*

Homemade, creamy macaroni and cheese with a crunchy crumb topping is king when it comes to comfort foods, and now we can enjoy it guilt free! Who would've ever thought you could make this indulgence with only four easy-to-find ingredients! Isn't life good! My teenage neighbor Joe Stone loved this!

Ingredients

4 cups chicken broth
3 cups elbow macaroni
24 Three Cheese Flavored Baked Crisp Snacks Crackers
2 (8-ounce) packages shredded fat-free cheddar cheese

Instructions for entrée:

▸ Preheat the oven to 400 degrees.
▸ In a 12-inch nonstick oven-safe saucepan, bring the chicken broth to a boil over high heat.
▸ Once the broth comes to a full boil, add the macaroni, stir, and make sure all of the pasta is covered by the broth.
▸ Bring the broth back to a full boil, then reduce to medium heat, keeping the broth at a medium-low boil. Stir occasionally. Boil for approximately 10 minutes or until the pasta is tender.
▸ While the pasta is boiling, crush the Three Cheese Flavored Baked Crisp Snack Crackers to make $1/2$ cup and set aside.
▸ When the pasta is tender, stir the cheese into the cooked macaroni. Do not drain the chicken broth. Constantly stir the cheese and pasta until the cheese is fully melted.
▸ Sprinkle the macaroni and cheese with the crushed crackers; then spray the crackers with butter-flavored cooking spray.
▸ Place in the oven on the top rack, and bake for 5 minutes.
▸ Remove from the oven and serve.

Yield: 8 (1-cup) servings **Calories per serving:** 267 (7% fat); **Total fat:** 2 g; **Cholesterol:** 10 mg; **Carbohydrate:** 35 g; **Dietary Fiber:** 1 g; **Protein:** 25 g; **Sodium:** 1109 mg **Diabetic Exchanges:** 2½ starch, 2½ very lean meat

Instructions to prepare the suggested meal

Set the timer for 25 minutes.

25 minutes before the meal

> ▸ Prepare the macaroni and cheese according to the directions.

5 minutes before the meal

> ▸ Place the macaroni and cheese in the oven.
> ▸ Prepare the Green Beans with Ham according to the directions.

MEAL SUGGESTION: 25 MINUTES FOR TOTAL MEAL: Green Beans and Ham (page 211)

HELPFUL HINTS:

❯ Keep your eye on the pasta, making sure to stir it occasionally so it will remain at a medium-low boil and not stick to the bottom of the saucepan.

❯ The Cheese Is King Macaroni and Cheese is best served right away.

❯ You can substitute whole-wheat pasta for this recipe, but it will take longer to cook.

Mushroom and Onion Beef Stew with Biscuits *30 minutes*

This recipe is the epitome of down-home cooking!

Ingredients

1 large sweet onion, chopped (to make 2 cups)
1 (8-ounce) package fresh, sliced mushrooms
2 (15-ounce) cans sliced new potatoes
2 (12-ounce) cans roast beef and gravy**
1/2 teaspoon rubbed thyme
1 teaspoon Canadian steak seasoning
1 (7-ounce) can home-style biscuits

Instructions for entrée:

▸ Place the oven rack on the top shelf of the oven. Preheat the oven to 400 degrees.
▸ Chop the sweet onion to make 2 cups.
▸ Generously spray an oven-safe 12-inch nonstick saucepan with nonstick cooking spray.
▸ Over high heat cook the mushrooms and onions in the prepared saucepan. Spray the mushrooms and onions with nonstick cooking spray. Cover and cook until the onions are tender, stirring occasionally.
▸ While the mushroom-and-onions mixture cooks, open, drain, and discard the juice from the cans of potatoes. Open the cans of Hormel roast beef and gravy. Set aside.
▸ Reduce the heat to medium once the onions are tender. Remove 1/2 cup of the cooked mushrooms and onions from the pan and set aside to use later.
▸ Spray the bottom of the saucepan with more nonstick cooking spray. Move the cooked mushrooms and onions to one side of the pan, spray with cooking spray, and do again to prevent the gravy from sticking.
▸ Stir in the roast beef with gravy, potatoes, thyme, and Canadian steak seasoning. Stir together until well mixed.
▸ Cook for about 5 minutes.
▸ Arrange the home-style biscuits on top of the stew.
▸ Sprinkle the reserved mushrooms and onions on top of the biscuits. Cover with a lid and let cook for 7 minutes.

SUPPLIES LIST FOR SUGGESTED MEAL
Oven
Cutting board
Oven-safe 12-inch nonstick saucepan with lid
12-inch nonstick saucepan with a lid
Timer

GROCERY LIST FOR SUGGESTED MEAL
Ingredients for the Mushroom and Onion Beef Stew with Biscuits

PRODUCE
*1 large sweet onion (2 cups chopped needed)
*1 (8-ounce) package fresh, sliced mushrooms

DAIRY
*1 (7-ounce) can home-style biscuits
Light butter

PACKAGED
*2 (15-ounce) cans sliced new potatoes
*2 (12-ounce) cans roast beef and gravy (Hormel)
2 (14.5-ounce) cans sliced carrots
1 box sugar-free spiced cider apple-flavor drink mix (10 pouches per box)

PANTRY
*Rubbed thyme
*Canadian steak seasoning
*Nonstick cooking spray
Ground black pepper (optional)

- Five minutes before mealtime, remove the lid, spray the top of biscuits with nonstick cooking spray, and place them in the preheated oven on the top rack to bake for 5 minutes.

Yield: 5 (1 cup stew with 2 biscuits) servings **Calories per serving**: 340 (13% fat); **Total fat:** 5 g; **Cholesterol:** 41 mg; **Carbohydrate:** 55 g; **Dietary Fiber:** 6 g; **Protein:** 21 g; **Sodium:** 1801 mg **Diabetic Exchanges:** 3½ starch, 1 vegetable, 2 very lean meat

---

Instructions to prepare the suggested meal

Set the timer for 30 minutes.

30 minutes before the meal

- Begin making the Mushroom and Beef Stew with biscuits according to the directions.

10 minutes before the meal

- Begin making the carrots according to the directions.

5 minutes before the meal

- Spray the top of the biscuits with nonstick cooking spray and place them in the preheated oven to bake for 5 minutes.

MAIN MEALS

**MEAL SUGGESTION:
30 MINUTES FOR
TOTAL MEAL:**
Candied Carrots (page 212)

HELPFUL HINT:

** I used Hormel brand of canned roast beef and gravy.

SUPPLIES LIST FOR
SUGGESTED MEAL
2 (12-inch) saucepans
with lids
Cutting board
1 medium microwavable
serving bowl
Medium-sized microwave-
safe bowl
Wax paper
Microwave oven
Timer

GROCERY LIST FOR
SUGGESTED MEAL
*Ingredients for the Beef
Stroganoff

PRODUCE
*1 (8-ounce) package fresh,
sliced mushrooms

MEATS
*1/2 pound any cooked
leftover lean steak or
hamburger

DAIRY
*Fat-free sour cream
(1 cup needed)

PACKAGED
*1 (12-ounce) package No
Yolks noodles, (dumpling
size) (4 cups needed)
3 (14.5-ounce) cans
asparagus cuts and tips
Fat-free Italian salad dressing
(3 tablespoons needed)
Pimento (optional)
French bread (optional)

PANTRY
*Beef broth made from
bouillon (4 1/2 cups needed)
*Minced garlic
Minced onion
Splenda granular
*Cornstarch
(1/4 cup needed)
Salt and pepper

Beef Stroganoff *25 minutes*

*Here's an excellent way to use and stretch leftover cooked hamburger or beef steak. Many
people like to dip their French bread into this sauce.*

Ingredients

4 cups beef broth made from bouillon
1 tablespoon minced garlic (from a jar)
4 cups No Yolks noodles, (dumpling size)**
1/2 pound any cooked leftover lean steak or hamburger
1/4 cup cornstarch
1 (8-ounce) package fresh, sliced mushrooms
1 cup fat-free sour cream

Instructions for entrée:

▸ In a 12-inch nonstick saucepan, bring the beef broth to a boil over high heat.
▸ Stir the minced garlic into the beef broth. Bring to a boil.
▸ Add the noodles to the boiling broth.
▸ Cover and return the broth to a boil; reduce the heat to medium and let cook at
a medium boil for 8 minutes.
▸ Cut the leftover meat into tiny pieces. Remove all visible fat.
▸ Remove 1/2 cup of broth from the pan and dissolve the cornstarch into the
removed broth.
▸ Stir the cornstarch broth back into the pan with the noodles, along with the
mushrooms, (cut-up) meat, and sour cream.
▸ Cover and cook for 5 minutes.
▸ Salt and pepper to taste if desired.
▸ Let sit for a couple of minutes before serving. As it cools, the sauce will thicken.

Yield: 7 (1-cup) servings Nutritional info using beef sirloin **Calories per serving:**
223 (10% fat); **Total fat:** 2 g; **Cholesterol:** 25 mg; **Carbohydrate:** 32 g; **Dietary
Fiber:** 1 g; **Protein:** 17 g; **Sodium:** 516 mg **Diabetic Exchanges:** 2 starch, 2 very
lean meat

186

Instructions to prepare the suggested meal

Set the timer for 25 minutes.

25 minutes before the meal

- ▸ Make the Beef Stroganoff according to the directions.

5 minutes before the meal

- ▸ Cover the stroganoff and turn off the heat.
- ▸ Make the European Asparagus according to the directions.

**MEAL SUGGESTION:
25 MINUTES FOR
TOTAL MEAL:**
European Asparagus
(page 215)
French bread (optional)

HELPFUL HINTS:

❯ You can use real beef broth, but it will add more calories.

187

Beef Pot Pie *30 minutes*

This light and flaky pot pie crust literally melts in your mouth; and the beef and vegetables are seasoned perfectly! This is down home goodness through and through!

Ingredients

4 to 5 celery stalks tops with leaves
1 medium sweet onion
1 (14.5-ounce) can peas and carrots
1 (14.5-ounce) can cut green beans, no salt added
2 (12-ounce) cans beef and gravy (Hormel)
1/4 teaspoon rubbed thyme
5 Filo dough sheets

Instructions for entrée:

▸ Place the oven rack on the top shelf. Preheat the oven to 350 degrees.
▸ Spray a 12-inch nonstick saucepan with nonstick cooking spray and preheat on medium-high heat.
▸ While the pan is preheating, finely chop the tops of celery stalks with the leaves to make 1 cup firmly packed. Finely chop the onion to make 1 cup.
▸ Cook the celery and onions in the pan over medium-high heat until tender, stirring frequently.
▸ While the celery and onions are cooking, drain the juice from the can of peas and carrots and the can of cut green beans. Set aside.
▸ Spray a 9 x 13-inch casserole dish with nonstick cooking spray and set aside.
▸ Once the onions and celery are tender, add the drained green beans and peas and carrots, beef and gravy, and rubbed thyme. Gently stir until well mixed; then cover and cook for about 5 minutes, stirring occasionally, until completely warmed through.
▸ Once the beef and vegetables are is fully heated, pour them into the prepared baking dish.
▸ One at a time, spray the tops of the filo dough sheets with butter-flavored cooking spray and layer on top of the beef and vegetables. There will be a stack of 5 filo sheets on top of the beef and vegetables to make the pot pie crust.
▸ Place in the oven on the top shelf for 10 minutes or until dough is golden brown and flaky.
▸ Cut into six servings.

Yield: 6 servings **Calories per serving:** 183 (15% fat); **Total fat:** 3 g; **Cholesterol:** 35 mg; **Carbohydrate:** 24 g; **Dietary Fiber:** 4 g; **Protein:** 16 g; **Sodium:** 1034 mg **Diabetic Exchanges:** 1½ starch, 1 vegetable, 1½ very lean meat

Instructions to prepare the suggested meal

Set the timer for 30 minutes.

30 minutes before the meal

> ‣ Preheat the oven to 350 degrees.
> ‣ Make the Beef Pot Pie according to the directions.

10 minutes before the meal

> ‣ Make the Citrus Salad according to the directions.

MEAL SUGGESTION: 30 MINUTES FOR TOTAL MEAL:
Citrus Salad (page 78)

HELPFUL HINTS:

❯ Filo dough is super easy to work with in this recipe! Don't hesitate to give it a try if you have never used it before; you will be pleasantly surprised!!!

❯ 1 teaspoon fresh thyme can be substituted for the dried rubbed thyme if desired, but fresh is a LOT more expensive.

**SUPPLIES LIST FOR
SUGGESTED MEAL**
Oven
12-inch nonstick saucepan
9x13-inch baking dish
Medium-sized serving bowl
Timer

**GROCERY LIST FOR
SUGGESTED MEAL**
*Ingredients for the Oriental
Chicken Pot Pie*

FROZEN
*2 (14-ounce) bags frozen
stir-fry vegetables
1 (8-ounce) container fat-free
dessert whipped topping
(3 tablespoons needed)
*Filo dough
(5 sheets needed)
1 (16-ounce) package frozen
berry medley

PACKAGED
*2 (12.5-ounce) cans chicken
breast in water
*1 (14-ounce) can bean
sprouts
*Teriyaki Baste & Glaze
(Kikkoman) (1/2 cup needed)
1 (20-ounce) can no-sugar-
added cherry pie filling

PANTRY
*Cornstarch (1/3 cup needed)
Almond extract
Splenda granular
*Nonstick cooking spray

Oriental Chicken Pot Pie *25 minutes*

Homestyle goodness unites with oriental flair!

Ingredients

2 (12.5-ounce) cans chicken breast in water
2 (14-ounce) bags frozen stir-fry vegetables
1 (14-ounce) can bean sprouts
1/3 cup cornstarch
1/2 cup Teriyaki Baste & Glaze (Kikkoman)
5 Filo dough sheets

Instructions for entrée:

▸ Place the oven rack on the top shelf. Preheat the oven to 350 degrees.
▸ Generously spray a 12-inch nonstick saucepan with nonstick cooking spray, and preheat the pan on high heat.
▸ Open the cans of chicken and drain the broth into the saucepan; leave the chicken in the cans.
▸ Add the bags of frozen stir-fry vegetables to the broth. Cover and cook on high, stirring vegetables occasionally.
▸ Spray a 9 x 13-inch baking dish with nonstick cooking spray and set aside.
▸ Drain the liquid from the can of bean sprouts into a large measuring cup to make approximately 3/4 cup liquid. Add the cornstarch to the liquid, and stir until the cornstarch is dissolved.
▸ Stir the cornstarch mixture into the boiling vegetables.
▸ Add the chicken and bean sprouts to the pan. Stir constantly, until a nice gravy forms.
▸ Stir in the Teriyaki Baste & Glaze (Kikkoman).
▸ Pour the mixture into the prepared baking dish.
▸ Spray the tops of the dough sheets with butter-flavored cooking spray and layer on top of the chicken and vegetables. There will be a stack of filo sheets on top of the beef and vegetables to make the pot pie crust.
▸ Place in the oven for 10 minutes or until the dough is lightly browned.
▸ Cut into 6 servings.

Yield: 6 servings **Calories per serving:** 260 (8% fat); **Total fat:** 2 g; **Cholesterol:** 50 mg; **Carbohydrate:** 31 g; **Dietary Fiber:** 4 g; **Protein:** 27 g; **Sodium:** 1079 mg **Diabetic Exchanges:** 1½ starch, 2 vegetable, 3 very lean meat

Instructions to prepare the suggested meal

Set the timer for 25 minutes.

25 minutes before the meal

 ▸ Place the oven rack on the top shelf. Preheat the oven to 350 degrees.
 ▸ Make the Oriental Chicken Pot Pie according to the directions.

10 minutes before the meal

 ▸ Make the Cherry Berry Fruit Salad according to the directions.

**MEAL SUGGESTION:
25 MINUTES FOR
TOTAL MEAL:**
Cherry Berry Fruit Salad
(page 79)

HELPFUL HINTS:

❷ Any frozen stir-fry vegetable combination is fine to use.

❷ Kikkoman Baste & Glaze can be found in the ethnic or condiments aisle.

191

Wet Pizza Burrito Casserole *25 minutes*

Why wait for the pizza delivery guy when you can easily make this satisfying recipe in half the time and at a fraction of the cost. This recipe will make everyone in the family happy!

Ingredients

1 (14.5-ounce) can Italian diced tomatoes
1 (6.5-ounce) can mushroom pieces and stems
2 (14-ounce) jars pizza sauce
7 fat-free flour tortilla shells
62 slices of pepperoni
1/2 cup shredded part-skim milk mozzarella cheese

Instructions

▸ Drain and discard the juice from the can of Italian diced tomatoes and the can of mushrooms.
▸ Place the tomatoes and mushrooms in a medium mixing bowl along with the jars of pizza sauce. Stir together to make tomato sauce.
▸ Spray a 2-quart microwavable baking dish with nonstick cooking spray.
▸ Place 1 fat-free flour tortilla shell in the bottom of the baking dish.
▸ Spread 1/2 cup prepared tomato sauce on top of the tortilla.
▸ Place 8 slices of pepperoni on top of the tomato sauce.
▸ Continue layering in that order until the tomato sauce is gone.
▸ For the last layer place 1/2 cup of tomato sauce, cheese, and 14 slices of pepperoni.
▸ Cover with wax paper and place in microwave oven on high for 10 minutes.

Yield: 6 servings **Calories per serving:** 282 (16% fat); **Total fat:** 5 g; **Cholesterol:** 30 mg; **Carbohydrate:** 41 g; **Dietary Fiber:** 6 g; **Protein:** 17 g; **Sodium:** 1486 mg **Diabetic Exchanges:** 2 1/2 starch, 1 1/2 lean meat

---

Instructions to prepare the suggested meal

Set the timer for 30 minutes.

30 minutes before the meal

> ▸ Make the Wet Pizza Burrito Casserole according to the directions.

20 minutes before the meal

> ▸ While the casserole is cooking, make the Tomato and Parsley Chopped Salad according to the directions.

MEAL SUGGESTION:
30 MINUTES FOR
TOTAL MEAL:
Tomato and Parsley Chopped
Salad (page 80)

HELPFUL HINT:

❯ Reduce the fat content by substituting turkey pepperoni.

clockwise from the top: Tomato Slices with Homemade Thousand Island Salad Dressing (page 213), Broccoli, Cauliflower, and Carrots (page 222), and European Asparagus (page 215)

Side Dishes

MINI INDEX

(continued on page 196)

Italian Green Beans and Sliced Potatoes *10 minutes*

This super-simple side dish complements most grilled meats.

Ingredients

2 (14.5-ounce) Italian cut green beans
2 (15-ounce) cans sliced potatoes
1 (8-ounce) package pre-sliced fresh mushrooms
1 teaspoon Italian seasoning
1 tablespoon butter-flavored sprinkles (Butter Buds)
20 slices turkey pepperoni

Instructions

▸ Drain and discard the liquid from the green beans and potatoes. Set aside.
▸ In a 12-inch nonstick saucepan combine the mushrooms, green beans, potatoes, Italian seasoning, and butter-flavored sprinkles. Stir together over high heat.
▸ Cover and let cook.
▸ Finely chop the pepperoni.
▸ Stir the pepperoni into the pan, cover, and cook until the pepperoni is heated.
▸ Serve.

Yield: 15 (1/2-cup) servings **Calories per serving:** 54 (8% fat); **Total fat:** <1 g;
Cholesterol: 3 mg; **Carbohydrate:** 11 g; **Dietary Fiber:** 2 g; **Protein:** 3 g;
Sodium: 381 mg **Diabetic Exchanges:** 1/2 starch

SIDE DISHES

SUPPLIES LIST
12-inch nonstick saucepan and lid
Cutting board
Grocery List

PRODUCE
8-ounces pre-sliced fresh mushrooms

MEATS/POULTRY
1 package sliced turkey pepperoni (20 slices needed)

PACKAGED
2 (14.5-ounce) cans Italian cut green beans
2 (15-ounce) cans sliced potatoes

PANTRY
Butter-flavored sprinkles
Italian seasoning

Green Beans and Potatoes *7 minutes*

The diversity and ease of this vegetable recipe will make it a favorite staple recipe for your family.

Ingredients

2 (14.5-ounce) cans green beans
1 (15-ounce) can diced potatoes
2 tablespoons diced pimientos
3 tablespoons butter-flavored sprinkles (Butter Buds)
2 tablespoons real bacon bits
2 tablespoons fat-free Italian salad dressing

Instructions

▸ Drain and discard the liquid from the green beans and diced potatoes.
▸ In a microwave-safe bowl stir together the green beans, potatoes, diced pimientos, butter-flavored sprinkles, real bacon bits, and fat-free Italian salad dressing.
▸ Cover the bowl with wax paper.
▸ Place in a carousel microwave and cook for 3 minutes or until fully heated.

Yield: 7 (2/3-cup) servings **Calories per serving:** 73 (7% fat); **Total fat:** 1 g; **Cholesterol:** 3 mg; **Carbohydrate:** 15 g; **Dietary Fiber:** 2 g; **Protein:** 3 g; **Sodium:** 792 mg **Diabetic Exchanges:** 1/2 starch, 1 vegetable

SUPPLIES LIST
Microwave oven
Microwave-safe bowl
Wax paper
Timer

GROCERY LIST

PACKAGED
2 (14.5-ounce) cans
green beans
1 (15-ounce) can
diced potatoes
Fat-free Italian
salad dressing

PANTRY
Diced pimentos
Butter-flavored sprinkles
Real bacon bits

Very Berry Spiced Applesauce *5 minutes*

This side dish also doubles as a healthy dessert that will curb your sweet tooth.

Ingredients

1 (20-ounce) can no-sugar-added apple pie filling, chilled
1/2 cup firmly packed dried mixed berries
1 (25-ounce) jar unsweetened applesauce, chilled
1/2 teaspoon allspice
1 tablespoon Splenda granular

Instructions

▸ Open the can of no-sugar-added apple pie filling. While the filling is still in the can, cut the apple slices into chunks.
▸ Finely chop the dried mixed berries; set aside.
▸ In a medium-size serving bowl, combine the pie filling, applesauce, allspice, berries, and Splenda. Stir until well mixed.

Yield: 8 (1/2-cup) servings **Calories per serving:** 90 (0% fat); **Total fat:** 0 g; **Cholesterol:** 0 mg; **Carbohydrate:** 23 g; **Dietary Fiber:** 2 g; **Protein:** 0 g; **Sodium:** 24 mg **Diabetic Exchanges:** 1 1/2 fruit

---

SUPPLIES LIST
Medium-sized serving bowl
Cutting board

GROCERY LIST

PACKAGED
1 (20-ounce) can no-sugar-added apple pie filling
1 (25-ounce) jar unsweetened applesauce
Dried mixed berries (1/2 cup needed)

PANTRY
Allspice
Splenda granular

HELPFUL HINT:

❷ Place the jar of unsweetened applesauce and the can of apple pie filling into the refrigerator as soon as you get home with the groceries so it will be nice and cold when you are ready to prepare this dish.

SUPPLIES LIST
Medium mixing bowl
Cutting board
Waxed paper
Microwave oven

GROCERY LIST

PRODUCE
3 fresh large pears

DAIRY
Nonfat vanilla yogurt
(¹/2 cup needed)
Finely crumbled
reduced-fat feta cheese
(2 tablespoons needed)

PACKAGED
Light balsamic vinaigrette
salad dressing
Finely chopped pecans
Raisins (¹/4 cup needed)

PANTRY
Ground allspice

Spiced Warm Pear Chutney *10 minutes*

This pear salad is warmed just enough to release the aromatic flavors of the allspice, enhance the the slight saltiness of the feta, and enlighten the sweetness of the pears.

Ingredients

¹/2 cup nonfat vanilla yogurt
2 teaspoons light balsamic vinaigrette salad dressing
¹/2 teaspoon ground allspice
¹/4 cup raisins,
1 tablespoon finely chopped pecans
2 tablespoons finely crumbled reduced-fat feta cheese
3 fresh large pears

Instructions

▸ In a medium mixing bowl, stir together the yogurt, vinaigrette salad dressing, and allspice. Set aside.
▸ Finely chop the raisins and add the raisins, pecans, and feta cheese to the mixture.
▸ Cut the pears into bite-size pieces and stir into the mixture.
▸ Cover with waxed paper and cook in the microwave for 1 minute on high.
▸ Remove the wax paper and stir.
▸ Replace the wax paper and return the chutney to the microwave to cook for an additional minute on high.

Yield: 9 (¹/2-cup) serving **Calories per serving:** 65 (12% fat); **Total fat:** 1 g; **Cholesterol:** 1 mg; **Carbohydrate:** 14 g; **Dietary Fiber:** 2 g; **Protein:** 1 g; **Sodium:** 50 mg **Diabetic Exchanges:** 1 fruit

HELPFUL HINTS:

❯ For added color and texture, use three different varieties of pears. I used Bartlett (yellow), Anjou (green), and Forelle (red).

❯ Don't plan on having leftovers. The pears will turn brown.

Pear Chutney *10 minutes*

Light, refreshing, cool, and tasty!

Ingredients

1/2 cup nonfat vanilla yogurt
2 teaspoons light balsamic vinaigrette salad dressing
Dash of Lite salt or sea salt
1/4 cup finely chopped raisins
1 tablespoon finely chopped pecans
2 tablespoons finely crumbled reduced-fat feta cheese
3 large pears

Instructions

▸ In a medium mixing bowl, stir together yogurt, salad dressing, a dash of salt, raisins, pecans, and feta cheese until well mixed. Set aside.
▸ Cut the pears into bite-size pieces and add to mixture.
▸ Stir well and serve.

Yield: 9 (1/2-cup) serving **Calories per serving:** 65 (12% fat); **Total fat:** 1 g; **Cholesterol:** 1 mg; **Carbohydrate:** 14 g; **Dietary Fiber:** 2 g; **Protein:** 1 g; **Sodium:** 49 mg **Diabetic Exchanges:** 1 fruit

---

SIDE DISHES

SUPPLIES LIST
Medium mixing bowl
Cutting board

GROCERY LIST

PRODUCE
3 large pears

DAIRY
Nonfat vanilla yogurt
(1/2 cup needed)
Crumbled reduced-fat
feta cheese (2 tablespoon
needed)

PACKAGED
Light balsamic vinaigrette
salad dressing
Finely chopped pecans
Raisins (1/4 cup needed)

PANTRY
Lite salt or sea salt

HELPFUL HINTS:

❷ For added color and texture, use three different varieties of pears. I used one yellow Bartlett, one Green Anjou, and one red Forelle pear.

❷ Store the pears in the refrigerator so they are already chilled for the recipe.

Tart Cherry Applesauce *5 minutes*

This tart yet sweet applesauce is sure to be a complement to any dish you choose to serve it with.

Ingredients

1 (20-ounce) can no-sugar-added cherry pie filling, chilled
1 (25-ounce) jar unsweetened applesauce, chilled
1 teaspoon almond extract
2 tablespoons Splenda granular**

Instructions

▸ In a medium-size serving bowl, mix together the pie filling, applesauce, almond extract, and Splenda.
▸ Serve.

Yield: 8 (1/2-cup) servings **Calories per serving:** 70 (0% fat); **Total fat:** 0 g; **Cholesterol:** 0 mg; **Carbohydrate:** 17 g; **Dietary Fiber:** 2 g; **Protein:** 0 g; **Sodium:** 10 mg **Diabetic Exchanges:** 1 fruit

---

SUPPLIES LIST
Medium-sized mixing bowl

GROCERY LIST

PACKAGED
1 (20-ounce) can no-sugar-added cherry pie filling
1 (25-ounce) jar unsweetened applesauce

PANTRY
Almond extract
Splenda granular

HELPFUL HINTS:

❷ Place the ingredients that need to be chilled in the refrigerator when you bring them home from the grocery store. That way they will be sure to be nice and chilled.

** Splenda granular measures like sugar. You can substitute the packets of Splenda, but it is concentrated, so start out using a teaspoon.

Mixed Greens *10 minutes*

Even people that are not fans of mixed greens like this recipe.

Ingredients

1 (14-ounce) can turnip greens
2 (14-ounce) can mustard greens
1 teaspoon onion salt
1 tablespoon butter-flavored sprinkles (Butter Buds)
1/2 teaspoon liquid smoke
1 teaspoon Splenda granular
1 1/2 tablespoons honey

Instructions

▸ Drain and discard the juice from the turnip greens and mustard greens.
▸ In a large microwave-safe bowl, stir together the turnip greens, mustard greens, onion salt, butter-flavored sprinkles, liquid smoke, Splenda, and honey until well mixed.
▸ Cover with wax paper and cook in the microwave for 2 to 3 minutes or until heated through.

Yield: 6 (1/2-cup) servings **Calories per serving:** 48 (8% fat); **Total fat:** 1 g; **Cholesterol:** 0 mg; **Carbohydrate:** 10 g; **Dietary Fiber:** 4 g; **Protein:** 4 g; **Sodium:** 878 mg **Diabetic Exchanges:** 1 vegetable, 1/2 carbohydrate

---

SIDE DISHES

SUPPLIES LIST
Large microwave-safe bowl
Microwave oven
Wax paper

GROCERY LIST

PACKAGED
1 (14-ounce) can turnip greens
2 (14-ounce) can mustard greens

PANTRY
Onion salt
Butter-flavored sprinkles (Butter Buds)
Liquid smoke
Splenda granular
Honey

HELPFUL HINT:

❯ Liquid smoke is usually in the condiment aisle.

SUPPLIES LIST
12-inch or larger nonstick
saucepan with lid

GROCERY LIST

PACKAGED
1 (12-ounce) can roast beef
(I used Hormel)
2 (14.5-ounce) cans whole
green beans
Diced pimento

PANTRY
Minced garlic
Butter-flavored cooking spray
Salt and pepper

HELPFUL HINT

** I used Hormel canned
roast beef.

Beefy Green Beans   *10 minutes*

These would be good served with a brunch or a meat loaf.

Ingredients

¹/₂ tablespoon minced garlic
1 (12-ounce) can roast beef**
2 (14.5-ounce) cans whole green beans
1 teaspoon diced pimiento

Instructions

▸ Spray a 12-inch or larger nonstick saucepan with butter-flavored cooking spray.
▸ Add the minced garlic and roast beef to the pan, breaking the meat up with your hands. Bring to a boil over high heat.
▸ Drain the green beans, then stir them into the beef, along with the diced pimiento.
▸ Cover and let cook until heated through, over medium heat, stirring occasionally.
▸ Salt and pepper to taste.

Yield: 6 (¹/₂-cup) servings **Calories per serving:** 76 (16% fat); **Total fat:** 1 g;
Cholesterol: 17 mg; **Carbohydrate:** 9 g; **Dietary Fiber:** 1 g; **Protein:** 7 g;
Sodium: 855 mg **Diabetic Exchanges:** 2 vegetable, ¹/₂ very lean meat

---

Mashed Pumpkin *7 minutes*

The flavors of Australia inspired this dish. In Australia, pumpkin is served as a vegetable not a dessert.

Ingredients

1 (29-ounce) can pure pumpkin
2 tablespoons butter-flavored sprinkles**
1¹/2 teaspoon steak seasoning (McCormick Montreal)
2 tablespoons light butter, divided

Instructions

‣ In a medium microwave-safe serving bowl, stir together the pumpkin, butter-flavored sprinkles, steak seasoning, and 1 tablespoon of the butter.
‣ Cover and heat in the microwave for 2 minutes.
‣ Take out and stir. Place the remaining 1 tablespoon butter on top. Cover and heat in the microwave for an additional 2 minutes or until fully heated.

Yield: 7 (1/2-cup) servings **Calories per serving:** 59 (28% fat); **Total fat:** 2 g; Cholesterol: 4 mg; **Carbohydrate:** 11 g; **Dietary Fiber:** 5 g; **Protein:** 2 g; Sodium: 281 mg **Diabetic Exchanges:** 1/2 starch, 1/2 fat

SIDE DISHES

SUPPLIES LIST
Medium microwave-safe
serving bowl
Microwave oven

GROCERY LIST

PACKAGED
1 (29-ounce) can pure
pumpkin

PANTRY
Butter-flavored sprinkles
Steak seasoning
(McCormick Montreal)
Light butter
Butter-flavored
cooking spray

HELPFUL HINTS:

** Popular brand names of
imitation butter-flavored
sprinkles are Molly McButter
and Butter Buds.

❯ I used McCormick
Montreal steak seasoning.

SUPPLIES LIST
Medium-sized microwave-
safe serving bowl
Microwave oven

GROCERY LIST

MEATS
1 package sliced turkey
pepperoni (15 pieces
needed)

PACKAGED
3 (14.5-ounce) cans Italian
cut green beans
1 (6.5-ounce) can mushrooms
stems and pieces
Italian salad dressing
(1/4 cup needed)

Pepperoni and Mushroom Green Beans *10 minutes*

Here's a fun way to get children to eat their green vegetables. Another good name for this recipe could be pizza style green beans.

Ingredients

15 slices turkey pepperoni
3 (14.5-ounce) cans Italian cut green beans
1 (6.5-ounce) can mushroom stems and pieces
1/4 cup fat-free Italian salad dressing

Instructions

‣ Julienne the turkey pepperoni and set aside.
‣ Drain and discard the liquid from the green beans and the mushrooms; then stir them together in a medium-size microwave-safe serving bowl, along with the pepperoni and Italian salad dressing, until well mixed.
‣ Cover and microwave for 5 minutes.

Yield: 6 (2/3-cup) servings **Calories per serving:** 61 (10% fat); **Total fat:** 1 g; **Cholesterol:** 6 mg; **Carbohydrate:** 9 g; **Dietary Fiber:** 2 g; **Protein:** 4 g; **Sodium:** 1034 mg **Diabetic Exchanges:** 2 vegetable

---

Variation:

‣ For a vegetarian side, make the recipe according to the directions, but omit the turkey pepperoni.

HELPFUL HINT:

❂ To julienne means to cut it into very thin strips.

Southwestern–Inspired Beans *10 minutes*

Southwestern flavors unite with the wholesome goodness of green beans from the Midwest for a flavor combination that you can't go wrong with.

Ingredients

12 ripe black olives
2 (14.5-ounce) cans whole green beans
1 (14.5-ounce) can wax beans
1 (10-ounce) can diced tomatoes and green chilies (mild)

Instructions

▸ Thinly slice the black olives. Set aside.
▸ Drain and discard the liquid from the green beans, wax beans, and tomatoes; then stir them together with the black olives in a medium-size microwave-safe bowl.
▸ Cover and microwave for 5 minutes or until heated through.

Yield: 8 (2/3-cup) servings **Calories per serving:** 38 (15% fat); **Total fat:** 1 g; **Cholesterol:** 0 mg; **Carbohydrate:** 7 g; **Dietary Fiber:** 2 g; **Protein:** 2 g; **Sodium:** 706 mg **Diabetic Exchanges:** 1 vegetable

SUPPLIES LIST
Medium-sized
microwave-safe bowl
Microwave oven

GROCERY LIST

PACKAGED
Black olives (12 needed)
2 (14.5-ounce) cans whole green beans
1 (14.5-ounce) can wax beans
1 (10-ounce) can diced tomatoes and green chilies (mild)

Sweet Cherried Pears *5 minutes*

Simply stated and to the point: these are just delicious!

Ingredients

2 (15-ounce) cans no-sugar-added Bartlett pear halves
10 maraschino cherries, plus 2 tablespoons maraschino cherry juice
1 pouch sugar-free spiced cider apple flavor drink mix (from a box of 10 pouches)

Instructions

▸ Open and drain the juice from the cans of pears.
▸ In a 4-quart saucepan on medium heat, add the drained pears, maraschino cherries, drink mix, and cherry juice. Stir together to heat.
▸ Reduce the heat to low to keep warm.

Yield: 5 (1/2-cup) servings **Calories per serving:** 99 (0% fat); **Total fat:** 0 g; **Cholesterol:** 0 mg; **Carbohydrate:** 24 g; **Dietary Fiber:** 2 g; **Protein:** 0 g; **Sodium:** 11 mg **Diabetic Exchanges:** 1 fruit, 1/2 carbohydrate

---

Lemon-Peppered Asparagus *10 minutes*

Slaw dressing and lemon pepper lightly kiss the asparagus for a heavenly combination!

Ingredients

2 (14.5-ounce) cans asparagus cuts and tips
1/2 teaspoon lemon pepper seasoning
2 tablespoons low-fat slaw dressing (I use Marzetti)

Instructions

▸ Discard the liquid from the asparagus.
▸ In a microwave-safe bowl, add the asparagus, lemon pepper seasoning, and slaw dressing and very gently stir together so as not to break up the asparagus.
▸ Cover and place in the microwave for 2 to 3 minutes until completely warmed through.

Yield: 5 (1/2-cup) servings **Calories per serving:** 43 (24% fat); **Total fat:** 1 g; **Cholesterol:** 3 mg; **Carbohydrate:** 6 g; **Dietary Fiber:** 2 g; **Protein:** 4 g; **Sodium:** 578 mg **Diabetic Exchanges:** 1 vegetable

SUPPLIES LIST
Microwave-safe bowl
Microwave oven

GROCERY LIST

PACKAGED
2 (14.5-ounce) cans
asparagus cuts and tips
Low-fat slaw dressing
(Marzetti)

PANTRY
Lemon pepper seasoning

HELPFUL HINT:

❷ Fresh asparagus can be used; however, it will have to cook a lot longer.

SUPPLIES LIST
4-quart nonstick saucepan
with lid

GROCERY LIST

PACKAGED
2 (15-ounce) cans no-sugar-
added chunky mixed fruits
1 (15-ounce) can mandarin
oranges in light syrup
1 box sugar-free spiced cider
apple flavor drink mix
(10 pouches per box)
1 (6-ounce) jar maraschino
cherries (10 needed)

Warm Fruit Cocktail *10 minutes*

This warm, sweet fruit dish melts in your mouth and is a perfect dessert for diabetics!

Ingredients

2 (15-ounce) cans no-sugar-added chunky mixed fruits
1 (15-ounce) can mandarin oranges in light syrup
1 (.14-ounce) pouch sugar-free spiced cider apple-flavor drink mix
10 maraschino cherries

Instructions

▸ Drain and discard the juice from the chunky mixed fruits and mandarin oranges.
▸ Add to a 4-quart nonstick saucepan over medium-high heat the mixed fruits, oranges, drink mix, and maraschino cherries. Stir to blend all ingredients.
▸ Cover and continue cooking until the fruit is heated through.

Yield: 7 (1/2-cup) servings **Calories per serving:** 89 (0% fat); **Total fat:** 0 g;
Cholesterol: 0 mg; **Carbohydrate:** 22 g; **Dietary Fiber:** 1 g; **Protein:** 0 g;
Sodium: 16 mg **Diabetic Exchanges:** 11/2 fruit

HELPFUL HINT:

❯ There are 10 individual pouches in one (1.4 ounce) box of sugar-free spiced cider apple flavor drink mix (by Alpine).

Green Beans and Ham *5 minutes*

These are anything but ordinary green beans; the flavor is delightful, and they are super easy to make!

Ingredients

4 slices 97% fat-free honey ham
3 (14.5-ounce) cans no salt added French-style green beans
1/4 cup low-fat slaw dressing (I used Marzetti)
1 teaspoon soy sauce
1/2 tablespoon minced garlic
1/2 teaspoon ground black pepper

Instructions

▸ Cut the ham into bite-size pieces. Set aside.
▸ Drain aand discard the liquid from the green beans; then stir them together in a 4-quart nonstick saucepan with the ham pieces, slaw dressing, soy sauce, minced garlic, and pepper until well mixed.
▸ Heat through and serve.

Yield: 7 (1/2-cup) servings **Calories per serving:** 67 (16% fat); **Total fat:** 1 g; **Cholesterol:** 10 mg; **Carbohydrate:** 10 g; **Dietary Fiber:** 3 g; **Protein:** 5 g; **Sodium:** 367 mg **Diabetic Exchanges:** 2 vegetable

---

SIDE DISHES

SUPPLIES LIST
4-quart nonstick saucepan

GROCERY LIST

MEATS
1 (16-ounce) 97% fat-free honey ham
(4 slices needed)

PACKAGED
3 (14.5-ounce) cans no-salt-added French-style green beans
Low-fat slaw dressing (Marzetti, 1/4 cup needed)

PANTRY
Soy sauce
Minced garlic
Ground black pepper

HELPFUL HINT:

❷ This can also be made in the microwave if desired. Heat for 2 minutes. Stir. Continue heating in one-minute intervals until fully heated.

Candied Carrots *10 minutes*

These carrots are like eating dessert with your dinner, but without the sugar. They are not too sweet, like some candied carrots. These carrots are just right!

Ingredients

2 (14.5-ounce) cans sliced carrots
1 (0.14-ounce) packet sugar-free spiced cider apple-flavor drink mix
1 tablespoon light butter
Ground black pepper, optional

Instructions

▸ Drain and discard the juice from the cans of sliced carrots.
▸ In a 2¹/2-quart nonstick saucepan over medium heat, stir together the carrots, drink mix, and light butter.
▸ Cover and cook over medium heat until heated through, stirring occasionally.
▸ Sprinkle with ground black pepper if desired.

Yield: 6 (¹/2-cup) servings **Calories per serving:** 39 (29% fat); **Total fat:** 2 g; **Cholesterol:** 3 mg; **Carbohydrate:** 8 g; **Dietary Fiber:** 2 g; **Protein:** 1 g; **Sodium:** 299 mg **Diabetic Exchanges:** 2 vegetable, ¹/2 fat

HELPFUL HINTS:

❷ The ground black pepper will decrease the sweetness of the carrots.

❷ These could also be done in the microwave. Add all ingredients together in a microwave-safe bowl, stir, cover, and cook for 2 minutes; stir and cook for an additional 2 minutes or until completely heated through.

❷ There are 10 individual pouches in one (1.4-ounce) box of sugar-free spiced cider apple flavor drink mix (by Alpine).

Tomato Slices with Homemade Thousand Island Salad Dressing *5 minutes*

These are good any time of year, but especially when homegrown tomatoes are in season!

Ingredients

2 fresh, large tomatoes
1 tablespoon light Miracle Whip
1 tablespoon fat-free Miracle Whip
1 tablespoon ketchup
1 teaspoon sweet relish
Dried parsley (optional)

Instructions

‣ Slice the tomatoes into 1/2-inch-thick slices.
‣ Arrange on a plate in single layer.
‣ In a small bowl add the light Miracle Whip, fat-free Miracle Whip, ketchup, and sweet relish. Mix together until well blended.
‣ Using a butter knife, frost the tomatoes with the homemade salad dressing.
‣ Sprinkle with dried parsley, if desired.

Yield: 4 (2 slices each) servings **Calories per serving:** 29 (27% fat); **Total fat:** 1 g; **Cholesterol:** 1 mg; **Carbohydrate:** 5 g; **Dietary Fiber:** 1 g; **Protein:** 1 g; **Sodium:** 119 mg **Diabetic Exchanges:** 1 vegetable, 1/2 fat

SUPPLIES LIST
Cutting board
Serving plate
Small bowl

GROCERY LIST

PRODUCE
2 fresh, large tomatoes

PACKAGED
Light Miracle Whip
Fat-free Miracle Whip

PANTRY
Ketchup
Sweet relish
Dried parsley (optional)

HELPFUL HINT:

❯ You can substitute the sweet relish for pickle relish. You can substitute the light Miracle Whip for the fat-free, but I do not like the flavor when using only fat-free.

Tomato Pudding *10 minutes*

This recipe is definitely old-fashioned. It brings back fond memories of generations past. Unlike the recipe Granny used to make, this home-style goodness is a lot healthier and quicker to make! Don't let the name of this recipe fool you; this pudding is sweet, but it is definitely a vegetable side dish.

Ingredients

6 egg whites
1 (6-ounce) can tomato paste
6 slices light potato bread
1/2 teaspoon celery salt
1 tablespoon Splenda Brown Sugar Blend

Instructions

▸ In a medium (2-quart) microwave-safe bowl, beat the egg whites, tomato paste, celery salt, and Splenda Brown Sugar Blend with an electric mixer until well blended, scraping the sides of the bowl often. Set aside.
▸ Cut the bread into bite-size pieces.
▸ Stir the bread pieces into tomato mixture, making sure the bread is completely saturated with the egg mixture.
▸ Cover with wax paper and cook in a carousel microwave for 5 to 6 minutes.

Yield: 7 (1/2-cup) servings **Calories per serving:** 75 (0% fat); **Total fat:** 0 g; **Cholesterol:** 0 mg; **Carbohydrate:** 14 g; **Dietary Fiber:** 3 g; **Protein:** 5 g; **Sodium:** 284 mg **Diabetic Exchanges:** 1 vegetable, 1/2 starch, 1/2 very lean meat

HELPFUL HINTS:

❷ Place the bread slices in a stack and cut the entire stack at once. This will help to make the bite-size pieces all the same size.

❷ To save money you can substitute regular white or whole-wheat bread for the light potato bread; however, remember it will be higher in calories.

❷ If you do not have a carousel microwave, turn the tomato pudding a quarter turn every 2 minutes.

European Asparagus *5 minutes*

This sure is a fancy name for something that is so simple to make. I like it because it is easy to prepare, and yet it has just the right amount of zip to add pizzazz.

Ingredients

3 (14.5-ounce) cans asparagus cuts and tips
2 teaspoons minced onion
3 tablespoons fat-free Italian salad dressing
2 tablespoons pimiento, optional
1 teaspoon Splenda granular

Instructions

▶ Drain and discard the liquid from the cans of asparagus. Place the asparagus in a medium-size microwave-safe bowl along with the minced onion, salad dressing, pimiento, and Splenda. Stir well.

▶ Cover with wax paper and cook in a carousel microwave oven for 2 to 3 minutes or until fully heated.

Yield: 7 (1/2-cup) servings **Calories per serving:** 39 (23% fat); **Total fat:** 1 g;
Cholesterol: 0 mg; **Carbohydrate:** 5 g; **Dietary Fiber:** 3 g; **Protein:** 4 g;
Sodium: 598 mg **Diabetic Exchanges:** 1 vegetable

SIDE DISHES

SUPPLIES LIST
Medium-size microwave-safe bowl
Wax paper
Microwave oven

GROCERY LIST

PACKAGED
3 (14.5-ounce) cans asparagus cuts and tips
Fat-free Italian salad dressing
(3 tablespoons needed)
Pimento (optional)

PANTRY
Minced onion
Splenda granular

SUPPLIES LIST
Medium-size mixing bowl
Microwave oven
Electric mixer

GROCERY LIST

DAIRY
Light butter spread

PACKAGED
2 (15-ounce) cans
diced potatoes
1 (14 1/2-ounce) can
sliced carrots

PANTRY
Fat-free chicken broth
(1/3 cup needed)
Celery salt
Butter-flavored sprinkles
(Butter Buds)

Mashed Potatoes and Carrots *5 minutes*

Here's a smooth and creamy old-fashioned recipe that Granny used to make, but ours is a lot faster to prepare, and a whole lot less fattening!

Ingredients

2 (15-ounce) cans diced potatoes
1 (14.5-ounce) can sliced carrots
1/4 cup light butter spread
1/3 cup fat-free chicken broth
1/2 teaspoon celery salt
1 tablespoon butter-flavored sprinkles (Butter Buds)

Instructions

▸ Drain and discard the liquid from the potatoes and carrots, and then put them in a medium-size mixing bowl.
▸ Stir the vegetables together with the light butter spread and chicken broth.
▸ Cover and cook on high in the microwave for 3 minutes or until fully heated.
▸ With an electric mixer beat on low speed until crumbly.
▸ Once the vegetables are broken down, add the celery salt and butter-flavored sprinkles, then increase the speed to high, and beat until smooth and creamy.

Yield: 6 (1/2-cup) servings **Calories per serving:** 136 (28% fat); **Total fat:** 5 g; **Cholesterol:** 10 mg; **Carbohydrate:** 24 g; **Dietary Fiber:** 4 g; **Protein:** 3 g; **Sodium:** 678 mg **Diabetic Exchanges:** 1 1/2 starch, 1 vegetable, 1 fat

---

Italian Green Beans with Black Olives and Mushrooms *10 minutes*

Take ordinary green beans to a new level of quality with simple ingredients that you probably already have in your pantry.

Ingredients

12 black olives
2 (14-ounce) cans Italian cut green beans
1 (7-ounce) can mushrooms, pieces and stems
1 teaspoon diced pimiento, optional
3 teaspoons Worcestershire sauce
1/2 teaspoon garlic salt

Instructions

‣ Cut the black olives into thin slices. Set aside.
‣ Drain and discard the liquid from the green beans and mushrooms.
‣ In a medium-size microwave-safe bowl stir together the olives, green beans, mushrooms, diced pimiento, Worcestershire sauce, and garlic salt.
‣ Cover with wax paper and heat in the microwave for 2 minutes.
‣ Stir and cook again for another 1 to 2 minutes or until heated thoroughly.

Yield: 7 (1/2-cup) servings **Calories per serving:** 35 (17% fat); **Total fat:** 1 g; **Cholesterol:** 0 mg; **Carbohydrate:** 6 g; **Dietary Fiber:** 2 g; **Protein:** 2 g; **Sodium:** 623 mg **Diabetic Exchanges:** 1 vegetable

SIDE DISHES

SUPPLIES LIST
Medium-size microwave-safe bowl
Wax paper
Microwave oven

GROCERY LIST

PACKAGED
2 (14-ounce) cans Italian cut green beans
1 (7-ounce) can mushrooms (pieces and stems)
Diced pimento
Black olives

PANTRY
Worcestershire sauce
Garlic salt

HELPFUL HINTS:

❍ Green beans can be substituted for Italian green beans.

❍ The diced pimento will make this dish more colorful.

SUPPLIES LIST
Medium-sized serving bowl
Cutting board

GROCERY LIST

PRODUCE
2 large Bartlett pears
1 large Red Delicious apple

PACKAGED
Fat-free Italian salad
dressing
(¹/4 cup needed)

PANTRY
Splenda granular
Dried chopped chives
Baco-bits (imitation bacon)

Pear and Apple Chutney *10 minutes*

The smoky bacon unites with the sweetness of the fruits and the tartness of Italian salad dressing to make an ideal salad to accompany most egg- or meat-based entrees.

Ingredients

¹/4 cup fat-free Italian salad dressing
1 tablespoon Splenda granular
2 teaspoons dried chopped chives
2 tablespoons Baco-Bits (imitation bacon pieces)
2 large fresh Bartlett pears
1 large Red Delicious apple

Instructions

▸ In the bottom of a medium serving bowl, mix together the salad dressing, Splenda, chives, and Baco-bits.
▸ Chop the pears and apple into bite-size pieces.
▸ Toss the chopped pears, apples, and dressing together, and serve.

Yield: 5 (1-cup) servings **Calories per serving:** 94 (6% fat); **Total fat:** 1 g; **Cholesterol:** 0 mg; **Carbohydrate:** 23 g; **Dietary Fiber:** 4 g; **Protein:** 1 g; **Sodium:** 205 mg **Diabetic Exchanges:** 1¹/2 fruit

HELPFUL HINTS:

❷ I don't use real bacon bits because I like the crunch of the Baco Bits.

❷ You can use real sugar if you like but it will increase the calories of the salad.

❷ If you'd prefer to use fresh chives you will need 4 teaspoons.

Cinnamon Syrup *10 minutes*

Special thanks to Isabel Reid for this delicious idea.

Ingredients

1 cup sugar-free butter-flavored syrup
1 teaspoon ground cinnamon

Instructions

▸ In a small saucepan over medium-low heat, combine the syrup and cinnamon. Whisk together until well blended.
▸ Cover and bring to a low boil.
▸ Once boiling, turn the heat off. Let the syrup rest on the warm burner for a few minutes.
▸ Just before serving whisk again. The syrup will be thick.

Yield: 4 (1/4-cup) servings **Calories per serving:** 58 (0% fat); **Total fat:** 0 g; **Cholesterol:** 0 mg; **Carbohydrate:** 12 g; **Dietary Fiber:** 0 g; **Protein:** 0 g; **Sodium:** 187 mg **Diabetic Exchanges:** 1 carbohydrate

---

SIDE DISHES

SUPPLIES LIST
Small saucepan with lid
Whisk

GROCERY LIST

PACKAGED
Sugar-free butter-flavored syrup (1 cup needed)

PANTRY
Ground cinnamon

HELPFUL HINT:

❯ The cinnamon will not dissolve in the syrup, so you will see cinnamon specks in syrup.

SUPPLIES LIST
Small serving pitcher

GROCERY LIST

PACKAGED
Sugar-free butter-flavored
syrup (1/2 cup needed)
Shredded

PANTRY
Coconut extract

Coconut Syrup (sugar-free) *5 minutes*

Not white in color, like the coconut syrup of the tropical Hawaiian Islands, and not nearly as fattening either!

Ingredients

1/2 cup sugar-free butter-flavored syrup
1 1/2 teaspoons coconut extract
1 tablespoon firmly packed shredded coconut

Instructions

▸ In a small serving pitcher mix together the syrup, coconut extract, and coconut.
▸ Serve immediately.

Yield: 4 (2-tablespoon) servings **Calories per serving:** 38 (9% fat); **Total fat:** <1 g; **Cholesterol:** 0 mg; **Carbohydrate:** 6 g; **Dietary Fiber:** 0 g; **Protein:** 0 g; **Sodium:** 97 mg **Diabetic Exchanges:** 1/2 carbohydrate

---

HELPFUL HINT:

❯ Serve this syrup at room temperature. Do not microwave; microwaving alters the flavor, making it less coco-nutty.

Strawberry and Kiwi Chutney *10 minutes*

Tart, tangy, and slightly sweet.

Ingredients

¹⁄₃ cup fat-free Italian salad dressing
1 teaspoon balsamic vinegar
1 tablespoon Splenda granular
1 pound fresh strawberries
3 fresh kiwis

Instructions

▸ In a medium-size serving bowl, combine the salad dressing, vinegar, and Splenda. Stir together and set aside.
▸ Wash and remove the stems from the strawberries.
▸ Slice the strawberries into thin slices and add to the bowl with the dressing.
▸ Peel the kiwis and dice into small pieces; add to the strawberries.
▸ Mix the ingredients together, place in the refrigerator to chill, or serve.

Yield: 4 (³⁄₄-cup) servings **Calories per serving:** 88 (0% fat); **Total fat:** 0 g; **Cholesterol:** 0 mg; **Carbohydrate:** 20 g; **Dietary Fiber:** 4 g; **Protein:** 2 g; **Sodium:** 295 mg **Diabetic Exchanges:** 1¹⁄₂ fruit

---

SIDE DISHES

SUPPLIES LIST
Medium-sized serving bowl
Cutting board

GROCERY LIST

PRODUCE
1 pound fresh strawberries
3 fresh kiwis

PACKAGED
Fat-free Italian salad dressing
(¹⁄₃ cup needed)

PANTRY
Balsamic vinegar
Splenda granular

HELPFUL HINT:

❯ Store the strawberries, kiwi, and salad dressing in the refrigerator so they are already chilled when you are ready to make this recipe. This recipe is also good at room temperature.

❯ This will only store well for about a day.

SUPPLIES LIST
Large nonstick Dutch oven
or soup pan with lid
Large mixing bowl
Timer

GROCERY LIST

DAIRY
Light butter

FROZEN
1 (32-ounce) package
frozen broccoli,
cauliflower, and carrot
blend

PANTRY
Butter-flavored sprinkles
(Butter Buds)
Honey

Broccoli, Cauliflower, and Carrots (lightly sweetened) *11 minutes*

The touch of honey removes any bitterness the vegetables might have and makes them taste more inviting. Honey is also a natural sweetener and is reported to contain natural healing properties.

Ingredients

1/2 cup water
1 (32-ounce) package frozen broccoli, cauliflower, and carrots blend
6 tablespoons butter-flavored sprinkles
2 tablespoons light butter
2 tablespoons honey

Instructions

▸ Add the water to a large nonstick Dutch oven or soup pan with lid.
▸ Add the frozen broccoli, cauliflower, and carrot blend to the water.
▸ Cover and cook on high for 10 minutes
▸ Drain the cooked vegetables and then place the vegetables in a large mixing bowl. Add the butter-flavored sprinkles and light butter. Carefully mix until the butter is combined.
▸ Drizzle the honey over the vegetables and mix well.
▸ Serve.

Yield: 8 (1-cup) servings **Calories per serving:** 75 (16% fat); **Total fat:** 2 g; **Cholesterol:** 4 mg; **Carbohydrate:** 15 g; **Dietary Fiber:** 4 g; **Protein:** 2 g; **Sodium:** 441 mg **Diabetic Exchanges:** 1 vegetable, 1/2 carbohydrate, 1/2 fat

---

Candied Applesauce *15 minutes*

Instead of cranberry sauce with your ham or turkey this holiday, try this! I like that it is sweet enough to do double duty as a side dish and curb my sweet tooth as a dessert at the same time.

Ingredients

1 (25-ounce) jar unsweetened applesauce
1/2 cup cinnamon-flavored candies (Red Hots)

Instructions

▸ Stir the applesauce and the cinnamon-flavored candies in a 2 1/2-quart saucepan, and cook over medium heat for 15 minutes, stirring occasionally.

Yield: 6 (1/2-cup) servings **Calories per serving:** 131 (0% fat); **Total fat:** 0 g; **Cholesterol:** 0 mg; **Carbohydrate:** 33 g; **Dietary Fiber:** 1 g; **Protein:** 0 g; **Sodium:** 2 mg **Diabetic Exchanges:** 1 fruit, 11/2 carbohydrate

---

SUPPLIES LIST
21/2-quart saucepan
Timer

GROCERY LIST

PACKAGED
1 (25-ounce) jar unsweetened applesauce
Cinnamon-flavored candies (1/2 cup needed)

Mushrooms and Cauliflower in Creamy Sauce *20 minutes*

This light sauce enhances the flavor of the vegetables but does not overpower it.

Ingredients

1 large head cauliflower
1 chicken-flavored bouillon cube
1 cup water
1 (8-ounce) package sliced fresh mushrooms
1/2 cup fat-free ranch salad dressing
1/4 cup crushed French-fried onions

Instructions

▸ Clean the cauliflower and cut into bite-size florets. Set aside.
▸ In a 12-inch nonstick saucepan over high heat, dissolve the bouillon cube in the water.
▸ Place the cauliflower florets into the bouillon. Place the sliced mushrooms on top of the cauliflower. Do not stir them together.
▸ Bring the bouillon to a boil, cover, and let cook for 2 minutes at a full boil.
▸ Turn the heat off and let the pan sit on the burner with the lid on for 10 minutes.
▸ After 10 minutes, drain and discard the liquid from the mushrooms and cauliflower, and put the vegetables in a pretty serving bowl.
▸ Gently stir the salad dressing into the mushrooms and cauliflower until well mixed.
▸ Sprinkle with the crushed French-fried onions, and serve.

Yield: 5 (3/4-cup) servings **Calories per serving:** 101 (17% fat); **Total fat:** 2 g; **Cholesterol:** 0 mg; **Carbohydrate:** 18 g; **Dietary Fiber:** 4 g; **Protein:** 4 g; **Sodium:** 589 mg **Diabetic Exchanges:** 2 vegetable, 1/2 carbohydrate, 1/2 fat

Spiced Baked Oranges *20 minutes*

This is much more satisfying than serving just a glass of orange juice for breakfast or brunch.

Ingredients

3 navel oranges
1/4 teaspoon ground allspice
2 tablespoons Splenda Brown Sugar Blend

Instructions

▸ Move the oven rack to the top shelf of the oven. Preheat the oven to 400 degrees.
▸ Slice the oranges in half horizontally. Segment each orange as you would a grapefruit. Place on a jellyroll pan (or a 9 x 13-inch baking dish)
▸ In a small bowl mix together the ground allspice and Splenda Brown Sugar Blend.
▸ Evenly sprinkle the mixture over the tops of the oranges.
▸ Place in the top rack of the oven and bake for 10 minutes.

Yield: 6 (1/2 orange) servings **Calories per serving:** 60 (0% fat); **Total fat:** 0 g; **Cholesterol:** 0 mg; **Carbohydrate:** 14 g; **Dietary Fiber:** 2 g; **Protein:** 1 g; **Sodium:** 0 mg **Diabetic Exchanges:** 1 fruit

---

SUPPLIES LIST
Oven
Cutting board
Small bowl
Jelly-roll pan
Timer

GROCERY LIST

PRODUCE
3 navel oranges

PANTRY
Allspice
Splenda Brown Sugar Blend

HELPFUL HINT:

❯ To segment the oranges, use a serrated knife, or you can buy a special citrus knife. Take the serrated knife and cut around the inside of the peel and the orange to separate the two from each other, leaving the orange in the peel.

Twice-Baked Deluxe Mashed Potatoes *20 minutes*

Here's a great quickie substitute for time-consuming traditional baked potatoes.

Ingredients

2 pounds red-skinned potatoes with skins on
1 (8-ounce) package fat-free cream cheese
1/4 cup light butter
2 tablespoons imitation butter-flavored sprinkles (Butter Buds)
1 1/4 to 1 1/2 cups skim milk
3 teaspoons garlic salt, optional

Instructions

▸ Wash the potatoes and poke several holes with a fork. Microwave the whole potatoes in a carousel microwave for 12 minutes, or until fully cooked.

▸ Using a fork and a sharp knife, cut the cooked potatoes into cubes, leaving the skins on.

▸ Put the potatoes in a medium-size mixing bowl. Add the cream cheese, butter, butter-flavored sprinkles, skim milk, and garlic salt.

▸ With a mixer, beat on medium speed for approximately 2 minutes or until you reach the desired creamy consistency.

▸ Microwave the bowl of potatoes in the microwave an additional 1 to 2 minutes to reheat before serving.

▸ Serve additional butter spread on the side if desired.

Yield: 8 (1/2-cup) servings **Calories per serving:** 145 (20% fat); **Total fat:** 3 g; **Cholesterol:** 13 mg; **Carbohydrate:** 20 g; **Dietary Fiber:** 2 g; **Protein:** 8 g; **Sodium:** 359 mg **Diabetic Exchanges:** 1 1/2 starch, 1/2 lean meat

---

SUPPLIES LIST
Microwave oven
Cutting board
Medium-sized mixing bowl
Electric mixer

GROCERY LIST

PRODUCE
2 pounds red-skinned potatoes

DAIRY
1 (8-ounce) package fat-free cream cheese
Light butter (1/4 cup needed)
Skim milk (1 1/4–1 1/2 cups needed)

PANTRY
Butter-flavored sprinkles (Butter Buds)
Garlic salt

HELPFUL HINTS:

❍ If you do not have a carousel microwave, turn the potatoes a quarter turn every 3 minutes.

❍ Butter Buds are found in the spice aisle. Molly McButter can also be used.

Broccoli and Onions
with Swiss Cheese *23 minutes*

Swiss cheese lightly complements the mild onion flavor in this recipe.

Ingredients

1 cup water
1 teaspoon onion salt
1 medium onion
1 (2-pound) package frozen broccoli
2 thin slices Swiss cheese *

Instructions

▸ In a medium nonstick saucepan over medium high heat, stir together the water and onion salt.
▸ Cut the onion into quarters and separate the layers. Add the onion pieces and frozen broccoli to the onion water mixture in the saucepan.
▸ Cover and cook over medium-high heat for about 10-15 minutes or until the vegetables are tender.
▸ Cut the Swiss cheese into small pieces. Set aside.
▸ Once the vegetables are cooked and tender, drain the water and place the vegetables back in the pan.
▸ Sprinkle the chopped cheese on top of the cooked vegetables. Cover and let sit on the warm burner until the cheese is melted (a couple of minutes).
▸ Once the cheese is melted, serve.

Yield: 5 (1-cup) servings **Calories per serving:** 84 (24% fat); **Total fat:** 3 g; **Cholesterol:** 8 mg; **Carbohydrate:** 11 g; **Dietary Fiber:** 6 g; **Protein:** 7 g; **Sodium:** 422 mg **Diabetic Exchanges:** 2 vegetable, 1/2 medium-fat meat

SUPPLIES LIST
Medium nonstick saucepan with lid
Cutting board
Timer

GROCERY LIST

PRODUCE
1 medium onion

DAIRY
1 (8-ounce) package natural deli-style sliced Swiss cheese (Sargento brand, 2 slices needed)

FROZEN
1 (2-pound) package frozen broccoli

PANTRY
Onion salt

HELPFUL HINT:

* I used Sargento brand natural deli-style sliced Swiss cheese; there are 12 thin slices in one (8-ounce) package.

Italian Seasoned Scones (page 245)

Breads and Biscuits

SUPPLIES LIST
Oven
Cookie sheet
Timer

GROCERY LIST

DAIRY
Shredded fat-free mozzarella
cheese (1 cup needed)
Shredded parmesan cheese
(1/4 cup needed)
Fat-free feta cheese
crumbles (1/4 cup needed)

PACKAGED
1 loaf fat-free multi-grain
whole-wheat bread
(7 slices needed)

PANTRY
Nonfat butter-flavored
cooking spray

Cheesy Triangles *10 minutes*

This presentation alone is impressive. They are like an open-face-grilled cheese.

Ingredients

7 slices fat-free multi-grain whole-wheat bread
Nonfat butter-flavored cooking spray
1 cup shredded fat-free mozzarella cheese
1/4 cup shredded parmesan cheese
1/4 cup fat-free feta cheese crumbles

Instructions

‣ Preheat the oven to 450 degrees.
‣ Generously spray both sides of the bread with cooking spray.
‣ Pile the slices of sprayed bread together and use a serrated knife to cut the pile from corner to corner and then corner to corner again to make triangles.
‣ Lay the triangles out on a cookie sheet.
‣ Sprinkle the triangles evenly with each of the cheeses. Spray the tops with cooking spray.
‣ Place on the top rack of the oven and bake for 5 minutes.

Yield: 9 (3-piece) servings **Calories per serving:** 112 (11% fat); **Total fat:** 1 g; **Cholesterol:** 4 mg; **Carbohydrate:** 16 g; **Dietary Fiber:** 2 g; **Protein:** 9 g; **Sodium:** 397 mg **Diabetic Exchanges:** 1 starch, 1 very lean meat

---

Garlic and Parmesan Rye Toast *10 minutes*

The mouth-watering and aromatic flavor of garlic toast is taken to a new height with this rye bread.

Ingredients

6 slices seeded hearty rye bread
1 teaspoon garlic salt
1/3 cup fancy shredded parmesan cheese blend

Instructions

▸ Place the oven rack on the top shelf and preheat the oven to 450 degrees.
▸ Generously spray both sides of the bread with cooking spray and place on a baking sheet.
▸ Evenly sprinkle the bread with the garlic salt and cheese.
▸ Put the garlic cheese bread in the oven, and bake for 4 minutes or until lightly browned.

Yield: 6 (1-slice) servings **Calories per serving:** 103 (15% fat); **Total fat:** 2 g;
Cholesterol: 0 mg; **Carbohydrate:** 18 g; **Dietary Fiber:** 2 g; **Protein:** 4 g;
Sodium: 478 mg **Diabetic Exchanges:** 1 starch

SUPPLIES LIST
Oven
Baking sheet
Timer

GROCERY LIST

DAIRY
Fancy shredded parmesan blend cheese
(1/3 cup needed)

PACKAGED
Seeded hearty rye bread
(6 slices needed)

PANTRY
Garlic salt
Butter-flavored cooking spray

HELPFUL HINT:

❯ For a prettier presentation, cut the slices of toast in half diagonally.

SUPPLIES LIST
Oven
2 Baking sheets
Timer

GROCERY LIST

PACKAGED
1 package fat-free flour
tortillas (4 needed)

PANTRY
Garlic salt
Dried parsley
(5 teaspoons needed)
Paprika
Butter-flavored cooking
spray

Homemade Seasoned Crackers *10 minutes*

These were a huge hit with my friend's children! They even made more later in the week for snacks, because they liked them so much

Ingredients

4 fat-free flour tortillas
1½ teaspoons garlic salt
5 teaspoons dried parsley
1 teaspoon paprika

Instructions

▸ Place the oven rack in the middle of the oven. Preheat the oven to 450 degrees.
▸ Cut each of the the fat-free flour tortillas into pie-shaped wedges. Arrange the wedges in a single layer on two baking sheets.
▸ Spray the wedges with butter-flavored cooking spray.
▸ Sprinkle garlic salt, dried parsley, and paprika evenly over the wedges.
▸ Place the seasoned tortillas in the oven. Bake until crispy, 3 to 4 minutes.

Yield: 16 (2 crackers) servings **Calories per serving:** 31 (0% fat); **Total fat:** 0 g; **Cholesterol:** 0 mg; **Carbohydrate:** 6 g; **Dietary Fiber:** 1 g; **Protein:** 1 g; **Sodium:** 168 mg **Diabetic Exchanges:** ½ starch

---

Homemade Butter-Flavored Crackers *10 minutes*

Crackers become a special treat when they are homemade like these! Kids especially love them!

Ingredients

6 fat-free flour tortillas
1½ tablespoons butter-flavored sprinkles
    (Butter Buds or Molly McButter)
Butter-flavored cooking spray

Instructions

▸ Preheat the oven to 450 degrees.
▸ Generously spray both sides of the tortillas with butter-flavored cooking spray.
▸ Place the tortillas in a stack and slice each tortilla into eight wedges.
▸ Arrange the tortilla wedges onto two baking sheets.
▸ Evenly sprinkle the wedges with butter-flavored sprinkles.
▸ Bake 3 to 4 minutes or until golden brown and crispy.

Yield: 12 (4 cracker) servings **Calories per serving:** 62 (0% fat); **Total fat:** 0 g; **Cholesterol:** 0 mg; **Carbohydrate:** 12 g; **Dietary Fiber:** 1 g; **Protein:** 2 g; **Sodium:** 237 mg **Diabetic Exchanges:** 1 starch

SUPPLIES LIST
Oven
2 baking sheets
Timer

GROCERY LIST

PACKAGED
1 package fat-free flour tortillas (6 needed)

PANTRY
Butter-flavored sprinkles
Butter-flavored cooking spray

HELPFUL HINT:

❯ Keep your eye on these when they are baking because they can get done quickly!

SUPPLIES LIST
Oven
2 cookie sheets
Timer

GROCERY LIST

DAIRY
Shredded cheddar cheese
(1/2 cup needed)

PACKAGED
4 whole-wheat bagels

PANTRY
Garlic salt
Dried chopped chives
Butter-flavored cooking
spray

Cheddar Chive Bagel Crisps *10 minutes*

Here's an ideal solution for a light bread.

Ingredients

4 whole-wheat bagels
2 teaspoons garlic salt
1/2 cup shredded cheddar cheese
2 teaspoons dried chopped chives

Instructions

▸ Preheat the oven to 450 degrees.
▸ Slice each of the bagels into 4 slices horizontally to make 16 slices.
▸ Place slices on two cookie sheets.
▸ Spray both sides of the bagel slices generously with butter-flavored cooking spray.
▸ Evenly sprinkle garlic salt, shredded cheddar cheese, and dried chopped chives on top of all the bagel slices.
▸ Bake for 4 to 5 minutes or until the cheese is melted and the bagels are crispy.

Yield: 16 (1 bagel crisp) servings **Calories per serving:** 57 (24% fat); **Total fat:** 2 g; **Cholesterol:** 4 mg; **Carbohydrate:** 9 g; **Dietary Fiber:** 2 g; **Protein:** 2 g; **Sodium:** 182 mg **Diabetic Exchanges:** 1/2 starch

---

HELPFUL HINT:

❯ These are best eaten fresh from the oven.

Salt and Pepper Baked Corn Tortilla Chips   *10 minutes*

A spin off on salt and pepper potato chips, these are just as tasty and a lot less fattening!

Ingredients

9 (6-inch) corn tortillas
1 teaspoon light salt
Ground black pepper

Instructions

- Preheat the oven to 450 degrees.
- Cut each of the corn tortillas into 6 wedges.
- Spread the wedges out on two jelly-roll pans. Spray the tops of the wedges with nonstick cooking spray.
- Evenly sprinkle the tops of the wedges with salt and pepper.
- Bake for 3 to 4 minutes or until lightly golden brown.

Yield: 9 (6 tortilla chips) servings **Calories per serving:** 31 (0% fat); **Total fat:** 0 g; **Cholesterol:** 0 mg; **Carbohydrate:** 7 g; **Dietary Fiber:** 1 g; **Protein:** 1 g; **Sodium:** 145 mg **Diabetic Exchanges:** 1/2 starch

SUPPLIES LIST
Oven
2 cookie sheets or jelly-roll pans
Timer

GROCERY LIST

PACKAGED
1 package (6-inch) corn tortillas (9 needed)

PANTRY
Light salt
Ground black pepper
Nonstick cooking spray

HELPFUL HINTS:

❷ As the chips cool they will be crispy on the outside and tender on the inside.

❷ A super quick way to cut all of the tortillas at once is to stack them, then cut them into wedges with a sharp butcher knife.

235

SUPPLIES LIST
Oven
2 cookie sheets or jelly-roll
pans
Timer

GROCERY LIST

PACKAGED
1 package (6-inch) corn
tortillas (9 needed)

PANTRY
Light salt
Taco seasoning
Nonstick cooking spray

Southwestern Corn Tortilla Chips *10 minutes*

These will add a kick of zest to your day for sure!

Ingredients

9 (6-inch) corn tortillas
1 teaspoon light salt
4 teaspoons taco seasoning

Instructions

▸ Preheat the oven to 450 degrees.

▸ Cut each of the corn tortillas into 6 wedges.

▸ Spread the wedges out on two jelly-roll pans. Spray the tops of the wedges with nonstick cooking spray.

▸ Evenly sprinkle the tops of the wedges with the salt and taco seasoning.

▸ Bake for 3 to 4 minutes or until the edges are lightly golden brown.

Yield: 9 (6-tortilla-chip) servings **Calories per serving:** 34 (0% fat); **Total fat:** 0 g; **Cholesterol:** 0 mg; **Carbohydrate:** 7 g; **Dietary Fiber:** 1 g; **Protein:** 1 g; **Sodium:** 212 mg **Diabetic Exchanges:** 1/2 starch

---

HELPFUL HINTS:

❷ As the chips cool, they will be crispy on the outside and tender on the inside.

❷ A super-quick way to cut all of the tortillas at once is to stack them, then cut them into wedges with a sharp butcher knife.

Mushroom Parmesan Muffin Toppers *11 minutes*

Toasted English muffins halves are topped with fresh chopped mushrooms and finely shredded parmesan cheese, then sprinkled lightly with garlic salt. I've turned what is normally thought of as a breakfast bread into a delicious dinner bread fit for a king!

Ingredients

4 English muffins
1/2 teaspoon garlic salt
4 ounces fresh mushrooms
1/4 cup finely shredded parmesan cheese

Instructions

▸ Place the rack in the oven on the highest shelf, as close to the heat element as possible.
▸ Preheat the oven to 450 degrees.
▸ If the English muffins are not already pre-cut, then slice them in half horizontally, making 8 halves.
▸ Spray both sides of the halves with nonfat butter-flavored cooking spray. Place on the baking sheet.
▸ Finely chop the fresh mushrooms.
▸ Sprinkle the garlic salt and the mushrooms evenly over the English muffins.
▸ Evenly sprinkle the cheese over the mushrooms.
▸ Place in the oven on the top rack and bake for 7 minutes or until crispy.

Yield: 8 servings **Calories per serving:** 80 (14% fat); **Total fat:** 1 g; **Cholesterol:** 2 mg; **Carbohydrate:** 14 g; **Dietary Fiber:** 1 g; **Protein:** 4 g; **Sodium:** 235 mg **Diabetic Exchanges:** 1 starch

---

BREADS AND BISCUITS

SUPPLIES LIST
Oven
Baking sheet
Cutting board
Timer

GROCERY LIST

PRODUCE
4 ounces fresh mushrooms

DAIRY
Finely shredded parmesan cheese (1/4 cup needed)

PACKAGED
4 English muffins

PANTRY
Garlic salt
Butter-flavored cooking spray

SUPPLIES LIST
Oven
Muffin tin
Medium-sized bowl
Timer

GROCERY LIST

DAIRY
Light butter
100% grated parmesan cheese

PACKAGED
1 (7.5-ounce) can home-style biscuits

PANTRY
Italian seasoning
Garlic salt
Olive oil cooking spray or butter-flavored cooking spray

Italian Pull-Apart Muffins *15 minutes*

These muffins could be served at any fine Italian restaurant.

Ingredients

1 (7.5-ounce) can home-style biscuits
1/2 tablespoon Italian seasoning
1/2 teaspoon garlic salt
1 tablespoon melted light butter
1 tablespoon 100% grated parmesan cheese

Instructions

▸ Place the rack in the middle shelf of the oven and preheat the oven to 425 degrees.
▸ Spray 5 cups of a muffin tin with olive oil* cooking spray; set aside.
▸ Cut the biscuits into quarters .
▸ Separate the quartered biscuits and place them in a medium-size bowl. Add the Italian seasoning, garlic salt, and melted butter. Mix together with your hands.
▸ Divide the biscuit dough into five muffin tins, and then sprinkle the grated parmesan cheese evenly over the muffin tops.
▸ Bake for 7 to 8 minutes or until golden brown.

Yield: 5 muffins **Calories per serving:** 114 (22% fat); **Total fat:** 3 g; **Cholesterol:** 4 mg; **Carbohydrate:** 20 g; **Dietary Fiber:** 0 g; **Protein:** 3 g; **Sodium:** 489 mg **Diabetic Exchanges:** 1 1/2 starch, 1/2 fat

HELPFUL HINTS:

❯ To make quartering biscuits easier, stack the flat sides of the biscuits together and cut into quarters. Then separate the biscuits into the bowl.

* Regular or butter flavored cooking spray can be substituted for the olive oil cooking spray

Italian Cream Cheese Crescents *15 minutes*

These could easily be ranked as a top pastry at any fine gourmet bakery. You can make them in less than 15 minutes from start to finish.

Ingredients

4 ounces fat-free cream cheese
1 teaspoon dried minced onion
1¼ teaspoons Italian seasoning, divided
1 teaspoon minced garlic*
¾ teaspoon garlic salt, divided
1 (8-ounce) package reduced-fat crescent rolls

Instructions

▸ Preheat the oven to 350 degrees.
▸ In a medium mixing bowl, use a fork to combine the cream cheese, minced onion, 1 teaspoon of the Italian seasoning, the garlic, and ¹/₂ teaspoon of the garlic salt until well blended. Set aside.
▸ Separate the crescent rolls to make 8 triangles. Place on a baking sheet.
▸ Spread 1 tablespoon of cream cheese mixture on each of the crescent rolls starting at the large end and working toward the point.
▸ Roll the crescents according to the directions.
▸ Spray the tops of the crescents with cooking spray. Evenly sprinkle ¹/₄ teaspoon Italian seasoning and ¹/₄ teaspoon garlic salt over all of the tops of the crescents.
▸ Bake for 8 to 10 minutes or until golden brown.

Yield: 8 (1 crescent) servings **Calories per serving:** 117 (37% fat); **Total fat:** 5 g; **Cholesterol:** 3 mg; **Carbohydrate:** 13 g; **Dietary Fiber:** 0 g; **Protein:** 4 g; **Sodium:** 394 mg **Diabetic Exchanges:** 1 starch, 1 fat

SUPPLIES LIST
Oven
Medium mixing bowl
Baking sheet
Timer

GROCERY LIST

DAIRY
1 (8-ounce) fat-free cream cheese (4 ounces needed)

PACKAGED
1 (8-ounce) package reduced-fat crescent rolls

PANTRY
Dried minced onion
Dried Italian seasoning
Minced garlic (from the jar is fine)
Garlic salt
Butter-flavored cooking spray

HELPFUL HINT:

* Use minced garlic from a jar to save time.

SUPPLIES LIST
Oven
Medium mixing bowl
Baking sheet
Timer

GROCERY LIST

DAIRY
1 package fat-free cream
cheese (4 ounces needed)

PACKAGED
1 (8-ounce) package
reduced-fat crescent rolls
Sugar-free raspberry
preserves

PANTRY
Splenda granular
Granulated plain or red
colored sugar
Butter-flavored cooking
spray

HELPFUL HINT:

❯ Different-flavored
sugar-free preservatives
can be substituted.

Raspberry and Cheese Crescents *15 minutes*

It's hard to believe something this delectable can be made quickly, easily, and affordably in minutes! They look as if they were baked at a fine pastry shop.

Ingredients

4 ounces fat-free cream cheese
1 tablespoon Splenda granular
1 (8-ounce) package reduced-fat crescent rolls
8 teaspoons sugar-free Raspberry preserves
1 teaspoon granulated plain or red colored sugar, optional

Instructions

▸ Preheat the oven to 350 degrees; place the oven rack in the middle shelf of the oven.
▸ In a medium mixing bowl, stir together the cream cheese and Splenda. Set aside.
▸ Separate the crescent rolls to form 8 triangles on a baking sheet.
▸ Spread 1 tablespoon of cream cheese mixture down the center of each crescent triangle starting at the largest end, working your way toward the point.
▸ Spread 1 teaspoon of preserves on top of the cream cheese mixture on each crescent roll.
▸ Roll the crescents according to the package directions.
▸ Spray the tops of the crescents with butter-flavored cooking spray.
▸ Evenly sprinkle the sugar over all of the crescent rolls.
▸ Bake for 8 to 10 minutes or until lightly golden brown.

Yield: 8 (1 crescent) serving **Calories per serving:** 121 (35% fat); **Total fat:** 5 g; **Cholesterol:** 3 mg; **Carbohydrate:** 15 g; **Dietary Fiber:** 0 g; **Protein:** 4 g; **Sodium:** 334 mg **Diabetic Exchanges:** 1 starch, 1 fat

Sugared Scones (soft) *15 minutes*

These soft, tender, and lightly sweetened scones melt in your mouth!

Ingredients

1 cup light fat-free vanilla yogurt
2 cups firmly packed Heart Smart Bisquick reduced-fat baking mix
1 teaspoon granulated sugar

Instructions

▸ Place the oven rack in the middle of the oven.
▸ Preheat the oven to 400 degrees.
▸ In a large mixing bowl, use a spatula to stir together the yogurt and baking mix. Stir until well mixed, making a stiff dough.
▸ Spray a large baking sheet with butter-flavored cooking spray.
▸ For each scone, place 2 heaping tablespoons of dough on the prepared baking sheet.
▸ Spray the tops of the scones with cooking spray.
▸ Sprinkle the granulated sugar evenly over the tops of the scones.
▸ Bake for 7 minutes or until golden brown.
▸ Serve immediately.

Yield: 10 (1-scone) servings **Calories per serving:** 97 (14% fat); **Total fat:** 1 g; **Cholesterol:** 0 mg; **Carbohydrate:** 19 g; **Dietary Fiber:** 0 g; **Protein:** 2 g; **Sodium:** 270 mg **Diabetic Exchanges:** 1 1/2 starch

SUPPLIES LIST
Oven
Large mixing bowl
Large baking sheet
Timer

GROCERY LIST

DAIRY
Light fat-free vanilla yogurt
(1 cup needed)

PACKAGED
Heart Smart Bisquick
reduced-fat baking mix
(2 cups needed)

PANTRY
Granulated sugar
Butter-flavored cooking
spray

HELPFUL HINTS:

❷ These are delicious hot, warm, or at room temperature.

Green Chile Scones *15 minutes*

These are light and fluffy with a little kick!

Ingredients

3/4 cup light fat-free vanilla yogurt
1/4 cup green chilies
2 cups Heart Smart Bisquick reduced-fat baking mix
1 tablespoon dried chopped chives
Paprika, optional

Instructions

▸ Place the baking rack in the middle of the oven, and preheat the oven to 400 degrees.
▸ In a large mixing bowl, stir together the yogurt, green chilies, baking mix, and chives until well mixed. The dough will be sticky. Set aside.
▸ Spray a baking sheet with nonstick cooking spray.
▸ For each scone, place 1 heaping tablespoon of dough onto the prepared baking sheet.
▸ Lightly sprinkle the tops of the scones with paprika, if desired.
▸ Bake for 8 minutes or until the bottoms are golden brown.

Yield: 12 (1-scone) servings **Calories per serving:** 84 (14% fat); **Total fat:** 1 g; **Cholesterol:** 0 mg; **Carbohydrate:** 16 g; **Dietary Fiber:** 0 g; **Protein:** 2 g; **Sodium:** 259 mg **Diabetic Exchanges:** 1 starch

SUPPLIES LIST
Oven
Large mixing bowl
Baking sheet
Timer

GROCERY LIST

DAIRY
Light fat-free vanilla yogurt
(3/4 cup needed)

PACKAGED
Green chilies
(1/4 cup needed)
Heart Smart Bisquick
reduced-fat baking mix
(2 cups needed)

PANTRY
Dried chopped chives
Paprika (optional)
Nonstick cooking spray

HELPFUL HINT:

❯ To substitute fresh chives for the dried chives, use 2 tablespoons of fresh chives.

Coffee Cake Mini Muffins *20 minutes*

You'll be able to make these almost effortlessly and so inexpensively that it will be easy to resist the high-fat and expensive coffee cake.

Ingredients

1 cup light fat-free vanilla yogurt
2 cups firmly packed Heart Smart Bisquick reduced-fat baking mix
1 cup Splenda Brown Sugar Blend
1 teaspoon ground cinnamon

Instructions

- Place the oven rack in the middle of the oven, and preheat the oven to 400 degrees.
- In a large mixing bowl, stir together the yogurt and baking mix until well mixed. Set aside.
- Spray the muffin tins with butter-flavored cooking spray. Set aside.
- In a small bowl mix the Splenda Brown Sugar Blend and cinnamon. Place $1/2$ teaspoon of the brown sugar mixture into the bottom of each mini muffin tin. Use your finger to make sure the sugar mixture covers the entire bottom of each mini muffin tin.
- Place 1 rounded tablespoon of the dough on top of the brown sugar cinnamon mixture in each muffin tin.
- Sprinkle the remaining brown sugar–cinnamon mixture evenly on top of the muffin dough.
- Generously spray the top of each muffin with butter-flavored cooking spray.
- Bake for 7 minutes or until golden brown.
- Let cool for a minute or two before serving.

Yield: 12 (2-muffin) servings **Calories per serving:** 166 (8% fat); **Total fat:** 1 g;
Cholesterol: 0 mg; **Carbohydrate:** 32 g; **Dietary Fiber:** 0 g; **Protein:** 2 g;
Sodium: 243 mg **Diabetic Exchanges:** 1 starch, 1 carbohydrate

SUPPLIES LIST
Oven
Large mixing bowl
Mini muffin tins
Timer

GROCERY LIST

DAIRY
Light fat-free vanilla yogurt
(1 cup needed)

PACKAGED
Heart Smart Bisquick
reduced-fat baking mix
(2 cups needed)

PANTRY
Splenda Brown Sugar Blend
(1 cup needed)
Ground cinnamon
Butter-flavored cooking spray

HELPFUL HINTS:

❯ These are scrumptious served hot, warm, or at room temperature.

❯ The easiest way to remove the muffins from the pan is to scoop them out with a spoon.

SUPPLIES LIST
Oven
Large mixing bowl
2 Large baking sheets
Timer

GROCERY LIST

FROZEN
1 (8-ounce) container fat-free
dessert whipped topping

PACKAGED
Heart Smart Bisquick
reduced-fat baking mix
(2 cups needed)
Mini semi-sweet chocolate
chips (1/4 cup needed)

PANTRY
Ground cinnamon
Cocoa
Splenda granular
Butter-flavored cooking
spray

HELPFUL HINT:

❯ These are full of flavor
served hot, warm, or at
room temperature.

Chocolate Chip Cinnamon Mini Scones *20 minutes*

These versatile mini scones are an original recipe combining the flavors of a chocolate chip cookie with the texture of a cinnamon biscuit or scone.

Ingredients

2 cups Heart Smart Bisquick reduced-fat baking mix
1 (8-ounce) container fat-free dessert whipped topping, thawed
1½ teaspoons ground cinnamon
1 tablespoon plus 1 teaspoon cocoa
2 tablespoons Splenda granular
1/4 cup mini semi-sweet chocolate chips

Instructions

▸ Preheat the oven to 400 degrees.
▸ In a large mixing bowl, combine the baking mix, whipped topping, cinnamon, cocoa, Splenda, and chocolate chips. Mix together to make a stiff dough.
▸ Spray two large baking sheets with butter-flavored cooking spray.
▸ Drop the dough by rounded teaspoonfuls onto the prepared baking sheets.
▸ Bake for 5 to 7 minutes.

Yield: 36 (1 mini scone) servings **Calories per serving:** 43 (18% fat); **Total fat:** 1 g; **Cholesterol:** 0 mg; **Carbohydrate:** 8 g; **Dietary Fiber:** 0 g; **Protein:** 1 g; **Sodium:** 81 mg **Diabetic Exchanges:** 1/2 starch

---

Italian Seasoned Scones *25 minutes*

These go great with any egg-based breakfast entrée or Italian-based pasta dinner! They are also a nice accompaniment for a ladies tea, instead of something sweet.

Ingredients

1 cup plus 2 tablespoons fat-free sour cream
6 egg whites (or $3/4$ cup Egg Beaters)
3 cups firmly packed Heart Smart Bisquick reduced-fat baking mix
3 tablespoons Italian seasoning
3 tablespoons dried minced onion
1 teaspoon garlic salt

Instructions

▸ Place the oven rack in the middle of the oven and preheat the oven to 400 degrees.
▸ In a large mixing bowl, whisk together the sour cream and egg whites until well blended.
▸ Using a stiff spatula stir in the baking mix, Italian seasoning, onion, and garlic salt; mix together well to form a sticky dough.
▸ Spray a large baking sheet with olive oil cooking spray.
▸ For each scone place two heaping tablespoons of dough onto the prepared baking sheet.
▸ Spray the tops of the scones with olive oil cooking spray, and then sprinkle each scone lightly with garlic salt.
▸ Bake in the oven for 7 minutes, or until golden brown.
▸ Serve immediately.

Yield: 16 (1-scone) servings **Calories per serving:** 104 (12% fat); **Total fat:** 1 g;
Cholesterol: 3 mg; **Carbohydrate:** 19 g; **Dietary Fiber:** 0 g; **Protein:** 4 g;
Sodium: 331 mg **Diabetic Exchanges:** 1½ starch

SUPPLIES LIST
Oven
Large mixing bowl
Whisk
Large baking sheet
Timer

GROCERY LIST

DAIRY
Fat-free sour cream (1 cup plus 2 tablespoons needed)
Eggs (6 needed)

PACKAGED
Heart Smart Bisquick reduced-fat baking mix (3 cups needed)

PANTRY
Dried Italian seasoning
Dried minced onion
Garlic salt
Olive oil cooking spray

HELPFUL HINT:

❷ These are tasty whether they're served hot, warm, or at room temperature.

Pineapple Cherry Delight (page 249)

Desserts

(continued on page 248)

Pineapple Cherry Delight *10 minutes*

This yields eight (1/2-cup) servings. I had the best of intentions to let my family eat this, but by the end of the day, I had eaten the whole thing myself!

Ingredients

1/2 cup plain nonfat yogurt
1 (20-ounce) can crushed pineapple (chilled)
2 tablespoons Splenda granular
1/4 cup finely chopped pecans
1 (10-ounce) jar maraschino cherries (chilled)
2 cups miniature marshmallows

Instructions

▸ Open and drain the juice from the pineapple and maraschino cherries. Set aside.
▸ In a medium mixing bowl, combine the yogurt, pineapple, cherries, Splenda, pecans, and marshmallows.
▸ Serve.

Yield: 8 (1/2-cup) servings **Calories per serving:** 144 (18% fat); **Total fat:** 3 g; **Cholesterol:** 0 mg; **Carbohydrate:** 27 g; **Dietary Fiber:** 1 g; **Protein:** 1 g; **Sodium:** 26 mg **Diabetic Exchanges:** 2 carbohydrate, 1/2 fat

SUPPLIES LIST
Medium mixing bowl

GROCERY LIST

DAIRY
Plain nonfat yogurt
(1/2 cup needed)

PACKAGED
1 (20-ounce) can
crushed pineapple
Chopped pecans
(1/4 cup needed)
1 (10-ounce) jar maraschino
cherries
2 cups miniature
marshmallows

PANTRY
Splenda granular

SUPPLIES LIST
9 x13-inch glass casserole
dish
Large mixing bowl

GROCERY LIST

FROZEN
1 (16-ounce) package
frozen blackberries
1 (16-ounce) bag frozen
blueberries (1 cup needed)
1 (8-ounce) container fat-free
dessert whipped topping

PACKAGED
1 (10-ounce) angel food cake
1 (12.75-ounce) jar sugar-free
red raspberry preserves

HELPFUL HINTS:

❷ A metal 9 x 13-inch pan
can be used, but using glass
is better, so everyone can
see the pretty colors.

❷ This dessert is good
when the berries are
still partially frozen or
completely thawed.

Very Berry Angel Food Dessert *10 minutes*

This recipe is light, fruity, and refreshing. Make it while the fruit is still frozen, and as the fruit thaws, the juices melt into the cake, giving the cake a pretty appearance. Perfect for diabetics.

Ingredients

1 (10-ounce) angel food cake
1 (16-ounce) package frozen blackberries, divided
1 cup frozen blueberries
1 (12.75-ounce) jar sugar-free red raspberry preserves
1 (8-ounce) container fat-free dessert whipped topping

Instructions

▸ Cut the cake into bite-size pieces and place in the bottom of a 9 x13-inch glass casserole dish. Set aside.
▸ Set aside 3 whole blackberries to use as garnish.
▸ In a large mixing bowl, gently stir together the remaining blackberries and blueberries with the preserves until well mixed.
▸ Spoon the mixed berries over the cake.
▸ With a spatula, spread the whipped topping over the frozen berries.
▸ Place the 3 whole blackberries in the middle of the whipped topping as a garnish.
▸ Cover and keep refrigerated until ready to serve.

Yield: 12 (1/2-cup) servings **Calories per serving:** 141 (0% fat); **Total fat:** 0 g; **Cholesterol:** 0 mg; **Carbohydrate:** 36 g; **Dietary Fiber:** 3 g; **Protein:** 2 g; **Sodium:** 188 mg **Diabetic Exchanges:** 2 1/2 carbohydrate

---

Cherry Pineapple Fruit Fluff *10 minutes*

This is a comfort food that reminds us of something our Mom's or Grandmother's used to make. Nowadays you can find them in the deli, but why would you buy this when it's so easy to make at home.

Ingredients

2 (20-ounce) cans crushed pineapple in unsweetened juice
1 (28-ounce) jar maraschino cherries, drained
1 (8-ounce) box fat-free cream cheese
1/3 cup Splenda granular
1/4 teaspoon light salt
1/4 cup chopped walnuts, 1 tablespoon reserved for topping
3 cups miniature marshmallows

Instructions

▸ Drain and discard one cup of juice from each can of crushed pineapple.
▸ Drain and discard the juice from the maraschino cherries. Set aside.
▸ In a large mixing bowl combine the cream cheese, Splenda, pineapple, and light salt with an electric mixer.
▸ Add the cherries, walnuts (minus 1 tablespoon for topping), and miniature marshmallows to the cream cheese mixture, and stir until well blended.
▸ Put in a pretty serving bowl and sprinkle the top with the remaining tablespoon chopped walnuts.

Yield: 14 (1/2-cup) servings **Calories per serving:** 167 (8% fat); **Total fat:** 1 g; **Cholesterol:** 3 mg; **Carbohydrate:** 32 g; **Dietary Fiber:** 1 g; **Protein:** 3 g; **Sodium:** 149 mg **Diabetic Exchanges:** 2 carbohydrate, 1/2 very lean meat

---

SUPPLIES LIST
Large mixing bowl
Electric mixer
Serving bowl

GROCERY LIST

DAIRY
1 (8-ounce) box fat-free cream cheese

PACKAGED
2 (20-ounce) cans crushed pineapple in unsweetened juice
1 (28-ounce) jar maraschino cherries
Chopped walnuts (1/4 cup needed)
Miniature marshmallows (3 cups needed)

PANTRY
Splenda granular (1/3 cup needed)
Light salt

Chocolate Cinnamon Pecan–Covered Marshmallows *5 minutes*

For people who like 100-calorie snack packs, this sweet treat fits the bill. The added touch of cinnamon gives it a unique twist.

Ingredients

1 (1.55-ounce) chocolate candy bar (Hershey's)
1/4 teaspoon ground cinnamon
3 cups miniature marshmallows
2 tablespoons finely chopped pecan pieces
1/8 teaspoon light salt

Instructions

▸ In a large mixing bowl, break up the candy bar. Place in the microwave and cook at 30-second intervals, stirring until completely melted.
▸ Add the cinnamon, and stir well.
▸ Stir in the marshmallows and pecans until the marshmallows are lightly coated with chocolate.
▸ Stir in the salt.
▸ Store in a zip-top bag.

Yield: 9 (1/3-cup) servings **Calories per serving:** 90 (25% fat); **Total fat:** 3 g; **Cholesterol:** 1 mg; **Carbohydrate:** 17 g; **Dietary Fiber:** 0 g; **Protein:** 1 g; **Sodium:** 33 mg **Diabetic Exchanges:** 1 carbohydrate, 1/2 fat

Cherry Coconut Cream Dessert *10 minutes*

This is the ideal solution for a quick homemade dessert to satisfy a dieter's craving. It's every bit as tasty as it is pretty! It tastes rich and fattening but it's not.

Ingredients

1 (8-ounce) container fat-free dessert whipped topping
1 (1.34-ounce) package of sugar-free French vanilla instant pudding mix
1/2 teaspoon coconut extract
3 tablespoons firmly packed angel flake sweetened coconut, divided
1/4 cup fat-free skim milk
1 (9-ounce) sugar-free angel food cake
1 (20-ounce) can no-sugar-added cherry pie filling

Instructions

▸ Using an electric mixer, beat together the whipped topping, pudding mix, coconut extract, 2 tablespoons coconut, and milk until smooth.
▸ Break up the cake into bite-size pieces.
▸ Mix the cake pieces into the pudding mixture.
▸ Press the mixture into a 9 x 9-inch glass casserole dish.
▸ Spread the pie filling over the top of the cake mixture.
▸ Sprinkle 1 tablespoon of coconut over the entire top.
▸ Cut into 9 squares to serve.

Yield: 9 servings **Calories per serving:** 136 (0% fat); **Total fat:** 0 g; **Cholesterol:** 0 mg; **Carbohydrate:** 33 g; **Dietary Fiber:** 1 g; **Protein:** 2 g; **Sodium:** 414 mg **Diabetic Exchanges:** 2 carbohydrate

---

DESSERTS

SUPPLIES LIST
Medium mixing bowl
Electric mixer
9 x 9-inch glass casserole dish

GROCERY LIST

DAIRY
Fat-free skim milk
(1/4 cup needed)

FROZEN
1 (8-ounce) container fat-free dessert whipped topping

PACKAGED
1 (1.34-ounce) package of sugar-free French vanilla instant pudding mix
1 (9-ounce) sugar-free angel food cake
1 (20-ounce) can no-sugar-added cherry pie filling
Angel flake sweetened coconut (3 tablespoons needed)

PANTRY
Coconut extract

HELPFUL HINTS:

❷ Place the can of cherry pie filling in the refrigerator when you get home from shopping so it will be nicely chilled.

❷ Different flavorings of (no-sugar-added fruit) pie filling can be substituted for the cherry pie filling.

253

Chocolate Cinnamon Dessert *10 minutes*

This is a great dessert for potlucks or last minute unexpected guests. This was a whopping winner with my neighbor's children Sally and Joe. It tastes every bit as good freshly made as it does the next day. Freshly made, the graham crackers are crispy and give the dessert a crunchy flavor; the next day the consistency of the graham crackers tastes more like a firm cake.

Ingredients

1 package cinnamon graham crackers, divided
2 (1.5-ounce) packages sugar-free chocolate instant pudding
1 1/2 cups fat-free milk
1 teaspoon ground cinnamon, plus extra for sprinkling on top
2 (8-ounce) containers thawed fat-free dessert whipped topping, divided
1 1/2 tablespoon mini semi-sweet chocolate morsels

Instructions

▸ Line a 9 x 13-inch baking dish with 6 whole cinnamon graham crackers (24 small crackers), cinnamon side down. Set aside.
▸ In a large mixing bowl, beat the pudding mix, milk, whipped topping, and cinnamon with an electric mixer until well blended.
▸ Spread the pudding mixture over the tops of the graham crackers.
▸ Place 6 whole cinnamon graham crackers (24 small crackers) on top of the pudding mixture, with the cinnamon side down.
▸ Spread whipped topping on top of the crackers.
▸ Lightly sprinkle the remaining ground cinnamon evenly over the top of the whipped topping.
▸ Sprinkle the chocolate morsels evenly over the top of the whipped topping.
▸ Cut into 15 servings with a sharp knife. Cover and refrigerate until ready to serve.

Yield: 15 servings **Calories per serving:** 124 (11% fat); **Total fat:** 1 g; **Cholesterol:** 0 mg; **Carbohydrate:** 24 g; **Dietary Fiber:** 0 g; **Protein:** 2 g; **Sodium:** 322 mg
Diabetic Exchanges: 1 1/2 carbohydrate

SUPPLIES LIST
9 x 13-inch baking dish
Large mixing bowl
Electric mixer

GROCERY LIST

DAIRY
Fat-free milk
(1 1/2 cups needed)

FROZEN
2 (8-ounce) containers fat-free dessert whipped topping

PACKAGED
1 box cinnamon graham crackers (1 package needed, 3 packages per box)
2 (1.5-ounce) packages sugar-free chocolate instant pudding mix
Mini semi-sweet chocolate morsels

PANTRY
Ground cinnamon

Pineapple Pudding *5 minutes*

Here's a quick dessert that is great anytime!

Ingredients

2 (20-ounce) cans crushed pineapple, chilled
1 (1.34-ounce) packet sugar-free French vanilla pudding mix
3 tablespoons chopped walnuts
1 cup fat-free dessert whipped topping,

Instructions

▸ Open and drain the juice from the cans of pineapple into a medium-size serving bowl. Be sure to squeeze as much juice out as possible. You will get approximately 1 cup of juice from each can. Leave the pineapple in the can; set aside.

▸ Whisk the pudding mix into the juice until thick and creamy.

▸ Add the reserved pineapple, walnuts, and whipped topping to the pudding mixture. Stir until well blended.

▸ If desired, sprinkle with additional chopped nuts.

Yield: 10 (1/2-cup) servings **Calories per serving:** 103 (13% fat); **Total fat:** 1 g;
Cholesterol: 0 mg; **Carbohydrate:** 21 g; **Dietary Fiber:** 1 g; **Protein:** 0 g;
Sodium: 170 mg **Diabetic Exchanges:** 1½ fruit

DESSERTS

SUPPLIES LIST
Medium-sized serving bowl
Whisk

GROCERY LIST

FROZEN
1 (8-ounce) container fat-free dessert whipped topping (1 cup needed)

PACKAGED
2 (20-ounce) cans crushed pineapple
1 (1.34-ounce) packet of sugar-free French vanilla pudding
Chopped walnuts (3 tablespoons needed)

HELPFUL HINT:

❷ Put the cans of pineapple in the refrigerator as soon as you get home from the grocery store to make sure they are nicely chilled to use in this recipe.

Fruit Fluff *15 minutes*

This would be great for potlucks and the holidays.

Ingredients

1 (16-ounce) can whole berry cranberry sauce
1 (8-ounce) tub strawberry-flavored Cool Whip
2 (20-ounce) cans unsweetened crushed pineapple,
1 (16-ounce) bag of miniature marshmallows
1/4 cup finely chopped pecans
4 Gala apples, chopped into bite-size pieces to make 4 cups

Instructions

▶ In a large mixing bowl, beat the cranberry sauce and Cool Whip with an electric mixer on high for 2 minutes.

▶ Discard $1\frac{1}{3}$ cups of juice from each of the cans of pineapple.

▶ Pour the remaining juice and crushed pineapple into the cranberry Cool Whip mixture.

▶ Add the miniature marshmallows, pecans, and chopped apples to the cranberry mixture.

▶ Serve.

Yield: 20 (1/2-cup) servings **Calories per serving:** 184 (15% fat); **Total fat:** 3 g; **Cholesterol:** 0 mg; **Carbohydrate:** 39 g; **Dietary Fiber:** 1 g; **Protein:** 1 g; **Sodium:** 27 mg **Diabetic Exchanges:** 2 1/2 carbohydrate, 1/2 fat

HELPFUL HINTS:

❂ Pre-chill your canned ingredients the night before.

❂ To save time you can purchase finely chopped pecans.

❂ You can substitute any sweet/tart apple for this recipe, but do not use Red or Golden Delicious apples.

Chocolate Minty Fudge   *15 minutes*

This dessert is a great way to curb your sweet tooth after dinner, without blowing your caloric intake for the day. And at a fraction of the cost of gourmet chocolates, this sweet treat is twice as nice!

Ingredients

7 tablespoons light butter, softened and divided
2 3/4 cups confectioners' sugar
1/2 cup powdered cocoa
1/4 teaspoon light salt
3 tablespoons fat-free sweetened condensed milk (not evaporated)
1 teaspoon mint extract
1/2 cup real semisweet mini-morsels chocolate chips (in baking aisle)

Instructions

▸ In a medium-size bowl beat 5 tablespoons of butter with the confectioners' sugar, cocoa, salt, sweetened condensed milk, and mint extract with an electric mixer on low speed until well blended. The mixture will be super stiff.

▸ *Do not do this next step until the first step is completely finished.* In a small bowl, melt the remaining 2 tablespoons of butter with the chocolate chips in a carousel microwave. Stir the chocolate and butter together after 1 minute until smooth and creamy. If needed, continue cooking for 30 seconds and then stir until the chocolate is completely melted. *Do not let it boil.* Simply cook enough to completely melt the chocolate.

▸ With a spatula, add the melted chocolate chips to the stiff mixture in the bowl. Stir with the spatula until the ingredients are well mixed, and then knead the fudge with your hands for about a minute longer.

▸ With your hands press the fudge into the prepared pan.

▸ Cut into 64 (1-inch) pieces.

Yield: 64 (1-inch) pieces **Calories per serving:** 37 (26% fat); **Total fat:** 1 g;
Cholesterol: 2 mg; **Carbohydrate:** 7 g; **Dietary Fiber:** 0 g; **Protein:** 0 g;
Sodium: 16 mg **Diabetic Exchanges**: 1/2 carbohydrate

DESSERTS

SUPPLIES LIST
Medium-size bowl
Electric Mixer
Microwave oven
Timer

GROCERY LIST

DAIRY
Light butter
(7 tablespoons needed)

PACKAGED
Fat-free sweetened
condensed milk
(3 tablespoons needed)
Semisweet mini-morsels
chocolate chips
(1/2 cup needed)

PANTRY
Confectioners' sugar
(2 3/4 cups needed)
Powdered cocoa
(1/2 cup needed)
Light salt
Mint extract

HELPFUL HINT:

❯ For added pizzazz gently press 2 crushed peppermint candy canes on top of the fudge with your hands before cutting into pieces.

SUPPLIES LIST
2¹/2-quart saucepan
Small bowl
Timer

GROCERY LIST

PACKAGED
1 (29-ounce) can no-sugar-
added yellow cling
sliced peaches
Cinnamon-flavored candies
(Red Hots) (¹/3 cup needed)

PANTRY
Cornstarch

Hot Spiced Peaches *15 minutes*

*The flavor of these Hot Spiced Peaches is every bit as wonderful as the vibrant color.
This wonderfully warm dessert is perfect for any cold winter day.*

Ingredients

1 (29-ounce) can no-sugar-added sliced yellow cling peaches
¹/3 cup cinnamon-flavored candies (Red Hots)
1 tablespoon cornstarch,
¹/2 tablespoon water

Instructions

▸ In a 2 ¹/2-quart saucepan, stir in the peaches and cinnamon-flavored candies.
  Cook on high heat. Bring it to a boil, and boil for 10 minutes, stirring
  occasionally.
▸ In a separate small bowl, make a paste of cornstarch and water. Stir into the
  boiling peaches.
▸ Remove from the heat and let sit for three minutes.
▸ Serve.

Yield: 6 (¹/2-cup) servings **Calories per serving:** 145 (0% fat); **Total fat:** 0 g;
Cholesterol: 0 mg; **Carbohydrate:** 35 g; **Dietary Fiber:** 1 g; **Protein:** 0 g;
Sodium: 22 mg **Diabetic Exchanges:** 1¹/2 fruit, 1 carbohydrate

---

Chocolate Almond Dessert *15 minutes*

Now you can enjoy a chocolate almond candy bar wrapped up in a creamy dessert without any guilt. Isn't life good!

Ingredients

1 (1.5-ounce) box sugar-free instant chocolate pudding mix,
1 1/2 cups fat-free skim milk,
1/2 teaspoon almond extract
1 (9-ounce) sugar-free angel food cake,
2 1/2 tablespoons mini semi-sweet chocolate morsels, divided
20 whole almonds, divided
1 1/2 cups fat-free dessert whipped topping,

Instructions

▸ In a large mixing bowl, beat the pudding mix, milk, and almond extract with an electric mixer on high speed for 2 minutes or until well blended.
▸ Tear the cake into pieces and add it to the pudding mixture along with 2 tablespoons chocolate morsels. Stir with a spatula until well mixed.
▸ Finely chop the almonds to make 2 tablespoons. Add 1 tablespoon to the pudding and cake mix. Reserve 1 tablespoon for later.
▸ Spread the mixture into an 8 x 8-inch baking dish.
▸ Spread the whipped topping on top of the cake and pudding mixture.
▸ Sprinkle the remaining chocolate morsels and almonds on top of the whipped topping.
▸ Keep chilled until ready to serve.
▸ Cut into 9 servings.

Yield: 9 servings **Calories per serving:** 125 (15% fat); **Total fat:** 2 g; **Cholesterol:** 1 mg; **Carbohydrate:** 26 g; **Dietary Fiber:** 1 g; **Protein:** 4 g; **Sodium:** 430 mg **Diabetic Exchanges:** 1 1/2 carbohydrate, 1/2 fat

---

DESSERTS

Supplies List
Large mixing bowl
Electric mixer
Cutting board
8" x 8" baking dish

GROCERY LIST

DAIRY
Fat-free skim milk
(1 1/2 cups needed)

FROZEN
1 (8-ounce) container fat-free dessert whipped topping
(1 1/2 cups needed)

PACKAGED
1 (1.5-ounce) box sugar-free instant chocolate pudding mix
1 (9-ounce) sugar-free angel food cake
Mini semi-sweet chocolate morsels
(2 1/2 tablespoons needed)
Whole almonds (need 20)

PANTRY
Almond extract

HELPFUL HINTS:

❷ Chocolate mini morsels are also known as mini chocolate chips, but some packages say morsels and some say chips.

❷ You can purchase slivered almonds instead of finely chopping whole almonds.

❷ For a variation add 1/2 cup shredded coconut to make this an Almond Joy dessert.

SUPPLIES LIST
Oven
Large mixing bowl
Baking sheet
Medium-size bowl
Timer

GROCERY LIST

DAIRY
Light fat-free vanilla yogurt
(Dannon Activia)
(1 cup needed)

FROZEN
1 (16-ounce) bag whole
frozen strawberries
2 (8-ounce) containers fat-
free dessert whipped topping
(2¹/2 cups needed)

PACKAGED
Heart Smart Bisquick
reduced-fat baking mix
(2 cups needed)

PANTRY
Granulated sugar
Splenda granular
Butter-flavored cooking
spray

HELPFUL HINTS:

❍ To serve at a later time,
store-baked shortcakes in
an airtight container or zip-
top bags and freeze.

❍ Sugar can be substituted
for the Splenda granular.

❍ Do not assemble the
shortcakes with the
strawberries until you
are ready to eat them;
otherwise the shortcake
will get soggy.

Easiest Strawberry Shortcake *15 minutes*

I'll never eat high-fat strawberry shortcake again! This is oh, so delicious! This shortcake recipe is yummy served warm, chilled, or at room temperature.

Ingredients

1 cup light fat-free vanilla yogurt (Dannon Activia)
2 cups firmly packed Heart Smart Bisquick reduced-fat baking mix
1 teaspoon granulated sugar
2 tablespoons Splenda granular
1 (16-ounce) bag whole frozen strawberries, thawed,
2¹/2 cups fat-free dessert whipped topping, thawed and divided,

Instructions

▸ Place the oven rack in the middle of the oven, and preheat the oven to 400 degrees.
▸ In a large mixing bowl, stir together the yogurt and baking mix. Stir until well mixed to make a stiff dough.
▸ Spray a baking sheet with butter-flavored cooking spray.
▸ For each shortcake, place 2 heaping tablespoons of dough onto the baking sheet.
▸ Spray the tops of the shortcakes with butter-flavored cooking spray. Sprinkle the sugar evenly over all of the shortcakes.
▸ Bake the shortcakes for 7 minutes or until the bottoms are golden brown.
▸ While the shortcakes are baking, gently stir the Splenda with the thawed strawberries in a medium-size bowl. Set aside.

Assembling the Shortcakes:

▸ Cut each baked shortcake in half horizontally.
▸ Place ¹/4 cup of sweetened strawberries on the bottom half of each shortcake.
▸ Place the top half of the shortcake on top of the strawberries.
▸ Place ¹/4 cup whipped topping on top of shortcake.
▸ Garnish with one sweetened strawberry from the bag.

Yield: 10 (1 strawberry shortcake) servings **Calories per serving:** 152 (10% fat); **Total fat:** 2 g; **Cholesterol:** 0 mg; **Carbohydrate:** 30 g; **Dietary Fiber:** 1 g; **Protein:** 3 g; **Sodium:** 303 mg **Diabetic Exchanges:** 1 starch, 1 carbohydrate

Apple and Cinnamon Spiced Dumplings *15 minutes*

Wow! If I had not created this myself I would have found it difficult to believe that a recipe like this (that is so full of down home goodness) is comfortably made in only 15 minutes! Keep the ingredients in your pantry for a last minute dessert that is sure to knock your guest's socks off!

Ingredients

2 (20-ounce) cans no-sugar-added apple pie filling
1 (0.14-ounce) packet sugar-free spiced cider apple-flavor drink mix, (Alpine)
1¼ teaspoon ground cinnamon, divided
1½ cups Bisquick Heart Smart reduced-fat baking mix
¾ cup fat-free vanilla yogurt
1 tablespoon Splenda Brown Sugar Blend
1¼ cups fat-free dessert whipped topping,

Instructions

▸ Spray a 12-inch nonstick saucepan with nonstick cooking spray.
▸ Add the apple pie filling, drink mix, and ¹/₂ teaspoon cinnamon to the pan and stir together. Cover and cook on medium-high heat. Bring to a boil.
▸ In a medium-size mixing bowl, stir together the baking mix, yogurt, the remaining ³/₄ teaspoon ground cinnamon, and the Splenda Brown Sugar Blend with a fork. A sticky dough will form. Set aside.
▸ Once the apple filling comes to a boil, drop the dough by heaping teaspoons onto the apple filling to form 10 dumplings on top.
▸ Cover and let cook for 5 to 7 minutes or until the dumplings are cooked through.
▸ If desired, sprinkle the tops of the dumplings lightly with additional ground cinnamon.
▸ Put a 2-tablespoon dollop of whipped topping on top of each serving.

Yield: 10 (1 dumpling plus ½ cup apple filling with 2 tablespoon dollop of fat-free whipped topping) servings; **Calories per serving:** 134 (8% fat); **Total fat:** 1 g; **Cholesterol:** 0 mg; **Carbohydrate:** 29 g; **Dietary Fiber:** 2 g; **Protein:** 2 g; **Sodium:** 240 mg **Diabetic Exchanges:** 2 carbohydrates

261

DESSERTS

SUPPLIES LIST
12-inch nonstick saucepan with lid
Medium-sized mixing bowl
Timer

GROCERY LIST

DAIRY
Fat-free vanilla yogurt (³/4 cup needed)

FROZEN
1 (8-ounce) container fat-free dessert whipped topping (1¹/4 cups needed)

PACKAGED
2 (20-ounce) cans no-sugar-added apple pie filling
1 box sugar-free spiced cider apple-flavor drink mix (10 pouches per box, Alpine brand)
Bisquick Heart Smart reduced-fat baking mix (1¹/2 cups needed)

PANTRY
Ground cinnamon
Splenda Brown Sugar Blend
Nonstick cooking spray

HELPFUL HINT:

❷ There are 10 individual pouches in one (1.4-ounce) box of sugar-free spiced cider apple-flavor drink mix (by Alpine).

Crepes *15 minutes*

I recommend making a bunch of these crepes ahead of time and layering them between waxed paper, then freezing them in a plastic zip-top bag so you have easy access to assemble impressive, homemade desserts within minutes for those unexpected guests.

Ingredients

1/2 cup Heart Smart Bisquick reduced-fat baking mix
3/4 cup fat-free skim milk,
2 egg whites

Instructions

▸ Preheat a 6- or 8-inch nonstick skillet over high heat.
▸ In a 4-cup measuring cup or mixing bowl, whisk together the baking mix, milk, and egg whites.
▸ When the skillet is hot, spray with nonstick cooking spray. Add the crepe batter to the skillet. Lift and tilt the skillet to spread the batter. Brown on one side. The top of the crepe will be full of bubbles. Lift the crepe from the pan with a fork and place on a plate with a paper towel. Watch closely, because it only takes about a minute for the crepes to cook. Place a paper towel between crepes to keep them from sticking together.

Yield: 10 crepes **Calories per serving:** 32 (0% fat); **Total fat:** 0 g; **Cholesterol:** 0 mg; **Carbohydrate:** 5 g; **Dietary Fiber:** 0 g; **Protein:** 2 g; **Sodium:** 88 mg **Diabetic Exchanges:** 1/2 starch

---

Pumpkin and Toffee Trifle *20 minutes*

The sweet and crunchy buttery bits of English Toffee within the creamy filling takes pumpkin dessert to a whole new level!

Ingredients

1 (10-ounce) angel food cake
2 cups pumpkin pie filling
1/4 cup plus 2 teaspoons crushed English toffee bits (Heath bar)
2 (1.7-ounce) packages sugar-free, fat-free instant vanilla pudding mix
1 (8-ounce) package fat-free cream cheese,
2 cups fat-free low-carb milk*
4 ounces fat-free dessert whipped topping,

Instructions

- Cut the angel food cake into bite-size pieces, then mix the cake, pumpkin pie filling, and 1/4 cup crushed English toffee bits in a large bowl. Set aside.
- In another large mixing bowl, beat the vanilla pudding mix, cream cheese, milk, and whipped topping with an electric mixer.
- In a large trifle bowl or large glass bowl, put 1 1/3 cups of the pudding mixture on the bottom. Then place 1 1/2 cups of pumpkin mixture on top of the cream mixture. Repeat the layers, ending with 1 1/3 cups of the cream mixture.
- Sprinkle the top with the remaining 2 teaspoons English toffee bits.

Yield: 15 (1/2-cup) servings (Using low-carb milk) **Calories per serving:** 169 (10% fat); **Total fat:** 2 g; **Cholesterol:** 5 mg; **Carbohydrate:** 32 g; **Dietary Fiber:** 3 g; **Protein:** 5 g; **Sodium:** 647 mg **Diabetic Exchanges:** 2 carbohydrates, 1 lean meat

---

DESSERTS

SUPPLIES LIST
Large bowl
Electric mixer
Large trifle bowl or large glass bowl

GROCERY LIST

DAIRY
1 (8-ounce) package fat-free cream cheese
Low-carb or fat-free milk (2 cups needed)

FROZEN
1 (8-ounce) container fat-free dessert whipped topping

PACKAGED
1 (10-ounce) angel food cake
1 (29-ounce) can pumpkin pie filling
2 (1.7-ounce) packages sugar-free, fat-free instant vanilla pudding mix
English toffee bits (1/4 cups plus 2 tsp crushed needed)

HELPFUL HINT:

❯ Fat-free skim milk can be substituted for the low-carb milk.

263

Cherry Chocolate Chip Trifle *20 minutes*

Never in a million years would you expect the combination of so many sugar-free ingredients to taste and look so exceptional. You'll especially like the fact that there is no sugar-free aftertaste. This is an ideal dessert for diabetics.

Ingredients

1 (1.34-ounce) sugar-free French vanilla instant pudding mix
2 cups nonfat light vanilla yogurt
1¼ cups fat-free whipped topping, divided
¼ cup miniature semi-sweet chocolate chips;
    reserve 1 teaspoon for topping
1 (10-ounce) sugar-free angel food cake,
2 (20-ounce) cans no-sugar-added cherry pie filling,
1 (.3-ounce) box sugar-free raspberry gelatin mix,

Instructions

▸ In a large mixing bowl, beat the instant pudding mix, yogurt, 1 cup whipped topping, and chocolate chips with an electric mixer.
▸ Tear the cake into bite-size pieces. Stir into the pudding mixture.
▸ In a second large mixing bowl, stir together both cans of cherry pie filling and the box of raspberry gelatin.
▸ Using a stiff spatula or knife, spread 2 cups of pudding mixture on the bottom of a trifle bowl, and then spread 2 cups of the cherry mixture on top. Alternate layers of the pudding mixture and cherry mixture to reach the top of the trifle bowl.
▸ On top of the last cherry mixture layer add a ¹/₄-cup dollop of whipped topping, and sprinkle the reserved 1 teaspoon chocolate chips on top.

Yield: 16 (1/2-cup) servings **Calories per serving:** 126 (7% fat); **Total fat:** 1 g; **Cholesterol:** 1 mg; **Carbohydrate:** 28 g; **Dietary Fiber:** 1 g; **Protein:** 2 g; **Sodium:** 225 mg **Diabetic Exchanges:** 2 carbohydrate

---

HELPFUL HINT:

❷ This is a great dessert to serve at Christmas, Valentine's Day or even the Fourth of July—just add sparklers for decorations.

Cherry Berry Decadent Trifle *20 minutes*

This looks so rich and elegant. It is definitely a dessert that's dressed to impress! What's so amazing is that it is diabetic friendly, too!

Ingredients

1 (2-pound) container light fat-free vanilla yogurt
1 (1.34-ounce) packet sugar-free French vanilla instant pudding,
1 teaspoon almond extract
2 (9-ounce) sugar-free angel food cakes,
2 (20-ounce) can no-sugar-added cherry pie filling,
1 (16-ounce) bag frozen berry medley (strawberries, blackberries, blueberries, and red raspberries)
1 (.3-ounce) package sugar-free strawberry gelatin mix,

Instructions

‣ In a large mixing bowl, beat the yogurt, pudding mix, and almond extract together with an electric mixer on high speed.
‣ Tear the cakes into bite-size pieces and place in the pudding mixture. Stir with a wooden spoon or stiff spatula until well blended. Set aside.
‣ In a medium mixing bowl, stir both cans of pie filling, the berries, and the gelatin mix until well mixed. Set aside.
‣ Spread half of the pudding/cake mixture on the bottom of a trifle bowl.
‣ Next layer half of the berry mixture on top of the pudding/cake mixture.
‣ Alternate layers until all of the ingredients are used.
‣ Serve or cover and keep chilled until ready to eat.

Yield: 24 (1/2-cup) servings **Calories per serving:** 89 (0% fat); **Total fat:** 0 g;
Cholesterol: 1 mg; **Carbohydrate:** 22 g; **Dietary Fiber:** 1 g; **Protein:** 3 g;
Sodium: 251 mg **Diabetic Exchanges:** 1/2 fat-free milk, 1 carbohydrate

---

SUPPLIES LIST
Large mixing bowl
Medium mixing bowl
Electric mixer
Trifle bowl

GROCERY LIST

DAIRY
1 (2-pound) container light
fat-free vanilla yogurt

FROZEN
1 (16-ounce) bag frozen
berry medley (strawberries,
blackberries, blueberries and
red raspberries)

PACKAGED
1 (1.34-ounce) packet
sugar-free French vanilla
instant pudding mix
2 (9-ounce) sugar-free angel
food cakes
2 (20-ounce) can no-sugar-
added cherry pie filling
1 (.3-ounce) package sugar-
free strawberry gelatin mix

PANTRY
Almond extract

265

SUPPLIES LIST
Large microwave-safe mixing
bowl
Whisk
Microwave oven
Small nonstick saucepan

GROCERY LIST

DAIRY
Eggs (12 needed)

PACKAGED
Sugar-free French vanilla
creamer (1 cup needed)
Light potato bread
(8 slices needed)
Raisins (1/4 cup needed)

PANTRY
Ground cinnamon
Cornstarch
Splenda Brown Sugar Blend

HELPFUL HINTS:

❷ Regular white bread,
reduced-calorie white bread,
regular wheat bread, or
reduced-calorie wheat bread
can be substituted for
the potato bread.

❷ The cream sauce comes
together quickly, so keep
your eye on it at all times.

Busy Day Bread Pudding with Cream Sauce *20 minutes*

I vividly remember the soothing aroma and comforting flavors of bread pudding as a child. This quick and easy recipe lives up to those expectations. This is good warm or cold.

Ingredients

12 eggs (4 whole eggs and 8 egg whites)
1 1/4 teaspoon ground cinnamon, divided
1 cup sugar-free French vanilla creamer, divided
1/2 cup plus 1 tablespoon Splenda Brown Sugar Blend, divided
8 slices light potato bread
1/4 cup raisins,
1/2 tablespoon cornstarch,

Instructions

▸ In a large microwave-safe mixing bowl, add 4 whole eggs and 8 egg whites, 1 teaspoon cinnamon, 1/2 cup French vanilla creamer, and 1/2 cup Splenda Brown Sugar Blend. Beat together with a whisk until well blended.

▸ Cut the bread slices into bite-size pieces. Add to the egg mixture and stir until the bread is saturated.

▸ Place in the microwave for 10 minutes.

▸ While the bread pudding is cooking, make the cream sauce. In a small nonstick saucepan over medium-high heat, stir together the 1/2 cup creamer, 1/4 teaspoon cinnamon, 1 tablespoon Splenda Brown Sugar Blend, raisins, and cornstarch. Continuously stir until thickened and fully heated.

▸ When the bread pudding is finished cooking, spoon the cream sauce over the bread pudding and serve.

Yield: 9 (1/2 cup) servings **Calories per serving:** 193 (28% fat); **Total fat:** 6 g;
Cholesterol: 94 mg; **Carbohydrate:** 27 g; **Dietary Fiber:** 3 g; **Protein:** 7 g;
Sodium: 191 mg **Diabetic Exchanges:** 2 carbohydrate, 1 very lean meat, 1 fat

---

Peach and Cinnamon Spiced Shortcakes *20 minutes*

This is ideal for afternoon teas or when you want something sweet for dessert, but not too sweet.

Ingredients

1 cup Bisquick Heart Smart reduced-fat baking mix
1 teaspoon, plus 1 tablespoon Splenda Brown Sugar Blend
1/2 cup light, fat-free vanilla yogurt
1/2 teaspoon ground cinnamon
1 (29-ounce) can no-sugar-added sliced peaches
1 tablespoon cornstarch,
1 teaspoon allspice

Instructions

For the shortcakes:

- Preheat the oven to 400 degrees.
- In a medium mixing bowl, stir together the baking mix, 1 teaspoon Splenda Brown Sugar Blend, yogurt, and cinnamon with a spatula until a stiff dough forms a ball.
- Spray a baking sheet with nonstick cooking spray.
- With your hands, divide the dough into six pieces and place on the prepared baking sheet.
- Bake for 7 minutes or until the bottoms are golden brown.

For the peach topping:

- Drain the juice from the can of peaches into a 12-inch nonstick saucepan over medium heat. Add the cornstarch, 1 tablespoon Splenda Brown Sugar Blend, and allspice and whisk until the cornstarch is dissolved.
- Bring to a boil, stirring constantly.
- After the sauce comes to a boil, stir in the drained peaches.
- Cover and let cook until the peaches are warmed through.
- Serve the peaches warm over the shortcakes.

Yield: 6 (1/2 cup peaches over 1 biscuit) servings **Calories per serving:** 193 (6% fat);
Total fat: 1 g; **Cholesterol:** 0 mg; **Carbohydrate:** 41 g; **Dietary Fiber:** 2 g;
Protein: 2 g; **Sodium:** 265 mg **Diabetic Exchanges:** 1 starch, 1 1/2 fruit
The nutritional information does not include fat-free dessert whipped topping.

DESSERTS

SUPPLIES LIST
Oven
Medium-sized mixing bowl
Baking sheet
Timer
12-inch nonstick saucepan with lid
Whisk

GROCERY LIST

DAIRY
Light fat-free vanilla yogurt
(1/2 cup needed)

PACKAGED
Bisquick Heart Smart reduced-fat baking mix
(1 cup needed)
1 (29-ounce) can no-sugar-added sliced peaches

PANTRY
Splenda Brown Sugar Blend
Ground cinnamon
Cornstarch
Allspice
Nonstick cooking spray

HELPFUL HINT:

❷ Serve with a dollop of fat-free dessert whipped topping if you'd like.

SUPPLIES LIST
Oven
10 x 15-inch jelly-roll pan
Electric mixer
Large mixing bowl
Plastic wrap
Toothpicks
Timer

GROCERY LIST

DAIRY
Eggs (6 needed)

FROZEN
1 (8-ounce) container fat-free
dessert whipped topping

PACKAGED
1 (18.25-ounce) box sugar-
free chocolate cake mix
Confectioners' sugar
(1/4 cup needed)
1 (12.75-ounce) jar sugar-free
red raspberry preserves

PANTRY
Nonfat cooking spray

HELPFUL HINTS:

❷ A jelly-roll pan has a
1/2-inch raised edge. It is
often used as a baking
or cookie sheet.

❷ To prevent the plastic
wrap from touching the
cake, insert toothpicks into
the cake before covering
with plastic wrap.

Red Raspberry Chocolate Cake *30 minutes*

The slight tartness of the red raspberries combined with the sweet cake is a mouthwatering treat. People who prefer desserts that are not "too sweet" especially like this dessert.

Ingredients

1 (18.25-ounce) box sugar-free chocolate cake mix
6 egg whites (or $3/4$ cup Egg Beaters)
1/2 cup water
1/4 cup confectioners' sugar
1 (12.75 ounce) jar sugar-free red raspberry preserves
1 (8-ounce) container fat-free dessert whipped topping,

Instructions

▸ Preheat the oven to 350 degrees.
▸ Spray a 10 x 15-inch jelly-roll pan with nonfat cooking spray. Set aside.
▸ In a large mixing bowl, beat the cake mix, egg whites, and water with an electric mixer on low speed for 30 seconds.. Increase the speed to medium, and beat for another $1^{1}/_{2}$ minutes.
▸ Pour and spread the cake batter evenly into the prepared pan.
▸ Bake on the center rack for 13 to 15 minutes or until the cake springs back when touched.
▸ Let the cake cool for 3 to 4 minutes, and then place it in the freezer for 7 minutes to help it cool faster.
▸ Spread the red raspberry preserves over the cake, and then spread the whipped topping over the preserves.
▸ Cover with plastic wrap and keep chilled until ready to eat.

Yield: 15 servings **Calories per serving:** 174 (7% fat); **Total fat:** 2 g; **Cholesterol:** 0 mg; **Carbohydrate:** 42 g; **Dietary Fiber:** 1 g; **Protein:** 3 g; **Sodium:** 303 mg
Diabetic Exchanges: 3 carbohydrate, 1/2 fat

Cranberry Peach Dumplings *30 minutes*

This is a great dessert by itself, but if you need a little more sweetness, add a dollop of fat-free whipped topping or fat-free vanilla ice cream.

Ingredients

1 (16-ounce) can whole berry cranberry sauce
2 (29-ounce) cans yellow cling peach pieces in light syrup
1/2 teaspoon allspice
1 1/3 cups Heart Smart Bisquick reduced-fat baking mix
1/2 teaspoon ground cinnamon

Instructions

▸ In a large nonstick saucepan on high heat, combine the cranberry sauce, peaches, and allspice. Stir together until well mixed. Bring to a boil.
▸ Continue boiling over high heat.
▸ In a large mixing bowl, use a fork to stir the baking mix with the cinnamon and 1/3 cup plus 3 tablespoons of the boiling fruit broth. Mix together to make a stiff dough.
▸ Drop the dough by rounded tablespoons into the boiling broth. Makes 11 dumplings.
▸ Cook uncovered at a full boil for 10 minutes.
▸ Reduce the heat to medium, cover, and cook an additional 5 to 7 minutes until the dumplings are fully cooked.

Yield: 11 (1 dumpling with 1/3 cup cooked fruit) servings **Calories per serving:** 177 (5% fat); **Total fat:** 1 g; **Cholesterol:** 0 mg; **Carbohydrate:** 42 g; **Dietary Fiber:** 2 g; **Protein:** 2 g; **Sodium:** 185 mg **Diabetic Exchanges:** 3 carbohydrate

---

SUPPLIES LIST
Large nonstick saucepan with lid
Large mixing bowl
Timer

GROCERY LIST

PACKAGED
1 (16-ounce) can whole berry cranberry sauce
2 (29-ounce) cans yellow cling peach pieces in light syrup
Heart Smart Bisquick reduced-fat baking mix (1 1/3 cups needed)

PANTRY
Allspice
Ground cinnamon

SUPPLIES LIST
Oven
Large mixing bowl
3 cookie sheets
Timer

GROCERY LIST

DAIRY
Eggs (3 needed)

FROZEN
1 (8-ounce) container fat-free
dessert whipped topping
1 (18.25-ounce) dark
chocolate cake mix

PACKAGED
Confectioners' sugar
(2 tablespoons needed)

PANTRY
Mint extract
Cooking spray

Chocolate Mint Cookies *30 minutes*

Chewy, chocolaty and minty. . . . Mmm! Need I say more?

Ingredients

1 (8-ounce) container fat-free dessert whipped topping,
1 (18.25-ounce) dark chocolate cake mix
1 teaspoon mint extract
3 egg whites (or 6 tablespoons Egg Beaters)
2 tablespoons confectioners' sugar

Instructions

▸ Place the oven rack on the middle shelf in the the oven. Preheat the oven to 350 degrees.
▸ In a large mixing bowl, stir together the whipped topping, cake mix, mint extract, and egg whites until well blended. The dough will become very stiff.
▸ Spray three cookie sheets with cooking spray.
▸ Drop the dough by rounded tablespoons onto the prepared cookie sheets.
▸ Evenly sift the confectioners' sugar over the tops of the cookie dough.
▸ Bake two cookie sheets at a time for 7 to 8 minutes.
▸ Bake the remaining cookie sheet for 7 to 8 minutes.

Yield: 32 (1-cookie) servings **Calories per serving:** 79 (15% fat); **Total fat:** 1 g;
Cholesterol: 0 mg; **Carbohydrate:** 16 g; **Dietary Fiber:** 0 g; **Protein:** 1 g;
Sodium: 118 mg **Diabetic Exchanges:** 1 carbohydrate

Coconut Cherry Chocolate Squares *25 minutes*

My neighbors, Spencer and Peggy Niles loved these! Peggy called for the recipe before I'd even gotten home from delivering them to her! The next morning she called again to say they liked them so much that they ate more for breakfast, and she's making them for Christmas!

Ingredients

4 egg whites (or $1/2$ cup Egg Beaters)
1 (18.25-ounce) Duncan Hines Coconut Supreme cake mix
1 (10-ounce) jar maraschino cherries, drained
$1/4$ cup firmly packed shredded coconut,
$1/4$ cup mini semi-sweet chocolate chips/morsels

Instructions

▶ Preheat the oven to 350 degrees.
▶ in a large mixing bowl, stir the egg whites into the cake mix with a stiff spatula, to form a stiff ball.
▶ Spray an 11 x 15-inch jelly-roll pan with butter-flavored cooking spray.
▶ Spray your hands with butter-flavored cooking spray; then use your hands to press the dough into the jelly-roll pan (like you would pizza dough).
▶ Make 6 rows of cherries with 5 cherries per row on top of the dough.
▶ Sprinkle with the shredded coconut and chocolate chips/morsels.
▶ Bake for 10 to 11 minutes or until the edges are golden brown.
▶ Let cool for 5 minutes, then cut into 30 (1-inch) squares.

Yield: 30 (1 piece) servings **Calories per serving:** 91 (19% fat); **Total fat:** 2 g;
Cholesterol: 0 mg; **Carbohydrate:** 17 g; **Dietary Fiber:** 0 g; **Protein:** 1 g;
Sodium: 122 mg **Diabetic Exchanges:** 1 carbohydrate

SUPPLIES LIST
Oven
Large mixing bowl
11 x 15-inch jelly-roll pan
Timer

GROCERY LIST

DAIRY
Eggs (4 needed)

PACKAGED
1 (10-ounce) jar
maraschino cherries
1 (18.25-ounce) Duncan
Hines Coconut Supreme
cake mix
Shredded coconut
($1/4$ cup needed)
Mini semi-sweet chocolate
chips/morsels
($1/4$ cup needed)

PANTRY
Butter-flavored
cooking spray

SUPPLIES LIST
Oven
Pie plate
Sharp scissors
Timer
Cutting board
Medium-sized mixing bowl
Baking sheet
Microwave-safe mixing bowl
Wax paper
Microwave oven

GROCERY LIST

DAIRY
Light butter

FROZEN
Phyllo dough
(10 sheets needed)

PACKAGED
Oatmeal (1/2 cup needed)
1 (20-ounce) can no-sugar-
added apple pie filling
1 box spiced cider sugar-free
apple-flavor drink mix (10
pouches per box,
Alpine brand)

PANTRY
Splenda Brown Sugar Blend
Pumpkin pie spice
Butter flavor cooking spray
Nonstick cooking spray

Apple Pie with Granola Crumb Topping *30 minutes*

With a flaky crust, tasty filling, and a crumb topping that is both sweet and crunchy, this quick and easy home-style light apple pie is every bit as delicious as the high-calorie version, but a lot easier on the waist line!

Ingredients

10 phyllo dough sheets
1/2 cup oatmeal
1/3 cup Splenda Brown Sugar Blend
1 teaspoon pumpkin pie spice
tablespoons light butter
1 (20-ounce) can no-sugar-added apple pie filling,
1 (.14-ounce) pouch Alpine spiced cider sugar-free apple-flavor drink mix
  from a (1.4-ounce) box of 10 pouches

Instructions

▸ Preheat the oven to 425 degrees.

Make Pie Shell:

▸ Take 10 sheets of phyllo dough and lay them flat.
▸ Spray each sheet of dough with butter-flavored cooking spray. Individually stack the sheets into a pie plate, like tire spindles, crossing in the center. Allow the extra to hang over the sides of the pie plate.
▸ With sharp scissors, cut the dough hanging off the edges of the pie plate.
▸ Place the pie dough in the oven for 6 to 8 minutes or until golden brown.

Make Granola:

▸ Take the cut off dough and finely chop it. Place it in a medium-size mixing bowl.
▸ Add the oatmeal, Splenda Brown Sugar Blend, pumpkin spice mix, and light butter to the mixing bowl.
▸ Using a spatula, mix the ingredients together. Set aside.
▸ Spray a baking sheet with nonstick cooking spray.

- Spread the oatmeal mixture on the baking sheet. Bake for 4 to 5 minutes, just until the butter melts.
- Remove from the oven and stir the oatmeal mixture around the baking sheet with a spatula, making a caramelized granola.

Make Pie Filling:

- In a microwave-safe mixing bowl, combine the apple pie filling and the drink mix.
- Cover with wax paper and cook in the microwave for 2 minutes. Stir and heat for 1 additional minute.

Assemble Pie:

- Place the apple filling in the prepared pie shell.
- Top with the granola and serve.

Yield: 6 servings **Calories per serving:** 188 (15% fat); **Total fat:** 3 g; **Cholesterol:** 5 mg; **Carbohydrate:** 37 g; **Dietary Fiber:** 2 g; **Protein:** 2 g; **Sodium:** 125 mg
Diabetic Exchanges: 2¹/2 carbohydrate, ¹/2 fat

DESSERTS

HELPFUL HINTS:

● This pie needs to be eaten the same day it's made or the crust will become soggy.

● This pie comes together very quickly so have all of your ingredients sitting out.

● This pie does not freeze well.

● Phyllo Dough (also spelled Filo Dough) is in the freezer section. It comes in 1-pound boxes. Each box has about 40 sheets in one box of Phyllo dough. It is super simple to work with, so do not be intimidated by it if you've never worked with it before.

SUPPLIES LIST
Medium-sized mixing bowl
Whisk
Serving plate

GROCERY LIST

DAIRY
Fat-free skim milk
(1 cup needed)

FROZEN
1 (8-ounce) container fat-free
dessert whipped topping
(1 cup plus 10 tablespoons
needed)

PACKAGED
1 (1.5-ounce) box sugar-free
chocolate instant
pudding mix
1 (20-ounce) can no-sugar-
added cherry pie filling
(1¹/4 cups needed)

PANTRY
Sugar-free chocolate syrup
(3 tablespoons plus 10
teaspoons needed)

HELPFUL HINTS:

❯ I recommend serving this
dessert chilled. Have the
ingredients already chilled
by putting the cherries and
the chocolate syrup in the
refrigerator as soon as you
unpack your groceries.

Black Forest Cream Crepe Filling *30 minutes*

Dressed to impress, these lovely crepes will capture the attention of even the most discriminating diner.

Ingredients

1 (1.5-ounce) box sugar-free chocolate instant pudding mix
1 cup fat-free skim milk
1 cup, plus 10 tablespoons fat-free dessert whipped topping, divided
3 tablespoons, plus 10 teaspoons sugar-free chocolate syrup, divided
1¹/4 cup no-sugar-added cherry pie filling, chilled

Instructions

▸ Make the crepe recipe on page 262.
▸ In a medium mixing bowl, whisk together the pudding mix and the milk until well blended.
▸ Add 1 cup whipped topping and 3 tablespoons chocolate syrup to the pudding mixture. Whisk together until well blended.
▸ Assemble the crepes by placing 2 tablespoons of filling down the center of each crepe, rolling the ends up jelly-roll style.
▸ Place the crepes seam side down on the plate.
▸ Put 2 tablespoons of chilled, cherry pie filling on top of each crepe.
▸ Drizzle 1 teaspoon chocolate syrup on the top of the cherries.
▸ Place 1 tablespoon fat-free whipped topping on the center of each crepe, and top with one cherry.

Yield: 10 (1 dessert crepe) servings **Calories per serving:** 93 (0% fat); **Total fat:** 0 g; **Cholesterol:** 1 mg; **Carbohydrate:** 18 g; **Dietary Fiber:** 0 g; **Protein:** 3 g; **Sodium:** 323 mg **Diabetic Exchanges:** 1 starch

---

Chocolate Peanut Butter Crepes *30 minutes*

Satisfy your sweet tooth without breaking your calorie bank!

Ingredients

1 (1.5-ounce) box sugar-free chocolate instant pudding mix
1 cup fat-free skim milk
1 cup, plus 10 tablespoons fat-free dessert whipped topping, divided
3 tablespoons, plus 10 teaspoons sugar-free chocolate syrup, divided
2 tablespoons creamy peanut butter

Instructions

▸ Make the crepe recipe on page 262.
▸ In a medium mixing bowl, whisk together the pudding mix and milk. Blend until well mixed.
▸ Add 1 cup whipped topping, 3 tablespoons chocolate syrup, and peanut butter to the pudding mixture. Whisk together well to blend all ingredients together.
▸ Assemble the crepes by placing 2 tablespoons of cream filling down the center of each crepe, rolling the ends up jelly-roll style, seam side down on a plate.
▸ Drizzle 1 teaspoon chocolate syrup on top of each crepe.
▸ Place 1 tablespoon whipped topping on the center of each crepe and serve.

Yield: 10 (1 dessert crepe) servings **Calories per serving:** 97 (19% fat); **Total fat:** 2 g; **Cholesterol:** 1 mg; **Carbohydrate:** 16 g; **Dietary Fiber:** 0 g; **Protein:** 3 g; **Sodium:** 334 mg **Diabetic Exchanges:** 1 starch

DESSERTS

SUPPLIES LIST
Medium-sized mixing bowl
Whisk
Serving plate

GROCERY LIST

DAIRY
Fat-free skim milk
(1 cup needed)

FROZEN
1 (8-ounce) fat-free dessert whipped topping
(1 cup plus 10 tablespoons needed)

PACKAGED
1 (1.5-ounce) box sugar-free chocolate instant pudding mix
Creamy peanut butter
(2 tablespoons needed)

PANTRY
Sugar-free chocolate syrup
(3 tablespoons plus 10 teaspoons needed)

SUPPLIES LIST
Small nonstick saucepan
Serving plate

GROCERY LIST

FROZEN
1 (8-ounce) fat-free dessert whipped topping (10 tablespoons needed)

PACKAGED
1 (20-ounce) can no-sugar-added apple pie filling
1 box sugar-free spiced cider apple-flavor drink mix (10 pouches per box, Alpine brand)
Caramel syrup (10 teaspoons needed)

HELPFUL HINTS:

❍ I recommend serving these crepes warm. If using crepes that were premade and frozen, microwave the stack for 1 minute to warm them first before assembling the crepes.

❍ The sugar-free spiced cider apple flavor drink mix comes in a box of 10 individual pouches (Alpine by Krusteaz).

Caramel Apple Crepes *30 minutes*

Here's a great alternative for warm apple pie that's supper simple to assemble in a pinch.

Ingredients

1 (20-ounce) can no-sugar-added apple pie filling
1 (0.14-ounce) pouch sugar-free spiced cider apple-flavor drink mix
10 teaspoons caramel syrup
10 tablespoons fat-free dessert whipped topping,

Instructions

▸ Make the crepes according to recipe on page 262.
▸ Open the apple pie filling. While the filling is still in the can, insert a sharp, long knife into the can and cut the apple slices into smaller, bite-sized pieces.
▸ In a small nonstick saucepan over medium heat, stir together the apple pie filling and the drink mix.
▸ When the filling is completely heated, place 3 tablespoons of filling onto each warmed crepe.
▸ Roll the crepes up jelly-roll-style, placing the seam side up on plate.
▸ Drizzle 1 teaspoon caramel syrup over each crepe.
▸ Place 1 tablespoon of whipped topping on the middle of each crepe.

Yield: 10 (1 dessert crepe) servings **Calories per serving:** 74 (0% fat); **Total fat:** 0 g; **Cholesterol:** 0 mg; **Carbohydrate:** 16 g; **Dietary Fiber:** 1 g; **Protein:** 2 g; **Sodium:** 118 mg **Diabetic Exchanges:** 1 starch

---

Pumpkin Bread Pudding   *25 minutes*

Don't be surprised if this becomes one of your new favorite holiday recipes! It's just that good!It was a huge hit at the pot luck I took it to . . . it was the only dish that was completely gone!

Ingredients

8 egg whites
1 (15-ounce) can 100% pure pumpkin
2 teaspoons pumpkin pie spice
1/2 cup firmly packed, plus 2 tablespoons Splenda Brown Sugar Blend, divided
1/2 teaspoon light salt
6 cups crusty French bread cut into 1-inch cubes (approximately 2/3 loaf)

Instructions

▸ In a large microwave-safe mixing bowl, whisk together the egg whites, pure pumpkin, pumpkin pie spice, 1/2 cup firmly packed Splenda Brown Sugar Blend, and light salt. Whisk together until well blended. Set aside.
▸ Mix the bread cubes into the pumpkin mixture.
▸ Sprinkle 2 tablespoons Splenda brown sugar on top of the bread and pumpkin mixture.
▸ Cover with wax paper and cook in a carousel microwave oven for 8 minutes.
▸ Remove from the microwave and let sit for a couple of minutes before serving.

Yield: 12 (1/2-cup) servings **Calories per serving:** 147 (4% fat); **Total fat:** 1 g;
Cholesterol: 0 mg; **Carbohydrate:** 27 g; **Dietary Fiber:** 2 g; **Protein:** 6 g;
Sodium: 248 mg **Diabetic Exchanges:** 2 starch

SUPPLIES LIST
Large microwave-safe mixing bowl
Whisk
Cutting board
Wax paper
Microwave oven

GROCERY LIST

DAIRY
Eggs (8 needed)

PACKAGED
1 (15-ounce) can 100% pure pumpkin
Crusty French bread
(approx. 2/3 of a loaf)

PANTRY
Splenda Brown Sugar Blend
Pumpkin pie spice
Light salt

HELPFUL HINTS:

❷ 100% pure pumpkin does not have the pie spices or sugar in it like pumpkin pie mix.

❷ Brown sugar can be substituted for Splenda Brown Sugar Blend, if desired, but remember, brown sugar will add extra calories.

Triple Chocolate Four-Layer Cake *30 minutes*

This is so super moist and light that it literally melts in your mouth.

Ingredients

1 (18.25-ounce) box reduced sugar Devil's Food cake mix
6 egg whites (or $^3/_4$ cup Egg Beaters)
1$^3/_4$ cups applesauce,
1 (8-ounce) container fat-free dessert whipped topping
3 (.29-ounce) envelopes diet hot cocoa mix
$^1/_2$ cup chocolate syrup

Instructions
Cake:

▶ Preheat the oven to 350 degrees.
▶ In a large mixing bowl, beat the cake mix, egg whites, and applesauce with a whisk. The cake batter will be very thick.
▶ Spray four round 8- or 9-inch cake pans with nonstick cooking spray.
▶ Divide the batter equally between the four pans. Spread the batter evenly in the bottoms of the pans.
▶ Bake for 10 minutes or until a tooth pick inserted in the center comes out clean.

Frosting:

▶ While the cake is baking, stir the whipped topping with the diet hot cocoa mix in a large mixing bowl until well blended.
▶ Place in the refrigerator to keep cold until ready to frost the cake.

Baked Cake:

▶ Tear off 4 sheets of wax paper.
▶ When the cakes come out of the oven, immediately invert each cake from its pan onto a sheet of wax paper. Do not stack the cakes!
▶ Place the cakes in the freezer to help them cool quicker. Keep in the freezer for 5 minutes before assembling the four-layer cake.

SUPPLIES LIST
Oven
2 large mixing bowls
Whisk
4 round 8 or 9-inch cake pans
Timer
Wax paper
Cake plate

GROCERY LIST

DAIRY
Eggs (6 needed)

FROZEN
1 (8-ounce) container fat-free dessert whipped topping

PACKAGED
1 (18.25-ounce) box Pillsbury reduced-sugar Devil's Food cake mix
Applesauce, (1$^3/_4$ cups needed)
1 box diet hot cocoa mix (3 envelopes needed, 10 envelopes per box, Swiss Miss Sensible Sweets Diet)
Chocolate syrup (1/2 cup needed)

PANTRY
Nonstick cooking spray

Assembling the four-layer cake:

- The cakes will be slightly warm.
- Take one layer out of the freezer and place it on a cake plate; spread one-third of the frosting on top.
- Take the second layer of cake out of the freezer, and place it on top of the first layer. Spread another one-third of the frosting on top; continue layering until all of the layers of cake are used. There will be no frosting for the very top of the cake.
- Spread 1/2 cup chocolate syrup on the top layer of the cake, letting some of the syrup ooze down the sides of the cake.
- Keep the cake refrigerated until time to eat.

Yield: 12 servings **Calories per serving:** 251 (7% fat); **Total fat:** 2 g; **Cholesterol:** 0 mg; **Carbohydrate:** 56 g; **Dietary Fiber:** 2 g; **Protein:** 5 g; **Sodium:** 433 mg **Diabetic Exchanges:** 31/2 carbohydrate, 1/2 fat

HELPFUL HINTS:

● All diet hot chocolate mixes are not created the same! I recommend only using the Swiss Miss brand of cocoa mix. We tested this recipe using different brands, and this was the best.

● To save time cleaning, wash the bowl that you mixed the cake batter in and use it to make the frosting. Wash the bowl in hot water, but rinse it in cold water so you don't melt the Cool Whip when making the frosting.

● Make sure you have four level places in the freezer to cool the cake layers.

● You don't want to move this cake around too much. If taking it for a potluck, assemble the cake once you get there.

Strawberry Smoothie (page 283)

Beverages

MINI INDEX

Warm Italian Virgin Mary *4 minutes*

Here's a unique way to get your veggies, and it's so tasty too!

SUPPLIES LIST
Microwave-safe (4-cup glass) measuring cup or pitcher
Microwave oven
Wax paper

GROCERY LIST

PACKAGED
1 (33.8 fl. oz) bottle of virgin Bloody Mary Mix

PANTRY
Italian seasoning

Ingredients

1 (33.8 fluid ounce) bottle of virgin Bloody Mary Mix
1 teaspoon of Italian seasoning

Instructions

▸ Pour the bottle of virgin Bloody Mary Mix into a microwave-safe (4-cup glass) measuring cup or pitcher.
▸ Stir in the Italian seasoning.
▸ Cover with wax paper.
▸ Cook in the microwave for 3 minutes on high.
▸ Pour into champagne glasses. Serve warm.

Yield: 6 (5½-oz) servings **Calories per serving:** 39 (0% fat); **Total fat:** 0 g; **Cholesterol:** 0 mg; **Carbohydrate:** 8 g; **Dietary Fiber:** 1 g; **Protein:** 2 g; **Sodium:** 826 mg **Diabetic Exchanges:** 2 vegetable

Strawberry Smoothie *5 minutes*

I love being able to have a sweet treat that is guilt free and actually good for me! This thick and creamy strawberry smoothie fits the bill! It's excellent as a healthy snack, refreshing dessert, or as a meal replacement.

Ingredients

1 (16-ounce) bag frozen whole strawberries (no-sugar-added),
1/2 cup fat-free plain yogurt
1/2 cup Splenda
1 cup water
2 tablespoons of 100% natural whey protein powder

Instructions

‣ In a blender, combine the strawberries, yogurt, Splenda, and water.
‣ Pulse, stirring occasionally, to make sure it is well blended.
‣ After well blended, add the whey protein powder. Blend well.
‣ Serve in a glass.

Yield: Meal Replacement – 2 (2-cup) servings **Calories per serving:** 168 (4% fat);
Total fat: 1 g; **Cholesterol:** 5 mg; **Carbohydrate:** 33 g; **Dietary Fiber:** 5 g; **Protein:**
10 g; **Sodium:** 74 mg **Diabetic Exchanges:** 2 fruit, 1 1/2 very lean meat

---

Yield: Snack/Dessert – 4 (1-cup) servings **Calories per serving:** 84 (4% fat);
Total fat: <1 g; **Cholesterol:** 2 mg; **Carbohydrate:** 16 g; **Dietary Fiber:** 2 g; **Protein:**
5 g; **Sodium:** 37 mg **Diabetic Exchanges:** 1 fruit, 1 very lean meat

SUPPLIES LIST
Blender

GROCERY LIST

DAIRY
Fat-free plain yogurt
(1/2 cup needed)

FROZEN
1 (16-ounce) bag frozen
whole strawberries
(no-sugar-added)

PANTRY
Splenda
whey protein 100% natural
powder (2 tablespoons
needed)

MEAL SUGGESTION:
Use this as a meal replacement
for breakfast or lunch.

(See photo on page 280)

HELPFUL HINTS:

❷ If you don't want to use
Splenda, you can use sugar
but sugar will add extra
calories.

❷ Wheat-free protein powder
can be substituted for the
whey protein powder.

❷ You can find whole-wheat
protein in the nutritional
supplement aisle.

❷ The secret to hiding the
flavor of the protein is to not
add it at the beginning of
making this smoothie. Only
add it at the end of blending.

SUPPLIES LIST
Blender

GROCERY LIST

DAIRY
Nonfat plain yogurt
(1/2 cup needed)

PACKAGED
1 (11-ounce) can of mandarin
oranges (in light syrup)
1 (14.5-ounce) can of sliced
peaches

PANTRY
Splenda granular
(1/4 cup needed)
Ground cinnamon

Spiced Nectar Smoothie *5 minutes or less*

Here's a light and creamy, refreshing substitute for plain fruit juice, and it's a delicious, sweet, healthy treat, too.

Ingredients:

1 (11-ounce) can of mandarin oranges in light syrup
1 (14.5-ounce.) can of sliced peaches,
1/2 cup of nonfat plain yogurt
3 cups ice cubes, divided
1/4 cup of Splenda granular (or sugar)
1/4 teaspoon ground cinnamon

▸ Place the mandarin oranges (undrained), sliced peaches, and yogurt into the blender.
▸ Add 1 cup of ice cubes (approximately 14). Pulse for 1 minute.
▸ Add in the Splenda, 2 more cups of ice cubes, and the cinnamon. Pulse for 1 more minute or until smooth and creamy.
▸ Pour into five (1-cup) glasses.

Yield: 5 (1 cup) servings (Nutritional information figured with Splenda) **Calories per serving:** 109 (0% fat); **Total fat:** 0 g; **Cholesterol:** 0 mg; **Carbohydrate:** 26 g; **Dietary Fiber:** 1 g; **Protein:** 2 g; **Sodium:** 36 mg **Diabetic Exchanges:** 1 fruit, 1 carbohydrate

---

Yield: 5 (1 cup) servings (Nutritional information figured with Sugar) **Calories per serving:** 143 (0% fat); **Total fat:** 0 g; **Cholesterol:** 0 mg; **Carbohydrate:** 35 g; **Dietary Fiber:** 1 g; **Protein:** 2 g; **Sodium:** 36 mg **Diabetic Exchanges:** 1 fruit, 1 1/2 carbohydrate

Christmas Cocktails (Virgin) *10 minutes*

We like being able to serve this special holiday cocktail that looks and tastes striking, while also being low in calories.

Ingredients

1 (.3-ounce) packet of sugar-free strawberry gelatin,
2 cups hot water
6 cups cold water
1 tub sugar-free raspberry ice flavored drink mix*
2 teaspoons almond extract
24 maraschino cherries (16 red and 8 green),
64 ice cubes
2 tablespoons of granulated sugar

Instructions
To make punch

▸ In a 2-quart pitcher, stir the strawberry gelatin into the hot water until dissolved.
▸ Stir in the cold water, drink mix, and almond extract until well mixed. Set aside.

To make maraschino skewers

▸ Cut off the bottom of 8 wooden skewers so that the skewers are only $2^1/_2$ inches taller than the glasses you are using.
▸ Alternate 3 cherries (red, green, red) on the end of each skewer. Set aside.

Assembling Christmas Cocktails

▸ Place $1/_4$ inch of water in the bottom of a small bowl. Set aside.
▸ Place the granulated sugar on a small plate. Set aside.
▸ One glass at a time, dip the rim of the glass in the plate of water and then into the plate of sugar (to give the glass a pretty sugared rim, like you'd see at a fancy restaurant).
▸ Fill each glass with ice cubes and 1 cup of punch.
▸ Place the maraschino cherry skewers in the punch glasses so that the cherries are sticking out of the glass. Serve.

Yield: 8 (1-cup) servings **Calories per serving:** 54 (0% fat); **Total fat:** 0 g;
Cholesterol: 0 mg; **Carbohydrate:** 9 g; **Dietary Fiber:** 0 g; **Protein:** 1 g; **Sodium:**
31 mg **Diabetic Exchanges:** 1/2 carbohydrate

SUPPLIES LIST
2-quart pitcher
8 wooden skewers
Small bowl

GROCERY LIST

PACKAGED
1 (.3-ounce) packet of sugar-free strawberry gelatin
1 tub sugar-free raspberry ice flavored drink mix
1 (6-ounce) jar red maraschino cherries (16 needed)
1 (6-ounce) jar green maraschino cherries (8 needed)

PANTRY
Almond extract
Granulated sugar

HELPFUL HINTS:

* There are 6 tubs in one container of sugar-free raspberry ice drink mix.

❯ Make sure the gelatin is completely dissolved in the hot water before adding the flavored drink mix and cold water to it.

❯ You can find colored sugars in the baking aisle.

285

GROCERY LIST

PACKAGED
1 tub sugar-free apple-
flavored drink mix
1 (15-ounce) can 100%
pumpkin
8 cinnamon sticks

PANTRY
Ground allspice
Ground cinnamon
Splenda Brown Sugar Blend

HELPFUL HINTS:

* There are 6 tubs in one
container of sugar-free
apple drink mix.

❷ You can make this ahead
and store in a container
in the refrigerator. When
ready to drink, simply stir
the beverage (the pumpkin
settles to the bottom as it
sits); then remove a cup of
Spiced Pumpkin Cider and
heat in the microwave for a
delicious and healthy snack.

Spiced Pumpkin Cider *10 minutes*

This sweet and smooth, warm, flavorful beverage can soothe any blues away. An added bonus is being able to drink your vegetables and having them taste like dessert! This has become one of my all-time favorite warm beverages!

Ingredients

7 cups hot water
1 tub sugar-free apple flavored drink mix* (6 tubs in a canister)
1 (15-ounce) can 100% pumpkin
¹/2 teaspoon ground allspice
1 teaspoon ground cinnamon, plus extra for garnish
¹/2 cup firmly packed Splenda Brown Sugar Blend
8 cinnamon sticks, optional

Instructions

▸ In a 4¹/2-quart saucepan stir together the hot water and drink mix over high heat until the mix is completely dissolved.
▸ Stir in the pumpkin, allspice, cinnamon, and Splenda Brown Sugar Blend until well mixed and fully heated.
▸ Pour 1 cup of cider into each mug or cup, and sprinkle the top with ground cinnamon before serving.
▸ If desired, garnish each beverage with a stick of cinnamon.

Yield: 8 (1-cup) servings **Calories per serving:** 84 (0% fat); **Total fat:** 0 g; **Cholesterol:** 0 mg; **Carbohydrate:** 16 g; **Dietary Fiber:** 2 g; **Protein:** 1 g; **Sodium:** 9 mg **Diabetic Exchanges:** 1 carbohydrate

Cinnamon and Spice Candied Peach Punch *10 minutes*

This is excellent hot or cold! Warm, it is very comforting and versatile. Instead of a tea, this would be nice for a ladies brunch. It's also nice on a chilly day. Served cold, it's refreshing and thirst quenching!

Ingredients

8 cups hot water
1 tub sugar-free peach drink mix
2/3 cup cinnamon candies (Red Hots)

Instructions

▸ Place the hot water in a 4^1/$_2$-quart saucepan with the beverage mix and cinnamon candies.
▸ Stir together and bring to a boil. Cook for a few minutes until the candies are completely dissolved.
▸ After the punch comes to a boil and the candies are dissolved, turn off the heat and serve.

Yield: 8 (1-cup) servings **Calories per serving:** 85 (0% fat); **Total fat:** 0 g; **Cholesterol:** 0 mg; **Carbohydrate:** 21 g; **Dietary Fiber:** 0 g; **Protein:** 0 g; **Sodium:** 7 mg **Diabetic Exchanges:** 1¹/2 carbohydrate

---

SUPPLIES LIST
4¹/2-quart saucepan

GROCERY LIST

PACKAGED
1 tub sugar-free peach drink mix
Cinnamon (Red Hots) candies (2/3 cup needed)

HELPFUL HINTS:

❷ This can be kept warm in a slow cooker on low for hours.

❷ There are 6 tubs in one container of sugar-free peach drink mix.

Cinnamon and Spice
Hot Chocolate *10 minutes*

Oh baby, it's hard to believe that something this mouthwatering and delicious is so low in calories!

Ingredients

4 cups water
6 packs diet hot cocoa mix (Swiss Miss Sensible Sweets)
1/4 cup cinnamon candies (Red Hots)
Ground cinnamon, for garnish

Instructions

▸ Add the water to the water bin of an automatic coffee maker.
▸ In the carafe of the coffee maker, combine the diet hot chocolate mix with the cinnamon candies.
▸ Turn the coffee maker on, to run the water through.
▸ Once the water is done dripping, take a whisk and stir the chocolate mixture and the candies together.
▸ Sprinkle the top of each serving with ground cinnamon.

Yield: 4 (1-cup) servings **Calories per serving:** 150 (9% fat); **Total fat:** 2 g; **Cholesterol:** 0 mg; **Carbohydrate:** 30 g; **Dietary Fiber:** 2 g; **Protein:** 3 g; **Sodium:** 277 mg **Diabetic Exchanges:** 1/2 fat-free milk, 11/2 carbohydrate

---

HELPFUL HINT:

❯ Actually use a measuring cup to measure the 4 cups of water because the measure on the coffee maker does not measure 8-ounce cups.

Citrus Cider (Hot) *10 minutes*

Here's a unique way to serve an ordinary beverage in an extraordinary way! The flavors are wonderful together!

Ingredients

1 (12-ounce) container frozen concentrated orange juice
3 cans of hot water
1/2 teaspoon ground allspice
1 teaspoon ground cinnamon, plus extra for sprinkling on top
2 tablespoons Splenda Brown Sugar Blend

Instructions

▸ In a large Dutch oven or saucepan, combine the orange juice with 3 cans of hot water, allspice, cinnamon, and Splenda Brown Sugar Blend. Stir together.
▸ Cooking over medium-high heat, bring to a full boil.
▸ For each serving, put 6 ounces in a tea cup, and sprinkle with ground cinnamon.

Yield: 8 (6-ounce) servings **Calories per serving:** 101 (0% fat); **Total fat:** 0 g; **Cholesterol:** 0 mg; **Carbohydrate:** 24 g; **Dietary Fiber:** 1 g; **Protein:** 1 g; **Sodium:** 6 mg **Diabetic Exchanges:** 1 1/2 fruit

BEVERAGES

SUPPLIES LIST
Large Dutch oven or saucepan

GROCERY LIST

FROZEN
1 (12-ounce) container frozen concentrated orange juice

PANTRY
Ground allspice
Splenda Brown Sugar Blend
Ground cinnamon

HELPFUL HINT:

➊ This is a good alternative to hot chocolate or apple cider.

SUPPLIES LIST
Toothpicks

GROCERY LIST

PACKAGED
24-ounce diet cranberry juice
1 (6-ounce) jar maraschino
cherries
(12 cherries needed)

PANTRY
Sugar-free hazelnut coffee
creamer

Cranberry Cream Cocktails (non-alcoholic) *5 minutes*

Slightly sweet, slightly tart, and slightly creamy.

Ingredients

32 ice cubes
24 ounces diet cranberry juice
4 teaspoons maraschino cherry juice
2 tablespoons sugar-free hazelnut coffee creamer
12 maraschino cherries

Instructions
To make 1 individual cocktail

▸ Put 8 ice cubes into a juice glass.
▸ Pour 1/2 cup diet cranberry juice over the ice cubes.
▸ Drizzle $1/2$ tablespoon maraschino cherry juice and 1 teaspoon hazelnut coffee creamer on top. DO NOT STIR.
▸ Put 3 maraschino cherries on a toothpick, and place on top of the ice cubes.

Yield: 4 (6-ounce) servings **Calories per serving:** 48 (21% fat); **Total fat:** 1 g; **Cholesterol:** 0 mg; **Carbohydrate:** 8 g; **Dietary Fiber:** 0 g; **Protein:** 0 g; **Sodium:** 11 mg **Diabetic Exchanges:** 1/2 carbohydrate

HELPFUL HINTS:

❷ Juice glasses vary in size and are approximately 7 to 8 ounces.

❷ Wine glasses can be substituted, if desired.

❷ Make these cocktails right before serving; do NOT make ahead of time, and do not stir.

❷ French vanilla creamer can be substituted for the hazelnut creamer.

Blueberry Lemonade *10 minutes*

What a fun and creative way to get your servings of fruit for the day. You may want to serve this beverage with a spoon so your diners can get every last bit of blueberries from their glasses.

Ingredients

1 (12-ounce) can frozen concentrated lemonade
3 cans water
1/3 cup Splenda granular
1 (16-ounce) bag frozen blueberries

Instructions

▸ In a large 2-quart pitcher, combine the frozen concentrated lemonade with cold water.
▸ Stir in the Splenda and the frozen blueberries.

Assembling each serving:

▸ Put 6 to 7 ice cubes in a tall glass.
▸ Pour the Blueberry Lemonade over the ice in the glasses.
▸ Serve immediately.

Yield: 6 (1 1/3-cup) servings **Calories per serving:** 176 (0% fat); **Total fat:** 0 g; **Cholesterol:** 0 mg; **Carbohydrate:** 45 g; **Dietary Fiber:** 2 g; **Protein:** 1 g; **Sodium:** 9 mg **Diabetic Exchanges:** 3 carbohydrate

---

BEVERAGES

SUPPLIES LIST
Large 2-quart pitcher

GROCERY LIST

FROZEN
1 (12-ounce) can frozen concentrated lemonade
1 (16-ounce) bag frozen blueberries

PANTRY
Splenda granular

HELPFUL HINTS:

❷ Be sure to use frozen blueberries in this recipe. They will thaw and help keep the beverage cold.

❷ The serving sizes are larger than the traditional 1-cup beverage size because you are getting your 1/2-cup serving of fresh fruit with this drink.

SUPPLIES LIST
Pitcher

GROCERY LIST

PACKAGED
1 (15-ounce) can tropical
fruit salad
1 (15-ounce) can whole
segment mandarin oranges
1 (20 ounce) can pineapple
in its own juice
Diet citrus-flavored green tea
(1¼ cups needed)

PANTRY
Coconut extract

Tropical Fruit Punch *5 minutes*

Mmm! Mmm! This is so smooth! To prevent being wasteful, this beverage is made using the juices that were drained from the cans of fruit in the Hawaiian Ham Breakfast Bake and the Polynesian Fruit Salad suggested meal menu.

Ingredients

³/4 cup juice drained from 1 (15-ounce) can tropical fruit salad, chilled
1 cup juice drained from 1 (15-ounce) can whole segment mandarin
    oranges, chilled
1 cup juice drained from 1 (20-ounce) can pineapple chunks in their own
    juice, chilled
1¼ cups diet citrus-flavored green tea, chilled
¹/2 teaspoon coconut extract

Instructions

▸ Pour the reserved juices from the tropical fruit salad, mandarin oranges, and pineapple into a pitcher.
▸ Add the diet green tea and the coconut extract.
▸ Stir and serve chilled.

Yield: 4 (1-cup) servings **Calories per serving:** 71 (0% fat); **Total fat:** 0 g;
Cholesterol: 0 mg; **Carbohydrate:** 19 g; **Dietary Fiber:** 1 g; **Protein:** 0 g;
Sodium: 9 mg **Diabetic Exchanges:** 1¹/2 carbohydrate

HELPFUL HINT:

❷ Have the ingredients already chilled by storing them in the refrigerator as soon as you unpack the groceries.

292

Almond Steamer *5 minutes*

Here's a comforting sweet drink to substitute for warm milk.

Ingredients

4 cups fat-free skim milk,
1 teaspoon almond extract
1/3 cup Splenda granular

Instructions

▸ In a large microwavable (4-cup) measuring cup or pitcher, whisk together the milk, almond extract, and Splenda granular until well blended.
▸ Microwave in a carousel microwave for 4 minutes or until fully heated and a frothy foam is on top.
▸ Pour into individual coffee cups or mugs.
▸ Serve immediately.

Yield: 4 (1-cup) servings **Calories per serving:** 94 (0% fat); **Total fat:** 0 g; **Cholesterol:** 5 mg; **Carbohydrate:** 14 g; **Dietary Fiber:** 0 g; **Protein:** 8 g; **Sodium:** 103 mg **Diabetic Exchanges:** 1 fat-free milk

Banana Cream Steamer

▸ Substitute 1 teaspoon banana extract for the coconut extract.

Yield: 4 (1-cup) servings **Calories per serving:** 94 (0% fat); **Total fat:** 0 g; **Cholesterol:** 5 mg; **Carbohydrate:** 14 g; **Dietary Fiber:** 0 g; **Protein:** 8 g; **Sodium:** 103 mg **Diabetic Exchanges:** 1 fat-free milk

---

BEVERAGES

SUPPLIES LIST
Large microwavable (4-cup) measuring cup or pitcher
Whisk
Microwave oven

GROCERY LIST

DAIRY
Fat-free skim milk
(4 cups needed)

PANTRY
Almond or banana extract
Splenda granular

HELPFUL HINT:

❯ Substitute other extracts for different flavors.

SUPPLIES LIST
2-quart pitcher
Cutting board

GROCERY LIST

PRODUCE
2 kiwis

PACKAGED
1 packet sugar-free instant
tea (to make 2 quarts)

Kiwi Tea *15 minutes*

This is an especially pretty beverage with the layers of kiwi floating with the ice cubes. Women especially like it!

Ingredients

1 packet sugar-free instant tea, (to make 2 quarts)
8 cups cold water
2 kiwis
24 ice cubes

Instructions

▸ Prepare the instant tea by stirring instant tea mix into cold water in a 2-quart pitcher until dissolved. It is very important that you do this step first, because the tea needs to be fully dissolved.

▸ Peel and cut each kiwi into 8 slices.

▸ Set out 8 drinking glasses (for best results, use tall glasses). In each glass, alternate putting ice cubes and slices of kiwi; put 3 to 6 ice cubes and 2 slices of kiwi per glass.

▸ Fill each glass with prepared tea, and let the beverages sit for at least 10 minutes. The kiwi will flavor the tea as it sits. Pieces of ice and kiwi should be floating in the glasses. It is very pretty.

Yield: 8 (1-cup) servings **Calories per serving:** 17 (0% fat); **Total fat:** 0 g; **Cholesterol:** 0 mg; **Carbohydrate:** 4 g; **Dietary Fiber:** 1 g; **Protein:** 0 g; **Sodium:** 11 mg **Diabetic Exchanges:** Free

---

Other books by Dawn Hall

Busy People's Diabetic Cookbook

Busy People's Down-Home Cooking Without the Down-Home Fat

Busy People's Fun, Fast, Festive Christmas Cookbook

Busy People's Low-Carb Cookbook

Busy People's Low-Fat Cookbook

Busy People's Slow Cooker Cookbook

Busy People's Super Simple 30-Minute Menus

7 Simple Steps to a Healthier You

Comfort Food for Your Soul

Recipe Index

Index

Photo by: Andy Grier

$\mathcal{D}$awn $\mathcal{H}$all self-published her first cookbook when she needed to raise money to pay for her late husband's cancer treatment. Since then over 1 million copies of her cookbooks have been sold. Her books contain simple, great-tasting dishes for busy people who like to eat real, everyday food. Her books also help to motivate and inspire healthy eating and healthy lifestyles. She is the host of *Cooking for Busy People TV Show* and is also a popular inspirational conference speaker; full of energy, insight and clever ideas.

Author Contact Information:

Dawn Hall
P.O. Box 53
Swanton, Ohio 43558
Office Phone: (419) 826-2665
E-mail: Dawn@DawnHallCookbooks.com
Website: DawnHallCookbooks.com

All of Busy People's Cookbooks are available for fund-raising, special sales incentives, donor gifts and promotional purposes.

For more information please e-mail: SpecialMarkets@ThomasNelson.com